The Book
of You

The Book of You

(formerly titled *What They Know About You*)

Bernard Asbell
with **Karen Wynn**

Fawcett Columbine   New York

A Fawcett Columbine Book
Published by Ballantine Books

Grateful acknowledgment is made to the following for permission to reprint previously published material:

AMERICAN PSYCHOLOGICAL ASSOCIATION AND MARK SNYDER: Table from "Self-Monitoring of Expressive Behavior" by Mark Snyder, from *Journal of Personality and Social Psychology*, 1974, v30, no4, p526. Copyright © 1974 by American Psychological Association. Reprinted by permission of the American Psychological Association and the author.
THE NEW YORK TIMES: Excerpt from "Forgetfulness Is Seen Causing More Worry Than It Should" by Daniel Goleman, July 1, 1986; "Social Chameleon May Pay Emotional Price" by Daniel Goleman, March 12, 1985; "Modifying Type A Behavior Reduces Heart Attacks" by Jane E. Brody, August 7, 1984. Copyright © 1984, 1985, 1986 by The New York Times Company. Reprinted by permission.

Library of Congress Catalog Card Number: 91-90633

ISBN 0-449-90717-1

Cover design by Dale Fiorillo
Cover photo: DPI, Inc.

Manufactured in the United States of America

First Ballantine Books Edition: August 1992

10 9 8 7 6 5 4 3 2

To Jean
and
To Jon

PREFACE

The idea for this book first glimmered twenty years ago while I was writing a biography of Franklin D. Roosevelt. Struggling to grasp that complex man's character, I stumbled across a psychological study that suggested a surprising linkage between two of his puzzling traits. The study was about people possessed by the fear of death. Such people are more likely than most, said the research report, to have suffered anguish in their early psychological separation from their mothers.

Reading the viscous text of that study, I recall, was hard going. But when I had finally slogged through its thick verbiage, it seized me for two reasons. First, I already knew that Roosevelt was as matter-of-fact about his own death as anyone could be. Years before he died, he had drawn a design for his tombstone and had prescribed the number of minutes for his funeral service, the precise departure time of the train bearing his coffin, and exactly which members of the government and press were to stand at his graveside. Certainly his separation from his mother—who was still bathing him after his eighth birthday—was gradual and secure in the extreme. Fascinating connection of those two traits. Imagine some researcher finding that out. Hmmm.

Which brought up the other reason the study interested me. If some scholar had researched his or her way to that insight, how many more glimpses into the mystery of the human soul had others turned up? Were all their studies tiny curlicued pieces of a great and fascinating jigsaw puzzle? How much of the whole picture had they put together?

They. Who are *they?* How is it that most of us know so little about what *they*—psychologists, social psychologists, sociologists, psychiatrists, even public opinion pollsters—have learned about *us?*

For years the thought nagged: Why not collect dozens—hundreds—of studies like the one I had come across, and put them in a book that would give *us*—those who are studied—some hints of the whole picture that *they* have been keeping to themselves?

True, not entirely to themselves. Those curlicued pieces do sometimes tumble out for the rest of us to see: in starkly simple items in *USA Today*, on *Donahue*. Those newsbits and pieces tickle us and trouble us and even push our lives around a bit. They may alter the ways we view our kids. They may make us wonder if our sex lives (that always *seemed* all right) meet some scientific standard of "good sex." Or they may help us explain to ourselves why we may not be popular with our peers ("How could I be? I was a firstborn child!").

My first experimental toe-dip into the library's vast pool of research was so discouraging, I still marvel that I didn't quit. Not because the scholars' works were hard to find or hard to understand. Not at all. On the contrary, what almost wore me out was that their simple insights, like small gifts disguised in oversize tissue-stuffed boxes, were often lost in billows of high-flown, overcontrived abstractions. The vocabulary! The sentences! The circumlocutory syntactical pretzels that passed for explanation and *thought*!

(I remember once chatting at a party with a sociologist about the exotic language of research. "Yes," he agreed, "it's very distantiating, isn't it?" "It's very what?" I asked. He looked at me queerly, as if I were a stranger in the dark. "Distantiating," he repeated, "you know—creating distance?" In contrast, the plainest language often throws their intellects off balance. I once mentioned to a social-psychologist friend a book in her field I had enjoyed. She said she had to read it twice. "The first time I didn't quite understand it," she said. "It was full of good ideas, but they were hidden—how shall I say?—hidden behind a wall of simple words.")

But for all the hard going, that early reading was surprisingly rewarding. Every time I successfully cracked the code of one of those research discoveries, do you know who I found hidden in the message? I found *me*. I found *you*. All that inscrutable talk is about *us*—and it's compelling stuff.

An example: A fairly typical study concluded that people of a certain personality type are likely to sprinkle salt on their food before they taste it; but people of the opposite personality type tend to taste their food first, and then salt it. For the moment, take my word that the distinction made between those two personality quirks may be very important in understanding the contrasting ways that I, you, your friends, and others around us experience the world. In fact, in a section near the end of this book called "Who's In Control Here?" (page 254), I suggest that that food-and-salting study may touch on the biggest little-known idea in all of psychology. In any case, for that study a team of University of Minnesota researchers visited four restaurants near campus, picked out twenty-four unsuspecting customers, and secretly watched as the customers salted their food. Then they approached the salters, asked them to volunteer for a psychological test, and matched the personality type of each against the salting habit. The results came out in the *Journal of Personality and Social Psychology,* a leading scholarly journal in its field. While the study itself is certainly simple enough, the *telling* of it is almost beyond the grasp of the ordinary mind.

It starts, as they all do, with an *abstract* in small type, a quick, easily digestible summary of the heart of the article, so that other scholars can just glance at it and decide whether to read the details or move on. Here is most of the "quick, easily digestible" summary of the food-and-salting experiment:

Two field observational studies were conducted to investigate the relationship between self-perceptions of situational versus dispositional causation of behavior and situational versus dispositional control of actual observed behavior. In each study it was found that individuals who ascribed relatively few traits to themselves (situational self-attribution) were particularly likely to salt their food after tasting it (situationally controlled behavior). By contrast, individuals who ascribed relatively many traits to themselves (dispositional self-attribution) were particularly likely to salt their food before tasting it (dispositionally controlled behavior). . . . The concepts of situational versus dispositional control of behavior are discussed and a reconceptualization proposed.

Wordy, you say? You wonder why they don't just tell us straight-out what they did and what the finding may mean?

My researchers and I, combing through indexes and computer searches for more, soon learned that university professors, under pressure from their deans to publish or perish, are churning out *more than 33,000 studies like that a year.* That's in the behavioral sciences alone.

One visible outcome of the publish-or-perish ethic has been a proliferation of *bubba* psychology. (That is a technical term borrowed from Yiddish to describe research results your grandmother could have told you without a federal grant.) There's a representative share of *bubba* psychology here, but don't let that turn you away. Some of the most trivial research findings on these pages may be the very ones that will most help you amuse and amaze the crowd at your next tea. One research grant helped establish (in case Bubba never told you) that two people in love tend to gaze directly into each other's eyes longer than two people who scarcely know each other. And a scholar at Loyola University in Chicago probed a panel of typical American women to determine their preferences in male body shapes. Science thus found that, by a significant margin, women prefer men shaped like Robert Redford to men shaped like Alfred Hitchcock. Another investigation demonstrated that 30 percent of bowlers, after scoring a strike or a spare, smile to themselves.

The discerning reader may also notice that an inordinate number of studies reported here are gleaned from a special subject population—people in their late teens or early twenties enrolled in college psychology courses. Does that suggest anything? Of course. They are the classroom students of the very professors who would rather publish than perish, but who are not about to venture dangerously into the outer world to do it. Thus, the college sophomore has become the Norway rat of American psychology. In 1974, someone even made a study of that, examining the three leading journals of social psychology, and found that college students were the subjects of 62 percent, 74 percent, and 87 percent, respectively, of all studies published in their pages that year. Most professorial researchers remain untroubled by this, however. When studying broad human characteristics, they argue, any human being is as valid a subject, more or less, as any other. Accept that or not, as you choose.

Despite those distractions, every study in these pages is a piece in the puzzle of human nature and some kind of clue to ourselves. If they don't fall readily into place to form a complete "big picture" of who we are, that should come as neither disappointment nor surprise. Psychology is an infant among sciences. Only a hundred years have passed since the pioneering publication, in 1890, of William James's *Principles of Psychology*, which "burst upon the world like a volcanic eruption." Sigmund Freud's *Studies in Hysteria* did not appear until 1895, followed by *The Interpretation of Dreams* in 1899.

So these studies are to be read and enjoyed not just as a search for *me* and for *you*. They are clues in a search for the character of the young science itself.

B. A.

ACKNOWLEDGMENTS

An important contribution to this book was made by Karen Wynn, who spent hundreds of hours in Pattee Library of Penn State University unearthing thousands of the original studies that led to my selection for these pages. She also made valuable suggestions toward forming the concepts of chapter and subchapter topics. To acknowledge those contributions, I happily add her name as a coauthor.

Regina Ryan, the book producer (a relatively new role in publishing), was as close to being a creative partner as I have had in a dozen previous books. Her enthusiasm for my initial idea and her editorial wisdom contributed to our long back-and-forth process of shaping a raw vision into what the book is today. By now, neither of us can quite tell which of us conceived this breakthrough idea or that one. I clearly remember, however, that the phrase "Look yourself up"—which crystallized the key concept of the book's structure—was hers. If, as author, I am this book's mother, she is its father.

A grant from the College of Liberal Arts of Penn State University helped finance computer searches and other research assistance, for which I am grateful.

I am indebted to Linda Friend, of the Pattee Library professional staff, for designing computer searches of the vast databases of social science research; also to Dr. Janet Swim, Dr. Judith Boswell, Doris Willens Kaplan, and Janet Sutta for reading portions of the manuscript and making helpful comments, as well as to Saramma Methratta and Eleanor Knight for additional research and editorial assistance.

At Random House I have not just one superb editor to thank, but two. Samuel S. Vaughan, old friend and partner in several books over many years, and Rebecca Saletan, the quickest mind in the East, collaborated in occasionally saving me from myself.

My devoted assistant, Nicki Caldwell, who knows her way as few do through the secret passageways of Pattee Library as well as those of my word-processing program, nursed this book through its every detail, every crisis, and every typed page.

B.A.

CONTENTS

WHAT THIS BOOK IS
AND HOW TO USE IT ...

. . . is what an introduction ought to explain. This introduction, however, needs also to explain what this book is *not* and how *not* to try to use it.

This is *not* a book of "pop psychology," although no doubt someone will call it that. Pop psychology melts the complex and subtle into the too-simple; it promises answers too large based on information too small. Worse, it offers facile rules for living where only difficult personal judgments will do. This book, on the other hand, is a survey of what human behavior researchers actually have been studying about us. You may criticize some of the studies here as too broad, too grand, too prying. You may take some to be so trivial as to seem like spoof or satire. If that's how they appear, so be it. This *is* what "they" have been studying. What has been changed is mainly the *language*—not to water down the research, but to raise it up to a more demanding level of clarity and avoidance of ambiguity.

While the "big picture" of human nature remains unrevealed (and may always remain so), the reader is invited to seek out surprising patterns of human tendencies and foibles that criss-cross and transcend the chapter topics. They abound here but, as in any good puzzle, you will have to find them yourself. One such pattern unexpectedly leaped at me—and the revelation may have altered my behavior.

The very first study reported in the first chapter might seem a curio—not too important. Look again. (You will see that all studies are categorized under a statement of some personal situation or condition. That is to help you locate yourself in all this research. Thus the heading "Look Yourself Up" is used to introduce the studies in each chapter.)

The book's opening "Look Yourself Up" study describes what

most often happens when a conversation starts among two or more strangers. Immediately, they engage in a game of "chicken" played with the eyes. One member of the group quickly establishes dominance by gazing the other(s) down. The others give way by averting their eyes. If the pair or group are of both sexes, the game is almost always won by a man. If the strangers are women only, one of them takes charge with *her* eyes, just as the man does when the pair is mixed. So this eye game that a man usually wins is apparently not about sex roles, but about power.

After reading that first item, read the second. Then the third. When I read them, something needled and gnawed at me. Under almost every chapter heading—whether the topic is your eyes, or your attractiveness, or your stresses, or your tendency to commit suicide, or your erotic responses, or your willingness to talk about yourself, or your marriage, or your divorce—the needle persisted. Almost every time men and women are studied as separate genders, the men come out as somehow taking over, and the women come out as accommodating or intimidated, in hidden, subtle ways that are far more insidious than daily life in a chauvinistic world had prepared me to expect.

Take another item, in the section "Your Willingness to Get (Physically) Close." A study there shows that when a man is seated next to a woman on an airliner, the odds are an overwhelming five to one that *he* takes over the armrest between them, no questions asked. Of course, there's an obvious explanation: He's probably bigger and needs the extra room. But hold on. The researchers separately observed couples in which the women were at least as sizeable as the men. What happens then? The men still take the armrest three to one.

Those are only two of dozens more that fill out a picture.

Organizing this book has raised my awareness as an army of evangelizing feminists might never have done. The pattern of such whole new levels of evidence—a pervasive, acrid mist of insidious, almost invisible acts of macho control—is more subtle, more stiletto-like, than I had ever imagined.

That's one hint of how this book has to be read. The picture of the culture is here for you to find—in your own way. It is not analyzed for you, not organized into big conclusions and answers. As in life, you have to fit the pieces into the "big picture" by yourself. But you may never have seen as many of the pieces in one place. If you are not a fan of jigsaw puzzles, jump in anyhow. Many of the pieces are surprises. Or provokers of shocks of recognition. Or objects d'art. Or rare bits of whimsy. Or knee-slappers.

One caution. Almost all the "Look Yourself Up" headings and almost all the studies here begin with the word *you*. You are admonished not to take *you* too literally. Which is to say, when the text says "you," it doesn't really mean *you*.

These studies are about *probabilities*, about *tendencies*. A study is about *you* personally only if you are perfectly average (and, of course, you are not). For example, a finding in these pages says that if you're tall and male, you tend to have higher self-esteem (also a higher salary!) than if you're short. That means that when a quantity of people take a psychological test measuring self-esteem, and when those same people are measured for height, more tall people get higher-than-average scores than short people do. High self-esteem is not the property of *all* tall people, and if you are tall, high self-esteem may not describe you. But statistically, it's more likely to than not to. In fact, the reason for your self-esteem may have more to do with the praise you got as a child for playing the violin than it has to do with your height. On the other hand, if you grew up being constantly criticized by your mother, and your father expected more of you than you could deliver, the chances are high that your self-esteem was battered, and your genes for tallness did little to help you.

Infinite, elusive, inscrutable complications like that—called *variables*—are what sometimes convince psychology majors to transfer to engineering. But these variables also keep life surprising, fresh, and, thank heavens, *unpredictable*, no matter how much "they" get to know about us.

The Book
of You

CHAPTER
1

Your Outer Self and What It Says About You

. . . No sooner met, but they looked;
No sooner looked but they loved.

SHAKESPEARE, *AS YOU LIKE IT*

YOUR EYES AND WHAT THEY EXPRESS

The human eye is called the "gateway to the mind." People come together by "seeing eye to eye." They read character by observing the shifty eye, the evil eye, the jaundiced eye.

Kingsley Amis, the novelist, once wrote about "the unspoken code which prohibits the eye from resting on a stranger for more than two seconds." Mark Cook of University College of Swansea, England, adds: "If someone is looked at by a stranger . . . he expects something to happen. . . . Indeed, in any situation, 'catching someone's eye' makes it almost obligatory to start an interaction: hence waiters and chairmen develop the ability to avoid eye contact."

Long before psychologists did—in fact, long before psychologists *were*—poets, playwrights, and just plain people knew that eye messages make us "expect something to happen," especially in courtship and sex. Casanova's lusty memoirs describe how, in the eighteenth century, the women of Madrid evaded the taboos of the day by relying on glances as covert invitations. To amplify, Stendhal, the nineteenth-century French novelist, pointed out that women invited men by gaze because the subtle message permitted denial of the invitation in case of change of mind or heart. Margaret Mead, in *Coming of Age in Samoa*, observed that courtship "conversation" on Bali consisted almost entirely of exchanges of furtive glances.

The eyes not only transmit but react. E. H. Hess, an eye-watching psychologist, found in 1965 that the pupils of the eye dilate when sighting something that stirs sexual arousal. He further found that men prefer photographs of women with enlarged pupils over those with smaller pupils (even if the enlargement has been brought about by retouching, and even though the men may be unconscious of the difference between them). Later studies showed that pupils enlarge at any pleasant sight and in fact whenever a person is involved in enjoyable thought, such as remembering a poem or solving a mathematical puzzle.

In the early 1960s, a few psychologists, particularly Ralph Exline of the University of Delaware, began to focus on the eyes as a medium of complex two-way wordless conversation. In fact, a major research field of social psychology—nonverbal communication—emerged from a decade of these studies, from 1965 to 1975, of what is called *gazing*—one person looking at another's eyes, or, more generally, at the upper half of the face.

These researchers have defined etiquettes for the eyes that vary from culture to culture. For example, white Americans and Europeans tend to look steadily at the talker while listening, but while talking, they look at the listener with short but frequent glances. American blacks do the opposite, averting the eyes while listening, making eye contact while talking. This could account for subtle discomforts sometimes felt between whites and blacks in conversation that can't reasonably be traced to prejudice, according to a study by Marianne La France and Clara Mayo of Boston University.

Another etiquette that varies from culture to culture is the use of eye contact in conversation as "turn-signals": a sign that a listener wants his turn to talk, or that a speaker has finished his turn.

Steady eye contact, or "mutual gaze," usually takes place during about one-third of conversational time. Such direct eye contact, however, soon becomes uncomfortable except where there is intimacy and deep trust.

One meaning of direct and sustained gazing has been enshrined by a study widely known and talked about among psychological researchers (and possibly also among the givers of ex-senator William Proxmire's Golden Fleece Awards, for research grants that make the eyes roll in disbelief). This study may be the most elaborate investigation of the obvious that science has ever turned loose. Three researchers at Illinois State University (see Goldstein et al) observed forty undergraduates (half of them male-female couples in "strong love" as tested by "Rubin's love scale" (see Chapter 5, "You and Your Lover"); the other half, male-female pairings who had just met). In addition, as the researchers meticulously specify, they employed two video cameras with zoom lenses, a split-screen viewer, two microphones, a "BRS/LVE Interact station controlled by a Data General Computer (Model 820) with a .01 second clock," and a specially designed and furnished conference room. The research platoon, thus armed, produced the following revelation: The "strong lovers," while sitting around idly waiting for some promised event to happen, conversed more with each other than the strangers did, and the lovers "spent more time in pure gazing" into each other's eyes than did the subjects who had just met.

Studies of gazing do, however, often suggest broader questions of human behavior. For example, this question: Are women, in general, truly more comfortable talking to other women than men are to other men, as modern folk wisdom often tells us? The answer seems to be yes. An Oxford University study by Michael Argyle and others found that two women conversing are likely to hold mutual gaze almost twice as long as two men (38 percent of the time versus 23 percent). In a gender-mixed conversation, the man and woman hold mutual gaze 31.5 percent of the time, no matter which one is doing the talking. And why does the longer gaze suggest greater comfort? In general, according to another British study by Mark Cook and J.M.C. Smith, the more a person is looked at during conversation, the more that person is likely to report feeling liked by the other. But there are limits to the lengths of the looks that we like. The longer gaze, ordinarily preferred, becomes oppressive when it exceeds the outside norm for lovers and trusting intimates of approximately three quarters of conversational time.

Eyes speak a language of displeasure and hostility as well as affection. An experimenter (Exline again, in partnership with Winters) interviewed college students, supposedly about "concept formation." Halfway through each interview, he interrupted to "evaluate" how the student was doing. He told one third (without relationship to how they really were "doing") that their performance was very poor; another third that they were doing very well; and to the rest remained noncommital. Meanwhile, the subjects' eye movements were being photographed on rapidly successive frames for later measurement. After being told they were "very poor performers," subjects, without a single exception, looked at the experimenter significantly less often than they had before receiving the bad news. Later on, most of these "poor performers" reported a strong dislike for the experimenter.

When we are challenged to think about something, we usually look slightly upward, and either to the right or to the left. Merle E. Day, a psychologist at the Downey Illinois Veterans Administration Hospital, reported in 1964 that each of us can be classified as a right-mover or a left-mover, in that each person tends to turn eyes in the same direction about 75 percent of the time. (Women are less consistent than men in this regard.) The number of right-movers and left-movers are about equal in any large group.

Day then discovered that the direction of the eye-turn appears to be a marker of a wide variety of psychological and physiological characteristics. Left-movers and right-movers differ in their degree of attention, use of language, brain-wave pattern, muscle tone, and response to psychotherapy.

A left-mover, according to Day, tends to have a heightened awareness of subjective, internal experiences. More recently, Paul Bakan of Simon Fraser University found that left-movers are significantly more susceptible to hypnosis than right-movers, as measured by the Stanford Hypnotic Susceptibility Scale, a standard test. Bakan has also found that left-movers score higher than right-movers in the verbal section of the Scholastic Aptitude Test (SAT) as well as show greater fluency in writing, while right-movers tend to score higher in the mathematics portion. Not surprisingly, therefore, right-movers are more likely to major in science and quantitative studies, while left-movers are more likely to study the humanities. Bakan further reports that right-movers are more likely to twitch and have tics than left-movers, spend less time asleep (if they're males), prefer cool colors, and make earlier choices of a career. Left-movers, on the other hand, tend to imagine more vividly, are more sociable, more likely to become alcoholics (if they're males), and are more likely to report themselves as musical and religious. Bakan reports tentatively that left-movers are more likely to have asthma, while right-movers are more prone to headache, especially migraine.

To find out whether you are a right-mover or a left-mover may be troublesome, because the simple effort of trying to find out may cause a self-consciousness that may stand in the way of an answer. Perhaps all you can do is to start becoming aware of the direction in which you usually flick your eyes when you confront a problem or question. Determining a friend's tendency ought to be easier if the friend doesn't know what you're trying to find out. Just face her/him fairly straight-on, and ask a few questions like the following:

1. How do you spell *perpendicular* (or, for that matter, *parallel*)?
2. What is the product of 11 by 15?
3. How would you define *virtue* (or *sin*, or *mashed potatoes*)?

Ignore the answers. Just watch the eyes.

LOOK YOURSELF UP

The following is a selection of key research conclusions on "Your Eyes and What They Express," translated into plain English. Some are listed because of their importance, others because they are surprising, curious, or even amusing. Any of them, however, may shed some unexpected light on you or someone you know. For that reason, these additional studies, here and in each section of the book, are organized and phrased to help you "look yourself up."

You are a woman or man in conversation with one or two strangers:

As soon as you meet, you and the other strangers spend your first few seconds in what looks like a game of "chicken," played with the eyes. One of you quickly, almost imperceptibly, speaks first and gazes the other(s) down, thus establishing dominance. If the group or pair is sex-mixed, the game is almost always won by a man, because women tend to avert their eyes from men when gazed at. In fact, if you are the rare woman who speaks first, you tend to avert your gaze as you do so. If you are the even rarer woman who offers a "gaze challenge," you don't have much chance of winning because a man usually refuses to accept it. When both members of a pair are women, one of them consistently uses her eyes to assume dominance, just as the man does when the pair is mixed. That suggests that the game is one of power rather than of sexual identification.

This was concluded from an experiment involving forty-two women and thirty-three men, sociology students aged eighteen to thirty, who were videotaped as they talked in groups of two or three. [Lamb] (Note to the reader: Lamb is the name of the researcher-author of this study. At the end of every study summary that follows in this book, the author's name will similarly appear in brackets. A list of published sources of all cited studies can be found, alphabetized by the principal researcher's name, beginning on page 271. The listings are grouped by chapter.)

If you score high in a test for social skills, you drop your eyes less and maintain your eye contact longer than someone who scores low; also, you ask more questions and use appropriate hand gestures more freely. [Royce]

If you are a woman, you probably gaze at others steadily (in the manner of dominant men) when you feel expert in a discussion subject. When the subject changes to one in which you do not feel expert, you will usually avert your gaze exactly as less dominant men or most other women do. [Ellyson, Dovidio, Corson]

You tend to maintain your eye contact longer with a stranger when you're attracted to him or her—or if you're trying to decipher his or her attitudes. [Rutter, Stephenson; British study]

The more closely you are required by the physical or social situation to stand near each other, the less eye contact you make and the shorter the duration of your glances, especially if you're of the opposite sex. [Argyle, Dean; British study]

You are conversing with a person of higher status than yourself:

You probably don't hold a steady gaze, but tend to glance at her or him dartingly. For that matter, the higher status person doesn't look straight at you very much, either. As the principal researcher of this study has pointed out, "Powerful people do not monitor the less powerful." [Exline, et al]

You converse with your spouse:

The more comfortable you are with your marriage, the less you and your husband or wife look at each other as you talk. If you are a poorly adjusted couple, on the other hand, you glance often, each of you seeming to monitor the other's reactions, particularly after a criticism or barb. [Noller]

You are a woman conversing with a man:

When a man holds steady eye contact with you, he probably feels one of three ways: He (a) considers you attractive, or (b) has a high opinion of himself, or (c) both, which contributes to a notably long, steady gaze. Not surprisingly, if he finds you unattractive and/or thinks little of himself, his eye contact is jumpy and brief. [Fugita, Agle, Newman, Walfish]

If you are meeting him for drinks in the company of others, before you down your first one you're apt to make more eye contact with another woman than with a man, at least if you act the way most people do in Finland. On the other hand, after a few drinks, you're likely to avoid eye contact with another woman. With the man or men, however, you're likely to continue eye contact at about the same rate after drinking as before. [Lindman; Finnish study]

You are a man conversing with a woman:

If she gazes dolefully into your eyes, she is more likely to win your sympathy, right? Right. The researchers determined this with the following "sympathy test": A woman (a confederate in the research project) "inadvertently" left a dime on the shelf of a phone booth—

in fact, she did so repeatedly, every time she saw the booth unoccupied. Twenty seconds after someone began a conversation, the confederate interrupted the caller, politely reporting the mislaid dime and asking for it back. She gazed directly into the eyes of half of the callers, and got many more dimes returned by them than from the "control group"—the half she didn't gaze at. (Incidentally, she also touched the arms of half the callers in each group while asking—and got more dimes back from those touched than those not touched. But gazing alone worked better than touching alone.) [Kleinke]

You see a woman or man in need of help:

If you are a woman, you are more likely—40 percent more likely—to help another woman if she "touches eyes" with you than if she doesn't. In this experiment, a research confederate (four were used in all: two women, age eighteen and twenty; two men, age twenty-one and twenty-four), dressed in jeans and a pullover and wearing an armsling, is waiting at a bus stop and trying to get coins out of a pants pocket on the same side as the sling, presumably a heart-plucking maneuver to watch. She or he finally does so, but drops about eight coins on the ground. In half the incidents, the confederate made momentary eye contact with a randomly chosen bystander, and in half the incidents did not.

If you are a man, and if a man needing help looks you right in the eye, in contrast to the woman above, you're *less* likely—28 percent less likely—to stop and help him if he "touches eyes" than if he doesn't. The researchers speculate that because men use their eyes as a tool of dominance, eye contact between men is threatening; for women, it's a signal of friendliness. [Valentine, Ehrlichman]

Someone whose trustworthiness you want to assess is looking you straight in the eye:

That's a good sign that the person is telling you the truth, right? Wrong. A man who is lying to another man is just as likely to keep steady eye contact as one who is telling the truth. When a man is lying to a woman, however, he is likely to gaze longer than when telling her the truth. Similarly, a woman lying to another woman is apt to gaze longer than when telling the truth, and *much* longer when lying to a man. [Burns, Kintz]

You tend to lower your eyebrows (as one does when glowering):

People perceive you as a more dominant person than someone who tends to raise his or her eyebrows. [Keating, Mazur, Segall]

You are driving and are stopped by a cop who gets out of his cruiser and approaches you:

You probably feel pronounced suspicion, hostility, and fear if the policeman is wearing mirrored sunglasses, thus preventing you from seeing his eyes. [Boyanowsky, Griffiths; Canadian study]

You are a male jogger:

If you jog past a park bench where a young woman sits facing your running path, you will speed up your running pace significantly even though she's showing no sign of looking at you. But you'll maintain your accustomed lope if her back is turned to the path. [Worringham, Messick]

You are eating alone in a cafeteria and, without saying a word or doing anything that would attract general attention, you'd like to cause a stranger alone at another table to get up and leave sooner than he or she ordinarily would:

Easy. Just stare at the person eating.
    Want to get especially fast results? Pick out a stranger who's overweight to stare at. [Lee, Goldman]

    Related to that finding comes this additional morsel of science, contributed by Stanford University: If you are standing at a street corner where cars are waiting for a light to change, you can cause a waiting driver to make a faster-than-average getaway by fixing an expressionless stare on him or her. If you stare at a pedestrian waiting for the light, she or he will cross faster, too. [Ellsworth, Carlsmith, Henson]

There's language in her eye, her cheek, her lip,
Nay, her foot speaks; her wanton spirits look out
At every joint and motive of her body.

SHAKESPEARE, *TROILUS AND CRESSIDA*

BODY LANGUAGE, TOUCHING, AND BEING TOUCHED

In 1872, years before social psychology was invented as a field of study, Charles Darwin observed that wherever he traveled in the world, facial expressions appeared to have universal meaning. Whether in Iceland or London or the Galápagos, gladness turns the ends of the mouth upward, and the face of anger everywhere looks like anger anywhere. The same for happiness, sadness, disgust, fear, surprise.

But while those expressions are the same all over the world, the rules vary as to when—or by whom and to whom—such displays are acceptable. A tribesman does not glare angrily at his tribal chief, nor a wise Westerner at her or his boss. Among traditional middle-class Americans, girls are pressured to learn never to show anger, while boys are supposed to learn never, never to be caught looking afraid. When a young beauty is crowned Miss America, people adore her if she sheds tears while all the world watches. But no crying allowed for runners-up.

Body language—posture, gestures, and touching—is as eloquent as the face, and also communicates beyond cultural boundaries, even though it has a more complex vocabulary and is often more subtle.

How powerful is nonverbal language? Powerful enough to wipe out completely the messages of speech. A study by Albert Mehrabian (of the University of California at Los Angeles) and S. R. Ferris shows that when something is expressed through facial expression or body gesture, *and* simultaneously through contradictory spoken words, the receiver will react almost entirely to the nonverbal message. For example, if a talker says, "Shut your mouth!" or even more rudely, "Drop dead!"—and if that slashing command is tempered by even the faintest smile—the message will be read not as what the words say, not even as a confusing or mixed message, but as an expression of humor and affection. The nonverbal language vetoes and transforms the verbal. The opposite, however, is generally not true: Words rarely cancel a message the body sends.

Like knowing any language, understanding the rudiments of body language can be valuable to anyone, either for "reading" or "talking." Everyone "reads" some amount of body language, picking up messages on at least an unconscious level. Becoming more conscious of it as a language is bound to increase anyone's "reading" accuracy. The other side, of course, is that fluency in body language can enable anyone to use it for sending powerful messages that instill impressions, that persuade, that cover and conceal attitudes and feelings a person may not wish to reveal. Yes, body language, the great truthsayer, probably can be used by an unusually skilled practitioner as a tool of concealment and deceit.

LOOK YOURSELF UP

You are conversing with an acquaintance or friend:

If your conversational partner leans his or her head or body in imitation of yours, or holds his legs or arms or hands in a way that imitates yours, that person is probably in tune with you, with how you are thinking, with what you are saying. The postures of you and your partner may be either "carbon copies" of one another or "mirror images." Such imitation is called "postural congruence," or "confluence," or, fancier still, "interactional synchrony." [Scheflen, 1974, summarizing many studies by himself and others]

The congruence of your postures (or absence of it) is more than a mere signal of harmony or disharmony. It is part of a complex and continuing mutual checking-out between the two of you that guides the conversational direction—especially guiding the one of you who may have an interest in "bringing the other around" to a particular point of view. The researcher suggests that the "conversation" of gestures and posture "provides one of the ways in which two people signal that they are 'open' to one another." (These observations were obtained from microanalysis of large quantities of sound film of people in conversation.) [Kendon]

A person leaning forward while talking to you probably likes you more than one who leans back while talking to you. A forward lean is likely to communicate "warmth" and "attentiveness" or "attention." That tendency is true regardless of sex. [Mehrabian, 1968 (2),

1969; Haase, Tepper, 1972; Tepper, 1973; Reece, Whitman, 1961, 1962; Genthner, Moughan, 1977; Rosenfeld, Hancks]

Another researcher found that this forward lean and body congruence, as well as steady eye contact, may mean just the opposite if the leaner's or looker's body language is accompanied by facial cues that bespeak wariness or skepticism. The expression of the face is the telltale clue that determines the real message of the body. [Waldron]

If your conversational partner is your psychotherapist—or if you're the shrink and the partner is your client—your congruence of gesture and posture, and the leaning-in signal, indicate that the two of you are probably feeling the kind of rapport that is likely to contribute to progress in therapy. [Trout, Rosenfeld]

If you are a teacher of a college seminar, the degree to which particular students mirror your posture tends to match their reports of how involved they feel in your class. [La France, Broadbent; La France, 1979]

If you maintain a steady level of vocal intensity and a regular rhythm of occasional silences, your partner, no matter what her or his usual speech habits, is highly likely to adapt to your pattern, moving toward imitating it. [Natale]

Once you know someone fairly well, you establish an "equilibrium level" of intimacy—some comfortable balance of distance and eye contact that seems right for the kinds of personalities and dealings you have. Once this is established, you will both carefully adjust your "distance" behavior with one another to maintain that equilibrium. Specifically, if one of you sits closer to the other than usual, the other will respond with more "distant" eye contact to rebalance the equilibrium. And vice versa: If one of you gazes at the other more steadily and intensely than usual, the other will rebalance by moving away. [Argyle, Dean]

You are trying to persuade somebody to your point of view:

You'll increase your likelihood of winning the other person over if you sit with an "open" body posture—elbows away from the body, legs stretched out, rather than elbows close and knees pressed together. [McGinley, LeFevre, McGinley]

You'll also help your cause by making direct eye contact, by keeping "body congruence" (see the previous item), by not shifting your posture nervously—and by picking a persuasion target who likes you to begin with.

You'll especially enhance your chances for successful persuasion if the other person is sitting down or reclining, rather than standing. Whether you're sitting or standing doesn't matter. [Petty, Wells, Heesacker, Brock, Cacioppo].

To touch is the beginning of every act of possession,
of every attempt to make use
of a person or thing.

SIGMUND FREUD (1856–1939), *TOTEM AND TABOO*

YOUR WILLINGNESS TO TOUCH AND BE TOUCHED

Touching someone seems a simple form of body language. *Simple?* Touching is fraught with possible interpretations and misinterpretations, conscious and unconscious.

Nancy Henley, of the University of California at Los Angeles, monitored the physical contact of large numbers of pairs of people in public places for her deliciously titled book, *Body Politics.* Among adults appearing to be under thirty, she found that men touched women with the hand significantly more often than women touched men. Henley went on to speculate that the reason for this asymmetry was that superior status gave men a "touching privilege."

That finding, published in 1973, and especially Henley's speculative explanation of it, generated a rash of "touching studies," the most consistent outcome of which has been their contradiction and uncertainty. In fact, in two later studies by Henley herself—one observing touchers appearing to be ten or more years older than those touched; the other, touchers and touchees appearing to be over thirty and roughly equal in age—she failed to find a significant difference in touching between men and women.

In 1984, two Harvard psychologists, Deborah Stier and Judith Hall, reviewed and analyzed forty-three touching studies (by others) that had taken place over the previous decade, and they came to a conclusion that directly contradicted Henley's: that women initiate touching more than men.

Henley's speculation about status and dominance does have support from other research. As early as 1967, Erving Goffman, a body-language pioneer, found that in a large hospital doctors touched people of lower rank, but lower ranks didn't dare initiate the touching of doctors.

Perhaps the most interesting finding about male-female touching arose from the questioning of men and women about what it would mean to them if a close friend of the opposite sex touched them in a certain manner (a stroke, say, as against a pat), and in various locations of the body. The researchers, Tuan Nguyen, Richard Heslin, and Michele Nguyen, found that men are considerably more sensitive than women about the manner of the touch. Women pay more attention to its location.

LOOK YOURSELF UP

You have been conversing with someone you've just met, and at the end of the talk that person lightly touches you:

If you're both men, you're more likely (in a questionnaire after the encounter) to give the other person a high rating as a "nice guy" if he patted you on the back than if he touched you on the arm. If you're both women, *or* if one of you is a woman and the other a man, you'll probably rate the other person as more likable if she or he touched you on the arm rather than patted your back. [Hewitt]

Where do you feel "safe" being touched? That depends on the sex of the toucher. Suppose the stranger who touched you after you'd just met (as above) "accidentally" dropped a sheaf of papers. Will you help pick up the papers?

If that person is a woman, you're more likely to help if the place she touched you was on the upper arm—more likely than if she touched you on the shoulder, on the lower arm, on the hand, or didn't touch you at all. Whether you, as the recipient of the touch, are a man or a woman makes no difference.

If the stranger is a man, you're *less* likely to help if he touches you than if he doesn't, especially if you're a woman. [Paulsell, Goldman]

You are a black man in a bowling alley, playing with other black men:

You are three times more likely than white bowlers to touch one of your companions during a game. Two thirds of your touches acknowledge a success, either yours or someone else's, such as scoring a strike. Fully 82 percent of the touches are hand to hand. [Smith, Willis, Gier]

You are a white man in a bowling alley, playing with other white men:

You and other white players not only touch each other less often than blacks (see previous item), but you're more likely to touch parts of the body other than hands. Only a quarter of the touches are related to success. [Smith, Willis, Gier]

You are a white woman in a bowling alley, playing with other white women and white men:

In an evening's play, you are likely to be touched ten times on the shoulder by a man, but you probably don't touch a man at all. (The survey doesn't report whether you touch other women or they touch you.) [Smith, Willis, Gier]

You watch a woman and man, both strangers to you, having a conversation:

You're likely to prejudge their personalities simply by whether you see them touch—and who touches whom. If you see the woman touch the man at the end of the conversation, the chances are you'll rate her as dominant or masculine, and you'll rate the man as passive or feminine. If he touches her, you're apt to judge him strong and properly manly.

For this study, college students watched three videotape versions of a conversation between a man and a woman and were then asked to rate the personalities of the two on a list of characteristics. The ratings varied consistently in accordance with one act: who touched whom at the end of the conversation. [Forden]

You are checking a book out of a library, and as the clerk returns your library card, his or her hand makes an "accidental" brushing contact with yours:

There's about a 50 percent chance you notice the touch (or so those who were touched reported on a questionnaire a few moments after the experimental incident). Regardless of whether you report noticing the contact or not, if you were touched you're more likely to say you liked the library and thought the clerk was nice than if you were in a "control group" who didn't get touched. (Obviously, the clerk was a research confederate.) Whether the clerk-toucher was a man or a woman doesn't make any difference in your reaction—although if *you* are a woman you're more apt to have reported liking the "accidental" touch than if you're a man. [Fisher, Rytting, Heslin]

You are chatting with a friend in a coffee shop:

If you are Americans chatting in a coffee shop in Gainesville, Florida, you probably touch each other twice an hour.

If you are English and chatting in a London coffee shop, you probably do not touch each other at all.

If you are French and chatting in a Parisian cafe, you touch each other 110 times an hour.

If you are Puerto Rican and chatting in a San Juan coffee shop, you touch each other 180 times an hour. [Jourard; British study]

Now my soul hath elbow-room.

SHAKESPEARE, *KING JOHN*

YOUR WILLINGNESS TO GET (PHYSICALLY) CLOSE

Each of us protects his feelings of safety and comfort by living in a "bubble" of protective space that we unconsciously maintain around ourselves—"an area with an invisible boundary . . . into which intruders may not come," says Robert Sommer, a leading researcher of "personal space."

The size of this protective bubble changes according to momentary circumstances, our feelings of trust toward an approaching person, our personality, previous experiences, age, sex, and ethnic origin. Anyone entering this buffer zone makes us feel jittery, particularly if the intruder is a stranger, and we hastily adjust our protective distance even as we carry on doing something else. Most people aren't particularly aware of a needed distance from another until the distance is "wrong." What fascinates researchers is when and how we shrink or enlarge or reshape the bubble in response to changed conditions. Every individual's demand for personal space keeps shifting, almost moment to moment. For example, when two people increase their distance from one another they often lengthen their duration of eye contact, as though adjusting an "equilibrium level," as described in "Body Language," earlier in this chapter.

At first, research interest in human personal space was intertwined with dramatic findings about crowding of animal populations, particularly rats and deer. When these animals collect too densely in confined areas, their social structures crumble in "behavioral sinks." They descend into unaccustomed violence, extremes of indolence, and attempts by males to overpower and sexually mount other males. These berserk reactions to crowding are attributable to a drain of adrenalin brought on by sustained crises of "fight or flight." In some groups of animals, such crowding has led to "population collapse"—mass deaths.

One of the first scholars to probe human requirements of space was not a psychologist, but an anthropologist. He was Edward T. Hall of Northwestern University whose 1959 book, *The Silent Language,* has become a landmark. In that and later works, Hall showed that the peoples of the world could be divided into two categories of modes of reaction to personal space: "contact cultures" (among them, Arabs and Latins), who like to talk and intermingle closely and who touch one another freely and frequently; and "noncontact cultures" (Northern Europeans and most North Americans), who shun touching, dislike high densities, and prefer to stand or sit with relative distance from non-intimates.

The most common way personal space preference is measured in the laboratory is by the researcher observing in designed rooms how subjects place their chairs and position their bodies; also, how close they let a researcher approach them before they somehow signal that they feel uncomfortable. Another way is to ask subjects of an experiment to place on a board, at distances that seem appropriate, paper dolls, drawings, miniature figures, or other representations of people.

The notion of a "proper distance" is so deeply trained into most people that these two widely different methods often (but not always) produce the same answers.

Learning one's own rules of "right distance" in particular situations can help people promote social comfort; it can also explain subtle discomforts felt by themselves and others. Developing sensitivity to needs for personal space can be of critical importance in arranging furniture for a comfortable "conversational distance" (a foot this way or that can make a big difference in encouraging relaxed and frank conversation), for choosing restaurant tables or seating for interviews, and for keeping the talk formal or promoting intimacy. All the social niceties or bright humor or solemnity one might invoke to make an occasion "right" may not make up for a distance—too large or too small—that feels "wrong" for a particular encounter.

LOOK YOURSELF UP

You are a student at work in a library:

You are likely to build barricades of books or clothing to keep strangers at a distance. If you are a woman, you usually pile your belongings to your sides. If you are a man you more probably block the area in front of you. [Fisher, Byrne]

You are riding in an elevator:

Whether you're a man or a woman, you're likely to stand closer to a stranger if he or she smiles at you. Also, you'll permit a short stranger to stand twice as close as a tall stranger. If you're a man, you'll stand closer to a woman than to another man. If you're a woman, you'll allow either a man or a woman to stand closer to you than will a man, and you will let a stranger stand closer to your sides than to your front. [Lockard, McVittie, Isaac]

You observe that a stranger in a room is gradually moving closer to you:

You'll show symptoms of alertness or anxiety sooner if the ceiling is low than if it is high. [Cochran, Urbanczyk]

You are standing and conversing with someone:

If you've been told in advance that that person and you have certain attitudes in common, you're likely to stand (or sit) closer than if you've been told the person has opposing attitudes. [Byrne, Ervin, Lamberth]

If the two of you are standing in a shopping mall almost blocking an escalator, shoppers are quite likely to barge between you to get to the moving stairs. An exception, however, is if either you or your companion is pregnant. In that case, shoppers are only half as likely to invade the personal space between you and your friend, stepping around you instead. [Davis, Lennon]

If the person you're talking to is a stranger of the opposite sex, you'll want more distance from him or her than from someone you know, or from a person of your own sex. This is true whether you are old or young, black or white, male or female. If you are a white woman, however, you're willing to get closer to the other person than if you're either a white man or a black woman. If you're a black man starting a conversation with a stranger, you're likely to move closer than a white man or either a white or black woman does, especially if the stranger is male. But if the stranger approaches you, you're likely to avoid closeness, especially if the stranger is a woman. Finally, the older you are, the less space you need around you to feel comfortable. This is particularly so if you are white. [Severy, Forsyth, Wagner]

If you are white, you prefer more space between conversational partners than blacks do, says a study by a doctoral candidate at the University of Iowa. In that study, subjects looked at photographs of people conversing, then chose pictures where the distance between speakers seemed "right." The choice ranged from 12 to 84 inches. Whites liked a distance of 26 to 28 inches best; blacks, 21 to 24 inches. When the distance exceeded 36 inches, blacks sensed the conversation was beclouded by trouble; whites didn't feel that way until 44 inches. Both blacks and whites picked the same "comfort" distances for depictions of the other race as for their own. [Connolly]

If your conversational companion is smoking a cigarette and you are a nonsmoker, you won't be surprised to learn that you probably stand at a greater distance from the smoker than you would from someone who is not smoking. However, if you're a smoker yourself, you're likely to stand at an even greater distance from the other smoker than a nonsmoker would. In fact, if you're a smoker, your choice of distance is so pronounced that the researchers speculate that your need for so much extra space might be a reason you took up smoking in the first place. [Kunzendorf, Denney]

If the person you're talking to is blind, either partially or totally, that person is likely to feel the distance is "right" or "wrong" in exactly the same ranges as sighted persons. The researchers, themselves surprised at their results, concluded that blind persons, without visual information as an aid, clearly develop the same sense of "proper" distance as everybody else. [Hayduk, Mainprize; Canadian study]

You are sitting and talking with someone you don't know:

If you're a man, the farther you sit from the other person (within a range of two to ten feet), the more willing you are to talk intimately about yourself. If you're a woman, the closer you sit together (within a range of two to ten feet), the more willing you are to tell intimate details about yourself. [Skotko]

Within that range of two to ten feet, whether you're a man or woman, you'll talk with a stranger longest and volunteer the most about intimate topics at a distance of five feet. [Stone, Morden; Canadian study]

If you're a woman talking to two men you don't know, and one of them is sitting noticeably closer to you than the other, you're likely to assume that the one sitting closer to you happens to be there by pure chance, but that the one further away has purposely rejected you. If you're a man in a similar arrangement with two women, you're likely to feel that the closer woman has been enticed to sit near you, while the one farther away just happened there by chance. [Deaux, Farris]

If you are a man sitting and conversing with someone who attracts you, either male or female, you're more comfortable sitting face to face than shoulder to shoulder. If you're a woman conversing with someone who attracts you, you're more comfortable sitting shoulder to shoulder than face to face. [Fisher, Byrne]

If you're a woman, you're also likely to think jokes are funnier when you're sitting side by side with the joke-teller than when you are face to face. [Yates, Miller]

If you're in a room with a total stranger, whether you are a man or a woman, the distance among chairs and sofas has no discernible bearing on whether you'll chat with the other person. But you're less likely to talk if the furnishings require that you sit side by side, as on a couch, than if the placement of furniture leads you to face one another. If either of you test out as highly sociable, the side-by-side sitting arrangement is especially inhibiting. Also, if you're the kind who feels sensitive to rejection, thus tending to keep to yourself, you're more likely to start talking in the presence of a conspicuous "conversation piece," like a sculpture, but less likely to do so if there's a puzzle lying around that might occupy you. [Mehrabian, Diamond]

You are a man seated next to a woman on an airliner:

The odds are an overwhelming five to one that you'll take over the armrest between you, no questions asked. Aha, you say, but men tend to be larger and therefore need the extra room. To check that out, the researchers divided the 426 men and 426 women they observed on twenty commercial airline flights into two subgroups: one in which the men were larger than the women, and the other in which the women were at least as sizeable as the men. When size difference was thus factored out, the men still took over the armrest three to one.

Is that another example of unconscious male domination? No. It seems that both the men and the women are quite conscious of their elbow war. One young man, interviewed at an airport, asserted, "I feel I deserve to have it. She doesn't." Of fifty-six men and forty-five women interviewed, the men under forty years of age surprised the researchers by expressing far more anger than their elders when they lost the armrest to a woman. [Hai]

You are a student choosing a seat in a college classroom:

If you are a white Anglo-Saxon Protestant, you are significantly more likely than others to take a seat near the center of the room. If you are black or Hispanic, you are more likely than others to choose a seat on the periphery of the room. If you are Jewish and your parents or grandparents were immigrants to the United States, you are more likely than a third-generation Jewish-American to choose a peripheral seat. If you are black, you tend to arrive at the classroom earlier than most whites; your reason for doing so, in the judgment of the researchers, is to make sure to get a seat on the periphery of the room.

Observations and questionnaires for this study were gathered in classes in fourteen separate disciplines at a summer session in a Maryland university. Each class had fifteen to forty students and at least one third of the seats were unoccupied, to insure free choice. [Haber]

You're talking with someone who has insulted and angered you:

Your "required space bubble" expands in size. It also expands, but not as much, in the presence of someone who is indirectly associated with the insult. [O'Neal, Brunault, Carifio, Troutwine, Epstein]

You are a male prisoner serving a sentence for a violent crime:

Your bubble of required personal space is larger than that of a nonviolent criminal, and will remain so after both of you are released from prison. More than the nonviolent man's, your space bubble bulges to the rear, as though to protect you from rear-flank attacks. [O'Neal, Brunault, Carifio, Troutwine, Epstein]

You are a roommate and sometimes feel crowded:

If you share a room for two in a university residence hall, your score on a standard psychological test called the Self-Perception Assessment is likely to be higher than that of someone who has lived squeezed into a room for three. The self-perception test measures your general feeling of control over situations in your life. The higher score, presumably a consequence of feeling less cramped, indicates that as a two-to-a-roomer you are less susceptible to feeling overly stressed, and that you feel a higher-than-average overall competence and a better ability to adapt to new situations. [Hughey]

In the United States there is more space
where nobody is than where anybody is.

GERTRUDE STEIN (1874–1946)

You are two years old and in day-care:

You keep greater distances from other children than you will at four or five years old, when you'll play more with others. At about six, you'll enlarge your required distance from others, especially if you're a boy. In fact, your need for distance will continue to enlarge until you are about twelve, when your personal bubble will have grown to the size you'll prefer as an adult. [Sarafino, Halmuth]

You are a man trying to urinate in a public lavatory:

You will start micturating (yep, that's the term the study uses) later and stop sooner if someone is similarly engaged two urinals away from you than you will if your nearest peer is at the third urinal away or even further.

That is the finding of a meticulous study conducted by a network of three professors in widely separated major universities (Oklahoma State, Ohio State, and Wisconsin). A few direct quotations from their six-page article in the leading scholarly publication of their academic discipline, *The Journal of Personality and Social Psychology*, provide insight into how rigorous and precise the demands of behavioral research can be; also into how the quest to verify a large-scale hypothesis may lead an imaginative researcher into hidden corners of specifics.

Their article first reviews many studies supporting their overarching hypothesis that "invasions of personal space are interpersonally stressful, increasing arousal and discomfort," as manifested in changes in blood pressure, sweatiness of palms, skin resistance to electricity, and more. But those findings all are suspect, write our micturation researchers, because they are all experimental, drawn from unrealistic laboratories in which subjects may be wired with instruments and the like, and in which they've been told either the true goal of the experiment or some cock-and-bull story to disguise it, either case leading to probable nervousness of the subject. Who can really trust such results? Therefore, our researchers write:

"As an alternative to the laboratory, a men's lavatory provides a setting where personal space violations can occur in a natural yet sufficiently standardized way. Although . . . the bathroom evokes concerns for privacy among members of the middle class, public facilities do not allow complete privacy, particularly in the case of men urinating. . . .

"A field observation conducted at a men's lavatory at a Western U.S. university provided evidence for a correlation between interpersonal distance and micturation times. Men entering a restroom to urinate were allowed to choose a urinal under prevailing ecological conditions. . . . The restroom contained two banks of five urinals, which were bowl-type receptacles jutting out of the wall and containing about 3 inches (8 cm.) of standing water, which the user flushed.

"An observer was stationed at the sink facilities and appeared to be grooming himself. When a potential subject entered the room and walked to a urinal, the observer recorded the selected urinal and the placement of the next nearest user. He also noted (with a chronographic wristwatch) and recorded the micturation delay (the time between when the subject unzipped his fly and when urination began) and the micturation persistence (the time between the onset and completion of urination). The onset and cessation of micturation were signaled by the sound of the stream of urine striking the water of the urinal.

"Of the 48 subjects recorded, none selected a urinal immediately adjacent to another user. Twenty-three were separated by one urinal from the nearest user, 16 were separated by two urinals, and 9 were separated by three or more. . . . Subjects standing one urinal away had a mean delay of 7.9 seconds, subjects two spaces away had a delay of 5.9 seconds, and subjects three or more spaces away had a delay of 5.7 seconds. . . .

"The pattern of results supports the hypothesis . . ." the researchers conclude triumphantly, that "both micturation delay and persistence were shown to be related to interpersonal distance." [Middlemist, Knowles, Matter]

What is beautiful is good,
And who is good will soon be beautiful.

SAPPHO OF LESBOS,
GREEK POET (C. 612 B.C.)

YOUR DEGREE OF ATTRACTIVENESS

Physical attractiveness, as everybody knows, is only skin deep, so serious researchers in human behavior can't be expected to take it seriously, can they? In fact, they didn't—until 1969.

That was the year, at a symposium in Nebraska, that Elliott Aronson, a prominent social psychologist, put beauty on the map.

Challenging his colleagues to look for more in fair features than meets the eye, Aronson declared: "Most psychologists implicitly *prefer* to believe that beauty is indeed only skin deep—and avoid the investigation of its impact for fear they might learn otherwise."

Reactions to such unexpected moments, when they take hold, are what can turn into research fads, or possibly trends, or even waves of history. Aronson's needle touched off an extended barrage of studies about the ways people unconsciously reward or punish good looks and homeliness. These studies leave no doubt that every person's life is importantly shaped by whether or not she or he is regarded as attractive.

The first post-Aronson wave began in 1972 with a study by three Midwestern psychologists (Karen Dion, Ellen Berscheid, and Elaine Walster). The title of their study, borrowed from Sappho, has become a precept of the field: "What Is Beautiful Is Good." They established that men and women who are rated by others as good-looking tend to be happier, more successful, more content with their marriages, more sought-out socially, more helped, more trusted, more just-about-everything-desirable. And even when they are not, they are perceived by others to be so.

That remained the consistent finding in follow-up study after study, until a few skeptical researchers began asking new kinds of questions, particularly about attractive and less attractive women—and began getting new kinds of answers. The second wave began with a 1975 study entitled "When Beauty May Fail" by Marshall Dermer and Darrel Thiel. It showed that, under certain definable circumstances, beauty, especially female beauty, may indeed be a detriment to success and happiness, evoking dislike or distrust, envy, and attributions of snobbishness and incompetence. (More about these findings in the specific studies reported below.)

This was followed in 1977 by a set of studies best described by the title of one of them—a reversal of Sappho—"What Is Good Is Beautiful." The researchers, A. E. Gross and C. Crofton, found that when people are rich or powerful, or if the observer finds them merely agreeable, those qualities may cause those people to be perceived as *physically* attractive. (More in the specific findings on that, too.)

Then in 1983 came another piece of an answer to what is attractive, and many beauty scholars found it surprising. Two researchers, Murray Webster and James Driskell, citing many studies involving hundreds of photographs of people rated by panels as attractive and unattractive, concluded that the most important component of beauty is *conventionality:* "The overall impression from these pictures is that very minor and superficial changes in hairstyle, weight, and, perhaps, clothing would be sufficient to make the unattractive people more attractive, or the reverse. In other words, the pretty ones probably looked the way their parents wanted them to, while the ugly ones had ignored one or more pieces of simple advice."

Webster and Driskell went on to lament what they perceived, fourteen years after Aronson, as a certain fluffiness and triviality in the growing mountain of research on attractiveness. These studies, they said, gave beauty "the status of magic." They proceeded to offer a theory of perceived beauty, suggesting that, like a person's race and sex and age, it is a characteristic that gives most of us an instant impression of a person's *status.*

Similarly, when a person sits in a meeting "dressed for success" and looks solemn, saying nothing, many people automatically attribute depth and wisdom to that person. That single fragment—any fragment—may cue our expectations about a person's competency, happiness, kindness, all manner of personal qualities. As study after study throughout this book will show, each of us makes our way around doing a powerful lot of attributing when what we think we're doing is making discerning judgments.

Yet beauty, even as a "status characteristic," Webster and Driskell pointed out, is significantly different from race or sex or age. Unlike those, attractiveness "is to some extent an achieved characteristic. Minor change can be effected through clothing or cosmetics, while reconstructive or plastic surgery is available for major alterations. . . . It may be that attractiveness will assume increasing significance as other characteristics such as race and sex fall into disuse."

All the preceding expert views and speculations leave a troublesome question hanging in the air, of course, and you're probably already asking it: Just what do these learned people mean by "attractiveness"? Who are they to decide that some people have it and others don't? And *how* do they decide?

Actually, they are not the ones who do. In conducting studies, the standard way of measuring "attractiveness" is to show panels of judges photographs or slides of individuals, usually waist-up unless the particular study requires a different view. The panels rate the subjects on a scale ranging from decidedly attractive to decidedly not attractive. These ratings usually come out with striking unanimity among panels, whether the judges are men or women, young or old. These judges are usually not told the purpose of the study, or even its topic.

Another way to measure attractiveness was developed by Michael Cunningham, a psychologist at the University of Louisville. He quantified—actually measured with a ruler—beauty as we rate it in the female face. Cunningham concluded that "conventionality appears to be the most important component of beauty." He asked 150 white male college students to rate the attractiveness of fifty women based on photographs of their faces. More than half of the pictures were of finalists in the Miss Universe contest. Most were white, but seven were black, and six Asian. Physical measurements of what was deemed attractive emerged with remarkable precision and consistency. From their ratings, Cunningham developed the following measurements of ideal beauty in the eyes of the white American male:

- The width of each eye of a perfect beauty is $3/10$ the width of the face at eye level.
- The length of her chin (from the lower lip down) is $1/5$ the height of her face.
- The distance from the bottom of her eyebrow to the center of the pupil of her eye is $1/10$ the height of the face.
- The width of each eye's iris is $1/14$ the distance between the cheekbones.
- The height of the visible portion of her eyeball is $1/14$ the height of her face.

- The total area of her nose is less than 1/20 the area of the face.
- The width of her mouth is 1/2 the width of her face at mouth level.

On Cleopatra's nose:
"If it had been shorter the face
of the whole world would have been changed."

BLAISE PASCAL,
FRENCH MATHEMATICIAN (1623–62)

Clearly, small variations make a lot of difference. Cunningham found that if the width of a woman's mouth is not the ideal 50 percent of face width, but 40 percent or 60 percent, research subjects voted her face much less attractive.

Surveys of women's reactions to men's faces are under way. But a University of Michigan psychologist, David Buss, is coming to the conclusion, as some studies below seem to confirm, that while a man attaches high significance to the physical attractiveness of a woman, a woman is more drawn by a man's social status and wealth—signs of his earning capacity. All of these qualities—attractiveness, status, and wealth—Buss says, have "evolutionary advantages," raising the chances of more successful reproduction. Beauty suggests that a woman is young and healthy, thus high in her likelihood of reproducing. A man is less limited by age in his capacity to reproduce, but his access to power and resources enhance his family's chances of survival, thus making him more desirable as a mate.

Buss has not yet won the day with that analysis. Ellen Berscheid, the pioneer in beauty studies, has told Daniel Goleman of *The New York Times* that she is "skeptical of these evolutionary arguments because there is a huge leap from the data to the explanation." But then she adds an impressive data-to-explanation leap of her own. Attractiveness in women, she speculates, may some day matter less in dating and marriage. That might be the result of women establishing a greater equality with men in their ability to attain power, wealth, and status.

Ellen Berscheid's point appears to be based on the assumption that the culture teaches us what human beauty is, that our taste for beauty is learned. But psychologist Judith H. Langlois and her colleagues at the University of Texas have come up with a surprising kind of contrary evidence. They studied the reactions of thirty infants who were only two to three months old and thirty-four more infants six to eight months old. Of them, thirty-seven were boys and twenty-seven were girls, all from middle-class families. These infants were shown color slides of sixteen adult Caucasian women. Half of those photo subjects had been judged moderately attractive and half moderately unattractive by a panel of several hundred undergraduate men and women. The slides were shown in pairs, one attractive and one unattractive, for ten seconds, then the slides in exchanged positions for another ten seconds to control any left-right tendencies the babies might have. About two thirds of the babies, both older and younger, gazed significantly longer at the attractive faces. In a second experiment, the babies were shown pairs of attractive faces side by side, followed by pairs of unattractive faces. Nearly the same proportion of older infants showed a marked preference for the attractive faces, as measured by a steady gaze (although in the second experiment the younger infants showed no measurable preference).

"For reasons we don't understand . . . there appears to be a predisposition among infants to discriminate attractive from unattractive faces," says Langlois, adding that the findings "seriously challenge the assumption that attractiveness is merely 'in the eye of the beholder.' "

LOOK YOURSELF UP

Physical beauty is the sign of an interior beauty,
a spiritual and moral beauty.

FRIEDRICH VON SCHILLER, GERMAN DRAMATIST
(1759–1805)

You are a man or woman whom others rate as attractive:

When you meet strangers of the opposite sex, they are likely to assume, on the basis of your good looks alone, that you share their attitudes. The more attractive they feel you are, the more that opposite-sex strangers are likely to make that assumption.

And contrary to what most people might assume, women are more inclined to be influenced in this direction by the attractiveness of men than are men by women. [Mashman]

The first finding stated above can also be turned around. Another researcher discovered that if you express an attitude shared by a stranger, that person will probably perceive you as more attractive than he or she would if your attitudes differed. This appears so whether or not you would otherwise be rated as attractive, and whether or not the observer is of the opposite sex. [Beaman, Klentz]

As a child, you probably received less punishment than an unattractive child received for making the same mistake.

This finding was determined by two companion studies. In the first, fifty-six women were deliberately provoked (or not) by a researcher, and then were maneuvered into disciplining a ten-year-old girl who had either an attractive or unattractive appearance. The women were significantly more likely to mete out more intense punishment to the unattractive child. In the second experiment, forty women were similarly provoked, then required to discipline a ten-year-old boy who was either good-looking or not—and either a normal speaker or a stutterer. Just as in the case of the girls, the unattractive boy was punished more severely than the good-looking one, and the stutterer got stronger punishment than the child of normal speech. [Berkowitz, Frodi]

You are less likely than an unattractive person to be perceived as having psychological problems. [Jones, Hannson, Phillips]

You are likely to be perceived as having a more active curiosity than an unattractive person—as well as being more complex, perceptive, careful, confident, assertive, happy, active, cooperative, friendly, candid, humorous, self-controlled, and flexible. [Miller]

You are also thought to be more capable than an unattractive person of flying an airplane. [Driskell]

Beauty is proof against spears and shields.
She who is beautiful is more formidable than fire and iron.

ANACREON, GREEK POET (582–485 B.C.)

You are a woman whom others rate as attractive:

Most people assume that you are more sociable than a less attractive woman; also happier, both socially and professionally; that you will marry (or have married) a man with a relatively better job; and that you are a better wife and bed partner. On the other hand, the same people expect you to be more conceited, more snobbish, and less sympathetic to unfortunates. Also, they regard you as more likely than an unattractive woman to have an affair. [Dermer, Thiel]

As a more attractive than average woman, you are likely to have a taller than average boyfriend. [Feingold]

Your attractiveness is likely to get you a husband of higher education and higher income than a less attractive woman is apt to acquire. But your attractiveness won't help you get a higher-status job or higher income for yourself. [Udry, Eckland, 1984]

If you grew up in a working-class family, your attractiveness increases the likelihood that you will marry (or did marry) a man from a class higher than your own. (If you're of the middle class, however, your education counts more than your attractiveness in getting a good catch.) [Elder]

If word gets around that you, as an attractive woman, slept with a man you had not previously met, most people will regard you as significantly less moral than an unattractive woman who did the same thing. If you knew the man more than six months, you'll still be deemed somewhat less moral than the unattractive woman. Incidentally, the researchers of this study think that the attractive woman is judged more harshly because she is perceived as having a wider than usual range in her choices of men. The researchers drew their conclusions after asking ninety-eight male and female undergraduates to read fictitious accounts of dating situations, then asking them to express their feelings about the characters in them. [Hocking, Walker, Fink]

While good-looking men almost always come out more liked, more respected, and more often chosen over their less handsome competitors, and good-looking women win most of the time, sometimes you, as a good-looking woman, may come out a loser *because* of your attractiveness. Recent refinements of research topics have begun to reveal that attractive women are favored for success *except* in roles not traditionally occupied by women. Here is one such study finding: If you are an executive in a traditional "man's world" job, you can expect to have a harder time than an unattractive woman in winning recognition for your capability and integrity, and in getting promoted (although your attractiveness would probably give you an advantage in a more typically "feminine" executive job, say, as a head dietician or women's wear buyer).

For this study, each of 113 working men and women in New York was shown a detailed résumé of a corporation executive, with an ID card and photograph attached. All résumés shown were essentially the same, but the attached photos varied. Half of them showed men, some attractive, some not attractive; half showed women, some attractive, some not attractive. Participants were asked to look at the photos of the "executives," read the résumé, and characterize the person portrayed, by selecting from various adjectives. [Heilman and Stopeck]

If you are an attractive female student, an essay you write will win a higher evaluation by your fellow students than the same essay by an unattractive woman student—provided your essay deals with a traditionally feminine topic, such as "How to Make a Quilt." But if it deals with a traditionally masculine topic, such as "How to Buy a Used Motorcycle," your essay will probably get a lower grade than an unattractive woman's. For this study, college freshmen were asked to rate essays they were told had been written by other freshmen. The essays were accompanied by photos of men and women, attractive and unattractive. Some essays dealt with stereotypical "masculine" topics, some with "feminine" topics. [Cash]

If you were to run for public office against an unattractive woman with exactly the same qualifications, you'd probably lose. (Inexplicably, you'd come out slightly better running for Congress than for another office, but you'd still probably lose to the less attractive woman.) [Bowman]

If you are convicted of a crime for which your good looks were probably irrelevant to success (for example, burglary), a jury is apt to let you off easier than it would less attractive defendants. But, conversely, if the crime was one in which your good looks may have helped you (for example, fraud or a con game), the jury is apt to throw the book at you, as compared to other convicted criminals.

To reach these conclusions, the researchers presented 120 male and female undergraduates with written accounts of a criminal case and asked them to "sentence" the defendant. One third of the students were led to believe that the defendant was physically attractive, one third that she was not attractive, and one third were given no characterization of the defendant's appearance. [Sigall, Ostrove]

You are a woman others rate as unattractive:

If you are young, your plainness may be a hazard to your health. For example, teenage and college-age women considered unattractive are likely to have significantly higher blood pressure (in fact, dangerously higher, say the researchers) than their peers who are considered attractive. (Note: Neither teenage boys nor older adults of either sex show the same correlation, according to this study of the blood pressure of 283 women and 369 men, aged fourteen to seventy-six.) [Hansell, Sparacino, Ronchi]

You are perceived, by both men and women, as more likely to be a virgin and more likely to masturbate than a woman considered attractive. [Durham, Grossnickle]

The chances are heightened that people will decide you're a feminist. [Goldberg, Gottesdiener, Abramson]

You are a woman whom others rate as average-looking:

When you are seen with attractive women, people perceive you as better-looking than when you are seen with unattractive women. If you are in the company of both attractive and unattractive women, people associate you with your more attractive companions. [Geiselman, Haight, Kimata]

You are perceived by both women and men as more attractive when your facial expression is happy—or even when your face is neutral—than when it is sad. [Mueser, Grau, Sussman, Rosen]

To find this out, Mueser and partners posed fifteen undergraduate women, randomly chosen, for five photos each: her whole person; her body only, from the neck down; her face only, relaxed and without expression; her face only, while thinking of being happy in the presence of a loved one; her face only, while thinking of a loved one dying. These photos were rated for attractiveness, according to a standard procedure called the Likert scale, by a panel of forty-five women and twelve men. Each panel member saw only one facial-expression photo of each model.

A Note on Your Inner Mood and Outward Beauty

Now, the foregoing study may, at first glance, appear to be a confirmation of what everybody already knows—as, in fact, many human behavior studies are.

But with a second look, and a moment's reflection, the finding may startle. Most often we think of beauty of face and body as the result of accident, like winning a genetic lottery. An attractive person is just plain lucky; a drab one is not. It's true, of course, that we can improve on our natural endowment with makeup, the right clothes, even careful posture. But how far can you really go in disguising ordinariness?

Now come these findings by Mueser and others to disturb us with evidence that we can *create* our own beauty (or ruin it) to some degree, simply by having a happy face—or better still, by *feeling* happy. It seems to say we can take at least partial responsibility for our looks and thus for the social rewards and punishments that follow. (See Chapter 6, "Who's In Control Here?")

"Beauty is the gift of God," reflected Aristotle.

And what this study seems to say in an offstage whisper is, "Yes, but God can use a little help. . . ."

You are a man whom others consider attractive:

You probably spend less time talking with other men and get less satisfaction out of it than the fellow who is considered not as attractive. Also, the better-looking you are, the more time you spend with women. Contrary to common belief, you are conscious of your attractiveness as a trading card in picking your friends, and use it even more than an attractive woman does.

For this study, seventy-one first year college students recorded and answered questions about every interaction of ten minutes or more that they had over an eight-month period. [Reis, Nezlek, Wheeler]

The more attractive a man you are, the more you are perceived as assertive and egocentric. How about being seen as kind? Your attractiveness is not likely to influence that judgment—unless you're *extremely* attractive. In that case, others are apt to perceive you as less kind than an unattractive man. [Gallucci]

If you are an executive, you are more likely than an unattractive man to be judged especially capable, deserving of promotion, and as having integrity. (Not necessarily so for attractive women. See above.) [Heilman, Stopeck]

You are more likely than an unattractive man to be hired for jobs that involve a lot of personal contact, such as personnel interviewer or counselor. But for jobs that involve little personal contact, such as personnel records manager or safety administrator, your good looks give you no advantage over the unattractive man in getting hired, according to this study. [*Academy of Management Journal*]

If you are a good-looking male student, an essay you write will probably be graded higher by your fellow students than will the same essay by an unattractive man—*regardless* of whether your essay deals with a "feminine" or "masculine" topic. (See contrast with attractive and unattractive women, above). [Cash]

If you were to run for public office against an unattractive man with exactly the same qualifications, you'd probably beat him. (See contrast with attractive and unattractive women, above.) [Bowman]

You are a man whom others rate as unattractive:

If you also had a notably homely face as a teenager (as adjudged by a relatively ugly mug in your high school yearbook), you may have reaped rich rewards for your trouble: You probably concentrated more than others on doing well in school, went further in your education, married a more highly educated woman, and now have a job of better-than-average prestige.

For this study, researchers interviewed 601 men fifteen years after high school graduation. The men were selected for the homeliness (and attractiveness) of their yearbook photographs. [Udry, Eckland, 1983]

If you were to run for public office against an attractive man with exactly the same qualifications, you'd probably lose. [Bowman]

> The awful thing is that beauty
> is mysterious as well as terrible.
> God and the devil are fighting there,
> and the battlefield is the heart of man.
>
> FYODOR DOSTOYEVSKI (1821–81),
> *THE BROTHERS KARAMAZOV*

You are a man or woman considered... well... partly attractive and partly not, and you wish you knew what parts counted most:

Suppose you're a woman with a pleasing face and dazzling smile but, despite that, you don't get many compliments about, say, your hips. Here's good news: Your face contributes more to the way men judge your overall attractiveness than the rest of your body does. (For this study, twenty-one undergraduate men in groups of seven viewed the photos of women, faces and figures combined; photos of their figures only; and still other photos of their faces only, in random order. The men rated each photo for attractiveness before seeing the next random-order photo.) [Mueser, Grau, Sussman, Rosen]

Here's how your facial features influence your attractiveness rating in order of decreasing significance:

- mouth
- eyes
- facial structure (what's left after other specific features are considered individually)
- hair
- nose

This was concluded from a complex procedure that involved having a panel of fifty white undergraduates (twenty-five males, twenty-five females) rate the photos of five males and five females, same age and race, both whole-face photos and closeups of facial parts. [Terry, Davis]

You are a man who has a babyface—big eyes, apple cheeks, unfurrowed eyebrows, and a soft, round chin:

The more those characteristics are present, the more you are perceived as naive and honest—as well as warmer and kinder—than a man with a more mature-looking face. [Berry, McArthur]

You are married to an attractive person:

If you're a man, you're perceived as more attractive than you would be if your wife were ugly. If you're a woman, however, you don't get the same benefit: People rate your attractiveness independent of your husband's. [Bar-Tal, Saxe; Israeli and American study]

You usually try to avoid catching sight of your reflection in a plate glass window:

You don't consider yourself good-looking. Want worse news? Others probably agree with you. [Lipson, Przybyla, Byrne]

Note: Important additional findings on the subject of attractiveness can be found in Chapter 5: "Your Dating" and "You and Your Lover."

"If I were as fat as you, I'd hang myself,"
George Bernard Shaw, tall and thin,
once said to corpulent G. K. Chesterton.

"And if I had it in my mind to hang myself,"
responded Chesterton,
"I'd use you as the rope."

YOUR WEIGHT, HEIGHT, AND BODY STYLE

FAT IS BEAUTIFUL, flaunts the bumper sticker from the rear end of an automobile.

So now that blacks and women and gays and lesbians have succes-sively raised consciousness and revised world attitudes, perhaps the next wave will belong to the obese.

Strong feelings about thinness and fatness are among the few traits that are spread throughout humankind. Anthropologists tell us that every culture known uses either thinness or fatness as a criterion for judging sexual attractiveness. Westerners may be surprised to learn that in most of the world's societies males consider obese females more attractive and desirable than thin ones. For example, a woman in the Karagwe kingdoms of East Africa requires the sexual splendor of extreme corpulence to qualify for a place in a king's harem. The Ekoi of Nigeria send young girls away, out of the sight of members of the tribe, to fatten them for the marriage market. This is not to say that in those cultures, or in our own, thinness or fatness, any more than prettiness of face or any other appealing trait, is the only, or even the major, criterion for choosing a desirable mate. But, like it or not, in all cultures people go to great lengths to make themselves thin or fat as a way of attracting and keeping sexual mates—and, in fact, for general social esteem.

In the West, researchers have consistently found that obese females are rated less desirable as sexual partners or wives. In the United States, even male medical students, for all their supposed training in emotional detachment, react negatively to overweight women on several dimensions including "seductiveness."

And do you know who feels the same way as those budding doctors? Overweight women do. A series of case studies reveal that obese women, far more frequently than others, have learned to think of themselves in nonsexual terms, and become confused, suspicious, and defensive when the subject of their sexuality is approached. But obese women are likely to be as active as others in developing friendships with other women, G. R. Adams has found, even though they have a noticeably higher fear of disapproval and more trouble accepting their own worth, thus creating obstacles in their relation-ships, even with women.

Does obesity really interfere with mate-finding and marital happi-ness, as many assume? "As spouses share a relationship and a house-hold over a period of time," says Jeff Sobal, a researcher on obesity at the University of Maryland School of Medicine, ". . . ideals for body weight are negotiated, expectations are created and modified, and fatness becomes a part of . . . a shared spousal value system about appropriate appearance, of which fatness is a component." Whether or not obesity disrupts a romance or marriage, concludes Sobal, is probably determined by *when* one of the partners first put on weight. If one partner was overweight during courtship and at the time of their wedding, making the weight a factor from the start, the relationship has the same likelihood of stability as any other. In fact, the obesity may even contribute to stability. The heavy partner may feel the other's acceptance as an assurance against having to seek a new partner in a marketplace that doesn't consider fat as beautiful.

LOOK YOURSELF UP

You are a woman:

You tend to dislike your body more than others do, thinking of yourself as fatter than you think men would prefer you to be. Furthermore, compared against your idea of the low weights you think men prefer in women, your own ideal of a body weight is even less than *that.* The surprising fact, according to this study of five hundred college-age men and women, is that men prefer women *fatter* than what most women think men like, and certainly fatter than what most women think is ideal. [Fallon, Rozin]

You don't have to be an American woman to mislead yourself that way. In a study of eighteen-year-old Swedish women of normal weight, 50 percent rated themselves as fat. [Nylander; Swedish study]

If you are a housewife, you are twice as likely as your husband (37 percent of married women versus 18 percent of married men) to be on a diet. That ratio holds regardless of your age. But if you're over fifty, the actual percentages of people on diets diminish to something like 25 percent of wives versus 12 percent of husbands. Apparently, as we get older, we're more apt to say, Oh, the hell with it. [U.S. Food and Drug Administration]

You are a man:

In contrast to women, you tend to think *better* of your body than others do.

This study of five hundred college-age men and women shows that you're apt to feel little or no discrepancy between the way you feel your body looks and what your notion is of an ideal body weight—or, for that matter, what you think women prefer in a man's body. You're happily deluding yourself. Women in this study prefer men lighter than your notion of an ideal—and lighter than what *you* think women like. [Fallon, Rozin]

If you are married, you are more likely than your wife to talk about food, offer food to her and others, and accept food when it is offered. Also, you are twelve times more likely to criticize your wife's eating behavior than she is to criticize yours. [Stuart, Davis]

If your wife is overweight, you may not like it exactly, but there's a good chance you harbor certain fears about her thinning down. For one thing, you're somewhat afraid that her consequent attractiveness will lead her to infidelity and the destruction of your marriage. Besides that, you're uneasy that her new attractiveness will increase her bargaining position and lead to her winning more arguments. [Stuart, Davis]

You are a woman with a large bust (37 inches or larger):

The first impression you convey to most people, whether they are male or female, is that you are relatively unintelligent, lazy, incompetent, immoral, and immodest. (The author of this study emphasizes that the finding is of *first impression,* not lasting judgment. [Kleinke, Staneski]

You are a woman with a small bust (less than 34 inches):

You give a first impression of being relatively intelligent, competent, ambitious, modest, and moral. [Kleinke, Staneski]

You are obese:

You probably overeat not because you're hungry, but to make yourself feel happier.

The snacks you wolf down between meals probably are high in carbohydrates. Such snacks increase your body supply of serotonin, a neurotransmitting chemical, which lifts your mood, makes you feel calmer, and helps your ability to concentrate. That's thought to be why you're drawn to choose those foods over other possible hunger-stavers.

For this study, twenty men and women, as a group about 40 percent overweight and therefore assumed to be heavy eaters, lived at the MIT Clinical Research Center, and were invited to eat whenever and as much as they wanted. At mealtimes, they ate moderately or little. But usually once a day, and most often in midafternoon or evening, they binged on snacks. Although protein foods were equally available, the overweight snackers almost always dived for the carbohydrates—candy, cake, breads, heavy-sugar jellies. Later the subjects were given an experimental drug called d-fenfluramine, which heightens the availability of serotonin, fooling the brain into thinking carbohydrates have been eaten. Their snacking was reduced by 41 percent.

A smart—and healthful—way for you to lose weight, the researcher surprisingly suggests, might be to make an addition to the traditional low-calorie diet: a daily snack such as a candy bar or an English muffin, to satisfy your craving for carbohydrates in an otherwise low-calorie regimen. [Wurtman]

If you are a woman, the more overweight you are, the lower your family income probably is. Even more pronounced statistically, the more overweight you are, the lower your husband's education probably is (although your weight does not appear related to your own education). These findings are based on a survey of 59,556 women, all members of a national weight reduction club. [Rimm, Rimm]

If you are married and dieting, you're likely to blame your husband or wife and your family for your fatness, and to complain that they don't support you properly in your efforts to lose weight. [Sussman]

If you are married nine years or more, the chances are that your spouse is also overweight. [Garn and others; several studies]

If you—and not your spouse—are considerably heavier now than when you married, there's a good chance your spouse is seriously disturbed about your added weight. That's especially likely if you are the wife and you're the one who has gained. You are more likely to take off weight in response to your spouse's disturbance if your marriage is relatively happy than if it's not. [Craddock]

If you are a married woman, your excess weight does not appear to inhibit your enjoyment of sex. You are likely to have coitus, masturbate, and achieve orgasm with the same frequency as other married women. [Schwartz, Hershenson, Shipman]

You are the subject of a "psychological profile" by an authority on obesity and eating disorders, Hilde Bruch, in her book *The Importance of Overweight.* If you resemble the archetype as drawn in her profile, you are the offspring of a dominant, overprotective mother who had mixed emotions about you as a child, and who compensated for her guilt over those emotions by feeding you excessively. You began to equate food with affection, thus learning to charge food with high emotional value. In addition, your mother (and perhaps both your parents) perceived you as someone whose successes could undo their disappointments in life. You sensed this special place in their hearts and needs, and you began to feel omnipotent. At the same time, you felt impelled to please your parents by doing everything perfectly. This perfectionism, of course, caused— probably still causes—you to feel frequent and easy disappointment. As an adolescent, you grew up holding visions of grandiosity, yet felt gripped with doubt about your ability to be perfect. You continually searched for new activities at which to be perfect, then would soon give each one up, feeling letdown either when you failed or succeeded. Your constant overriding fear has been that you would fail at fulfilling the grandiose ideal. So, reaching back for the comforting symbol of security and affection that was instilled in you by your parents (who also instilled the perfectionism), you gorge food, hoping it will help you escape the threat of disappointment. If you're a typical gorger, you may often perceive yourself as either fatter or thinner than you actually are, and you often have feelings that "sneaked" foods will not fatten you. [Bruch, as reported by Hoover]

Now that all that is said about obesity and overeating, as though they are interchangeable words, here comes Dr. Albert J. Stunkard, a psychiatrist and obesity specialist at the University of Pennsylvania, reporting in *The New England Journal of Medicine* that your fatness or thinness is programmed in your genes.

Dr. Stunkard studied 540 adopted adults in Denmark, where complete records are available on all adopted children and their biological families. He found that "family environment alone has no apparent effect." Adult fatness is most closely linked to that of the person's biological mother, and this is especially true for daughters of the biological mothers. [Stunkard]

You consider yourself overweight:

If you are single, you probably date less frequently than someone who feels his or her body is normal, and you have a harder time establishing relationships with members of the opposite sex. Although you also consider yourself less attractive than normal-weight people, a sexual relationship makes you feel more attractive than you feel when you're celibate. A sexual relationship also makes you feel more attractive than the virgins of the world, but less attractive than normal-weight people who are sexually active. [Kallen, Doughty]

If you're male and young, you have a stronger urge to smoke cigarettes than your counterparts with leaner, huskier bodies. At least, that's what a study of four hundred high school males determined. The researcher speculates that your greater desire to smoke may be an attempt to gain status and acceptance. [Tucker]

You are a man who considers himself too skinny:

You have essentially the same self-esteem hangups and dating problems as men and women who think they're too fat. [Kallen, Doughty]

You are a man who craves having a perfect body, shaped in the ideal "tapered V":

You're more likely than most men to have a negative attitude towards women, which, the researchers speculate, "may be related to a fear of femininity." Also, you probably have a more rigid personality than men who care less about having perfect bodies. Finally, you place more significance on the tapered-V male body than most women do. [Maier, Lavrakas]

You are a man who has a "beer belly":

People find you less attractive than a man with a flat abdomen. And if you care about that, you better pay attention: This study also shows that the condition of your middle plays a greater role in whether people consider you attractive than do your shoulders, neck, head, or other features of your physique. [Gitter, Lomranz, Saxe; Israeli and American study]

YOUR HEIGHT

After "Fat Is Beautiful," maybe the next wave of consciousness-raising will be "Short Is Beautiful." But if you're short you'll have to come a long way before gaining full social citizenship, if studies about attitudes in most Western countries are to be believed. (The author of this book makes that assertion from deep pits of sadness. He is short.)

Not much research has been done about the pains and rewards of shortness and tallness, perhaps because people feel less emotional about height than they do about weight. Yet the research findings show that we do react to height in pronounced ways.

"People are endlessly engaged in defensive strategies to cope with body experiences," says Seymour Fisher, a body image scholar. Upon suffering a failure, a person may feel physically smaller, the way a child feels physically shrunken while being scolded by the school principal. People who pride themselves on the power of their minds often have an enlarged notion of the size of their heads. "There is a constant process," says Fisher, "of feeling that one's body is growing larger or smaller as different life conditions are encountered."

LOOK YOURSELF UP

You are taller than average:

Whether you are a man or a woman, you have a slight tendency to have a higher IQ than a shorter person. That surprising finding is based on a statistically impressive study by Stanford University researchers of fourteen thousand youngsters between the ages of six and seventeen who were surveyed during the 1960s by the National Center for Health Statistics. The link between height and IQ held even after the researchers accounted for other possible influences, such as family size, wealth, birth order, and race. The clear finding so defies other explanations that one of the researchers, Darrell Wilson, a pediatrician, offers a psychological reason: "Perhaps people treat shorter children as if they were younger than they really are. These children may do less well on test scores as a result."

Wilson warns parents against artificially stimulating their children's growth, however. Synthetic growth hormones, he points out, may produce dangerous side effects in children who are not deficient in the hormones. Besides, the link between height and IQ appears to be forged very early in life, so trying to increase a child's height after his or her tendency to shortness reveals itself will not likely alter the IQ. [Wilson]

You are a taller-than-average woman:

You probably score higher on tests measuring general self-esteem— in other words, you like yourself more—than most women who are shorter than average. [Murrell, Lester]

You are a tall man—six feet or more:

You are more likely than a shorter man to rate yourself attractive. [Lucker]

You probably have a prettier-than-average girlfriend. [Feingold]

You're likely to earn more money than a shorter man. More specifically, if you're six-feet-two or taller, you're likely to start a new job at a salary 12.4 percent higher than that of a "shorty" under six feet. [*The Wall Street Journal*]

Still more specifically, each extra inch of height is worth an extra $600 a year on average, according to a survey of 1,200 MBAs who are graduates of the University of Pittsburgh's Graduate School of Business. Average salary of those surveyed in the year 1987: $43,000. Six-footers typically earned $4,200 more than men who were five-foot-five in comparable jobs, unless the six-footer was also fat. A man who was at least 20 percent overweight earned $4,000 less than a thin man in a similar job. It would seem to follow that if the tall man is trim and the short guy is overweight, the tall fellow has a double advantage, right? Right. The dollar spread between them almost doubled—from $4,200 to $8,200. On the other hand, in the fat-for-height tradeoff, overweight six-footers and skinny five-foot-fivers collected about the same. Of the 1,200 surveyed, 350 were women

MBAs; too few of them were significantly tall or heavy enough for shaping conclusions about women.

The Associated Press solicited a comment on all this from Eileen Lefebvre, president of the National Association to Aid Fat Americans, and she complied amply: "Finally the press and government are starting to listen to us. You can't discriminate against black people or women anymore, so the only people left are fat people. And if you're fat *and* short, you're really finished." [Frieze, Olson]

You have an advantage over a shorter man in getting a leadership job. For example, one survey (in which false résumés accompanied by photos were sent to school boards advertising vacancies) shows that if you are a candidate for a job as high school principal, you are apt to be judged more qualified than your competitors who are shorter. This is true even when the résumés of "short" and "tall" candidates are virtually identical. For this study, photos and résumés of mock candidates were sent to New York State school superintendents. [Bonuso]

If you ever run for president, your chances of winning are overwhelming if your opponent is even the least bit shorter than you. In twenty-two out of twenty-three elections since 1900, the taller of the two major-party candidates has won. The exception? Carter over Ford in 1976. (In fact, if you ever run for president, voters who support you will consistently overestimate your height, and those who are against you will consistently underestimate your height.) [Feldman; Kassarjian]

Where the hostess is handsome, the wine is good.

FRENCH PROVERB

YOUR STYLE OF DRESS AND GROOMING

Let's grant, then, that physical beauty and height can't just be dismissed as of superficial import. But surely the ways we clothe and primp ourselves are no more than state-of-the-art candy coating— hardly fit for scholarship.

Research seems to stand that notion on its head, too.

The preceding section showed that when we find a person attractive, we tend to attribute to that person our own opinions and attitudes, and vice versa: A person sharing our opinions looks better to us.

A similar two-way relationship apparently exists between (1) what we wear and (2) something that runs much deeper than opinions: a person's *values*. Mere opinions and attitudes are changeable. But a value, as defined by Milton Rokeach, author of a standard measure called the Rokeach Value Survey, is a "relatively enduring" belief that is "centrally located within one's total belief system about how one ought or ought not to behave, or about some endstate of existence worth or not worth attaining." Thus a value is a foundation belief from which opinions, attitudes, and behaviors arise.

As clothes express, also they are read. Studies on the way we adorn ourselves increasingly reveal that the ways we dress are read by others as statements of deep and subtle personal values—whether those who observe us consciously know it or not.

LOOK YOURSELF UP

You dress conventionally/unconventionally:

Yes, exactly as most people might suspect, the way you dress does tip off how you think about politics and social issues, at least if you're a male (this experiment was not done with women). If you wear clothes commonly regarded as conservative (jackets, neckties, tailored pants), the chances are highly likely (76 percent) that you'd score as a social and political conservative in a standard social attitudes test. If you dress in faded jeans, T-shirts, and sneakers, and wear an untrimmed beard, you would probably score as a liberal. For this study, one hundred male students at Penn State were classified by dress by the researchers, then given the Eysenck Social-Attitude Inventory. [Kness, Densmore]

You are neat/sloppy:

If you dress neatly, your good appearance most often makes others feel more trustful of you and more generous toward you than if you dress sloppily. Many experiments confirm this. In one typical study, a neatly dressed woman who approached strangers in an airport terminal to ask for a dime got it 81 percent of the time; when she was dressed sloppily, it was only 32 percent. Men, incidentally, gave her a dime 14 percent more often than women did. In still another dime-in-the-airport study, a woman repeatedly placed a dime conspicuously on the shelf of a phone booth. When someone entered the booth and started a call, she interrupted the caller to say she "accidentally" left a dime there. The experiment revealed that she was considerably more likely to get the dime back if she was neatly groomed than if sloppily dressed. Whether the interrupted caller was a man or woman did not make a significant difference. For these studies, four undergraduate women, two dressed neatly and two sloppily, approached strangers in Boston's Logan Airport. Incidentally, the students returned the dimes. [Kleinke; also Sroufe, Chaikin, Cook, Freeman]

You are a woman:

The shorter the skirt you wear is, the more youthful and outgoing you look. The longer your skirt, the more sophisticated you are taken to be. A narrow skirt, too, makes people rate you as sophisticated, but more arrogant and less friendly than if you are wearing a wide one. A "tank top" makes you look more youthful, outgoing, friendly, open-minded, and sexy than a T-shirt does. [Gibbins, Coney]

You know, of course, that wearing a well-chosen perfume is a shortcut to turning a man on, don't you? Well, don't rush to simple judgment about this complicated matter. The way your perfume spins a man's head, it turns out, depends on how you dress—and don't guess too hastily about that either. This Purdue experiment, supported by the National Science Foundation, used as confederates two undergraduate women who wore two different modes of clothing which they interchanged at intervals. One costume was "very neat" or "formal"—skirt, blouse, hosiery. The other was "informal"—jeans and a sweatshirt. It also used ninety-four male students as subjects. Each of the ninety-four men was paired with a "partner" (one of the women confederates) and interviewed by a Purdue professor with a series of innocuous questions about career goals and hobbies. For half of those "partnership interviews," each woman wore a perfume called Jungle Gardenia, which had been chosen by a five-man panel as "pleasant and potent." Later the men were asked to fill out a "first impression form" about their women "partners" and were then interviewed about them further. The experimenter states that he expected men would rate their partners as most attractive when the women were in the double condition of wearing perfume *and* high-tone clothes. But not so. The perfume, his study reports, "exerted such effects only when they were dressed informally. When the confederates dressed [more formally], in contrast, the presence of perfume actually seemed to reduce attraction." The men also were asked to rate their partners along scales for imagined personality characteristics: conceited/modest, neat/sloppy, unromantic/romantic, patient/impatient, energetic/lazy, generous/stingy. Again, perfume led to favorable shifts only when the women dressed in jeans and sweatshirts. When more fancily clothed, the women came off with negative ratings. Why? This may help explain: Many of the men later told the researcher in "debriefings" that when the women were perfumed *and* more dressed up, the men sensed the women as "aloof and unattainable." [Baron]

You are a man:

As most might guess, you're apt to be less interested in clothes than most women are—*unless* you're a highly self-conscious man. In that case, you're more likely than a highly self-conscious woman to be interested in clothes, more likely than she is to feel buoyant when you're buying new clothes, to report that the clothes you wear affect your mood, and to believe that others judge you by what you wear. [Solomon, Schopler]

You are a man with a beard:

You scare kids more than a man who's clean-shaven.

The researchers showed 132 boys and 121 girls, ages three to seven, four drawings of a man's face. They were all the same face, except one was clean-shaven, one had a full beard and mustache, and the remaining two wore different styles of sideburns and mustache, but no beards. When the kids were asked to point to "the nice man," most often they chose the clean-shaven face. When they were asked for "the scary man," the bearded fellow won, hands down. Mustaches made little difference. There may be a hidden lesson here, suggest the researchers: A man whose profession requires winning the trust of children may, if he wears a beard, be "creating problems in interpersonal relationships with his scary face." [Newman, Gale]

WHAT YOUR MANNER OF SPEECH SAYS

LOOK YOURSELF UP

You talk fast and intensely:

The way you talk may eventually kill you, especially if your baseline blood pressure tends to run higher than 155/95. And the source of your dangerous way of talking may be found in your infancy.

"The longer a newborn cries, the higher its blood pressure," says Dr. James J. Lynch, former co-director of the Psychophysiological Clinic of the University of Maryland School of Medicine in Baltimore. He adds, "I think that many adult hypertensives are using language in a way that masks their internal crying."

An intense manner of speech can raise blood pressure "anywhere from ten to fifty percent above resting levels," says Dr. Lynch, "and the higher your resting blood pressure, the more it goes up when you speak. . . . You can blame the renal system, salt, obesity, cholesterol, or anything else. Though these are crucially important, it is also important to understand the breakdown that's occurring in human beings when they talk to each other. . . . The entire body, even down to the microscopic levels of circulation and the exchange of blood gases in individual tissues, is involved in human dialogue."

Dr. Lynch, a psychologist, believes that the typical person with high blood pressure may disguise unexamined or unresolved anxieties by transforming them into intensity of speech. That person may "disconnect" from his or her most troublesome feelings, with potentially disastrous results.

The worst offenders against themselves, Dr. Lynch has written in his book, *The Language of the Heart*, are the so-called Type A's, those driving, impatient, impulsive workaholics (see Chapter 6) who are especially prone to heart attacks. While most people normally relax as they listen to others speak, Type A's and most hypertensives remain stressed, even "defensive," while listening, says Dr. Lynch. So their blood pressure stays high.

Since 1980, Dr. Lynch and his colleagues have been teaching

hypertensives, individually and through two-day workshops, to change their style of "misspeaking and mislistening," with frequent success in lowering blood pressure. First, with the aid of a computerized monitor that takes continuous readings, he demonstrates to patients how their blood pressure directly responds to their speech intensity. Then he teaches ways to talk that don't unduly strain the vascular system, even when private or painful matters are involved. [Fellman]

Your fast-talking manner may be an asset. If you're trying to persuade an audience or an individual, you're more likely to be judged credible if you talk fast than if you talk slowly. Despite the stereotype of the fast-talking used-car salesman, people prefer rapid speech, and learn measurably more from fast talkers in a fixed amount of time.* [Apple, Streeter, Krauss; Miller et al; MacLachlan]

A NOTE ABOUT INFANT CRIES AND SPEECH

The crying of a baby, more than a distress signal or a lung exercise, is the cradle of adult speech, and may be directly related to the anxieties that are reflected in an intense style of speech.

"Crying is a communicative act," says Dr. Michael Lewis, professor of pediatrics at Rutgers Medical School, a devoted student of the crying of babies, as quoted in *The New York Times*. "Ideally, crying should teach the child optimism about the environment, which he learns when his cries are answered. An infant as young as eight weeks is capable of understanding . . . that he can cause things to happen."

"The more responsive a mother is to her baby," observes Susan Crockenberg, associate professor of human development at the University of California at Davis, ". . . the more readily it develops trust."

---

*Important additional findings about intense talkers and cardiovascular disease may be found under "Type A or Type I?," a heading in "Your 'Type A' Anxiety" in Chapter 6.

The Master said . . . "Without knowing the force of words,
it is impossible to know men."

CONFUCIUS (551–479 B.C.)

You talk loud:

The impression given others by your high vocal volume is that you are assertive, aggressive, and possibly not too desirable to work with. [Page, Balloun]

But your loud voice (usually about 75 decibels) causes people to pay more attention to what you say than they do to others of lower volume (say, 70 decibels). [Robinson, McArthur]

We shall never understand one another
until we reduce the language to seven words.

KAHLIL GIBRAN (1883–1931),
SAND AND FOAM

You usually speak in short sentences, using lots of pronouns, and active verbs with vivid adverbs:

The impression you make on your audience is that you are informal, personal, and colorful. On the other hand, if you use long sentences connected by prepositions, many nouns and articles, and multiple adjectives, the impression you make is that you are formal, impersonal, conventional, and a little boring, that you don't much like your audience, and you don't want to be identified with the people in it. [Giles, Farrar; British study]

When you speak to a friend, you're far more likely to use shorter sentences than when you're speaking to strangers. You're also likely to allow longer silences to occur, and to speak more often but for shorter periods. [Rutter, Stephenson; British study]

You casually converse with friends of your own sex:

If you're like most people, among your most frequent topics of conversation, regardless of whether you are a woman or man, are, in order of frequency: work, movies, and television. But the similarity between the sexes seems to end there, according to a survey of 166 women and 110 men, age seventeen to eighty.

If you are a woman, you probably talk far more frequently than do men about relationship problems, family, health, sex related to having children, weight, food, and clothing. According to the results of this questionnaire, there's a 60 percent likelihood you'd say that you *often* talk with other women about "emotional" matters. You also talk often of sexuality and sex (not in direct relation to reproduction), but usually only with another woman. You talk about other women far more frequently than men talk about other men (except talking about them as athletes and public figures). What you find most rewarding about talk with other women is understanding and empathy, the feeling you're being listened to. (Sample reasons from the survey: "to know you're not alone," "the feeling of sharing and being understood," "sensitivity to emotions that men feel are unimportant.") There's a 63 percent probability you'd say that you not only like such same-sex conversations, but you *need* them (compared with only a 43 percent probability if you're a man). You're far likelier than a man (almost 50 percent more likely) to phone a same-sex friend at least once a week just to stay in touch. Only 14 percent of women say they never call a same-sex friend just to chat, while 40 percent of men say they never do.

If you're a man, you're more likely than women to talk about (in this surprising order) music, what's in the news, and sports. There's only a 27 percent chance you'd report that you often talk with other men about "emotional" topics. You, too, talk often about sexuality and sex, but usually only with other men. What you like best about man-to-man talk is its freedom and playfulness, the "buddyship" of it. Typical survey comments: "You don't have to watch what you say," "We teach each other practical ways to solve everyday problems, like about cars and taxes."

Oh, there's one additional matter, on which men and women seem to agree. Each sex feels that the other's favorite topics are frequently trivial. [Sherman]

. . . .

Note: You'll find more, much more, on the subject of intimate talk (or lack of it), in Chapter 3, under "Your Willingness to Reveal Yourself."

Speech is the mirror of the soul;
as a man speaks so is he.

PUBLILIUS SYRUS, SYRIAN-BORN
LATIN WRITER (1ST CENTURY, B.C.)

SECRETS OF OUR UNSECRET CODES

Almost all of us speak in a variety of languages and dialects, each reserved for special settings and special company.

To illustrate, Georgia Dullea of *The New York Times* recalled not long ago a special moment in the movie *Tootsie*, when Dustin Hoffman, batting "her" eyelashes in a bar, tells a waiter: "I'll have a Dubonnet on the rocks with a twist, please?"

"Women have been trained by the culture to talk like that," says Dr. Lillian Glass, who teaches speech pathology at the University of Southern California. "Like that" in this case means adding a "tag ending," a demure uptwisting of the sentence into a question mark, where the statement requires none. "Many casualties in the war between the sexes result from a failure to realize that men and women actually speak different languages," says Dr. Glass, who was hired to coach Hoffman to play Tootsie. That got her started unexpectedly in her interest in sex differences in speech—or, more precisely, in how subtle differences in speech help women express their sex roles.

Here are some findings about the "different languages":

You are a woman:

You are twice as likely as a man to end your sentences with a tag question (like "I'll sit here, O.K.?" or "This answer is right, isn't it?" or like Tootsie's request above, which isn't even a question). Tag questions defer and seem to convey uncertainty and a need for confirmation from the listener. You use tag questions more often in the presence of men than when you're talking only with other women.

You are three times more likely than a man to state imperative commands in question form (e.g., "Will you please close the door?" instead of "Please close the door").

You are almost twice as likely as a man to give your declarative statements a "modal construction," which means inserting unnecessary doubt into a perfectly factual statement ("I think I might have said that Joe likes to watch sports on Sundays"). Examples of words that help shape sentences into modal construction form are *could, should, would, may,* and *might.*

You are six times as likely to adorn your sentences with intensifiers—modifying words that don't add information or modify anything (like "that's *very* beautiful," "this leaves me *so* confused," "if I could *just* have one look at it"). Intensifiers signal emotional involvement and probably are intended to solicit involvement from the listener. [McMillan, Clifton, McGrath, Gale]

> *There is always the one right word;*
> *use it, despite its foul or merely ludicrous associations.*
>
> DYLAN THOMAS (1914–53)

You are a man:

You are more likely than a woman to react to profanity as humor.

When shown a cartoon with a caption that contains no profanity, your probable evaluation of its funniness is exactly the same as a woman's. (The survey's example: A child peruses a storybook at a school desk and says to his teacher who is standing over him, "Who thought up this Dick and Jane stuff anyway?")

When *mild* profanity is added ("Who the hell thought up this Dick and Jane crap anyway?"), you are both likely to rate the cartoon funnier than without the mild profanity, but you're slightly more likely to rate it funnier than a woman will.

When *strong* profanity is added ("Who the fuck thought up this Dick and Jane shit anyway?"), you are considerably more likely to rate it funnier than a woman will. [Sewell]

There's a 61 percent chance that when speaking of the sex act you sometimes use the word "fucking," compared to a 5 percent probability for women. On the other hand, there's only a 13 percent chance that as an alternative you may use the word "screwing," compared to a 34 percent likelihood for women. [Sanders, Robinson]

You make requests of people:

If you are a woman, you are expected by women and men alike to make requests in polite form, most clearly typified by use of the word "please" or a softening phrase like "if you don't mind."

If you're a man, the acceptable form of the request depends on what you're requesting. You are not only permitted but expected to use a blunt, "nonpolite" form if you're asking for something that is typically masculine (like "Get me a hammer," or "Buy me a pair of tickets to the game"), especially if you're addressing another man. But if you're asking for a cup of tea or a recipe for a casserole, an act or item that is associated with femininity, you're expected to append a polite "please"—or "to speak like women" (in the phrase of the female researcher).

Of course, these "rules" are not always obeyed. When you violate them, however, whether you're a man or woman, you run a high risk of disapproval by both men and women. A woman who "speaks like a man" is likely to be sensed as rude, aggressive, or domineering. A man who "speaks like a lady" may be viewed as weak or effeminate. [Kemper]

AND WHO DO YOU THINK YOU ARE?

Finally, there's one special "language" that would appear to carry the least psychological freight, yet it almost always transmits an immediate and powerful impression-making message: the speaker's accent, dialect, and/or vocal placement.

Anthony S. Kroch of Temple University has specialized in trying to find out what we're really saying through variations in speaking manner—and what others "hear" in those changes. He has come up with the striking conclusion that some of the ways we pronounce and vocally place our words may be a class assertion of who we think we are in relation to other people. The root of such speech differences, he says, may be found "in ideology."

"Dominant social groups," concludes Kroch, "tend to mark themselves off" from the groups they dominate, using speech and other marks (dress, body carriage, food) "as evidence of superior moral and intellectual qualities." Lower-status or certain popular dialects, he says, use "simplified articulation," tending to drop or soften the "weak" details of speech (like saying "somethin' ") and to slide along with "natural" vowel shifts ("tomorra's a'right"). In contrast, Kroch produces experimental and historical evidence "that prestige dialects require special attention to speech, attention motivated not by the needs of communication but by status consciousness."

The British have long used the phrase "BBC English" to describe the perfect manner of speech that instantly marks a person of high breeding and status—witness Eliza Doolittle and her success at the queen's ball. After enunciating a few words, no further social credential is necessary. Studies have shown that perfect British English accomplishes its social magic in Australia, New Zealand, and Canada as well as in the United Kingdom. And more recently, three scholars from two sides of the Atlantic (Stewart, Ryan, and Giles) established that the United States, too, is enthralled by BBC English. A speaker with what the researchers choose to call "network English" is taken by Americans to have higher status *and greater competence* than speakers of any regional American dialect or any foreign accent, "even though British speech was considered less intelligible and aroused more discomfort."

HOW YOUR NAME AFFECTS YOUR LIFE

A name and a person . . . share an identity, although it takes a while before they cling to each other. . . . I remember feeling a sense of inappropriateness when a friend once referred to my newborn son as Ian. It did not seem he was yet enough of a person to warrant being called by his name. . . .

A curious taboo exists involving women's names in Jewish law. A man may not marry a woman who has the same Hebrew name as his mother. This law can easily be construed as an incest taboo. . . . The name and person share an identity. . . .

It is hard to get away from believing what we know for certain is not true: the name and the person are one and the same. For in the end, all that remains is the name.

MYRNA FROMMER,
KINGSBOROUGH COMMUNITY COLLEGE,
BROOKLYN, NEW YORK

LOOK YOURSELF UP

You have a "socially desirable" first name:

If you are a woman, people are apt to think of you as more physically attractive than if you had an undesirable name. This was learned in a poll of male and female students from Tulane and Loyola Universities (New Orleans) who were asked to choose a beauty queen from six photos. The photos were preselected (in a separate poll) for equal ranking in attractiveness. Then, fake first names, three of standard desirability and three "undesirables," were randomly assigned to the photos. "Kathy," "Jennifer," and "Christine," the beauties desirably named, combined to win more than 80 percent of the votes for beauty queen. They got 158 votes (96 from males, 62 from females) over the combined total of only 39 for "Ethel," "Harriet," and "Gertrude" (20 from males, 19 from females). [Garwood, Cox, Kaplan, Wasserman, Sulzer]

If you are a woman, the higher yours rates among best-liked women's names, the more likely you're assumed to rank high—on the basis of your name alone—in qualities of femininity. If you're a man who's nicely named, you're similarly expected to rank high in masculinity.

But, whether you're a man or woman, having a less desirable name doesn't lead to people assuming you're deficient in feminine or masculine traits. [Garwood, Baer, Levine, Carroll, O'Neal]

Now let's hold on here! How does anyone know if her/his name is "socially desirable"? Who decides? By what standard?

This has been the subject of study after study, each researcher asking different questions, testing different standards, coming up with different lists, or different concepts of what makes a name advantageous, or even just well liked. So there is no master list of right names. But have they got little lists! Get this:

If your parents have inflicted upon you—oh, how to say it without hurting?—one of those drab, *ordinary* names, meaning the kind that turns up most frequently in the phone book or the census, like Anne or Mary or Michael or John, you can just relax. That's the surest sign that your name turns up high in almost any measure of "social desirability." The following could easily pass as lists of most common female and male names. But they're actually the names nominated by four classes at Tulane University as those they liked most:

1. Susan	1. David
2. Anne	2. Michael
3. Jennifer	3. Steven
4. Elizabeth	4. John
5. Mary	5. James
6. Katherine	6. Mark
7. Laura	7. Thomas
8. Deborah	8. Robert
9. Linda	9. Christopher
10. Julia	10. Paul

The ten highest votes at Tulane for *disliked* female names (some are the same as those most liked): Gertrude, Mary, Susan, Martha, Bertha, Betty, Margaret, Jane, Sally, Ann, Patricia.

The top ten for disliked male names: Frederick (or Fred), Harry, George, Harold, Joseph, Albert, Ralph, Samuel, Frank, Dick, Henry, Howard. [Garwood, Baer, Levine, Carroll, O'Neal]

Further evidence that it's nice to have one of those unbearably ordinary names: Dr. Thomas V. Busse of Temple University found, in a study of 2,212 Philadelphia school children, that *no* highly common name received an undesirable rating.

Another finding: A girl is significantly more likely to be popular with boys if she has a desirable first name. An advantage also applies to well-named boys in their popularity with girls, but less markedly. [Busse, Seraydarian, 1978, 1979]

If your name is *John,* you're commonly assumed (by someone who has nothing but your name to go by) to be trustworthy and kind, at least according to a poll in England reported in 1976. *Robin?* You're young. If you're *Tony,* you're sociable. *Agnes* is old. *Agnes* and *Matilda* are unattractive. *Ann* is nonaggressive.

If your first name is *Sargent, Baxter, Otto, Shepard,* or *Bruno*—this time, according to an American poll of about the same time—you're likely to be seen (if your name is all there is to go by) as active. If it's *Aldwin, Winthrop, Alfred, Milton,* or *Wendell,* you come off as passive.

If you like your name, according to a New Zealand study, you probably score well in a standard test for self-esteem. If you don't like your name, according to an American study, you don't score too well in that test of liking yourself. [Marcus]

> *The name of a man is a numbing blow*
> *from which he never recovers.*
>
> MARSHALL MCLUHAN (1911–80)

You have an unusual or unique first name:

You're likely to be black and/or poor, and more likely to be a woman than a man, a wide variety of surveys agree. Also, you're less likely than the average person to be a professional. [Willis, Willis, Gier]

But don't conclude from the preceding item that an unusual name will impede your entering a profession or rising socially. If you were born in the upper class to begin with, or have somehow passed its barriers, your likelihood of outstanding success is higher than average. Of the blue-bloods with unusual or unique names listed in the *Social Register*, a considerably higher-than-chance proportion are listed in *Who's Who in America*, to which achievement is the ticket of admission. [Zweigenhaft]

You have a slightly better-than-average chance of becoming a college professor (or graduating from West Point and becoming an army officer, as William Gaffney found in an informal study). Want to aim higher? Edwin Newman concluded in his book *Strictly Speaking* that a first name easily usable as a surname gives you a leg up in becoming head of a university or foundation (Kingman Brewster of Yale; Derek Bok of Harvard; Bryce Jordan of Penn State; Clark Kerr of the University of California; McGeorge Bundy of the Ford Foundation, and many more). [Marcus]

You are a man called by a diminutive form of your name:

If you're making a first impression, a shortened form of your first name (say, Dave) probably contributes to a different image of you than would your formal name (David)—sometimes a better one, sometimes more negative, depending on the name. But a nickname form (Davey) almost always creates a lesser impression. [Lawson]

After you're introduced, strangers often can't recall your name:

That's not because of your name or you, but because you were introduced by name too soon. If your name were spoken about five minutes into the conversation (after you've become more than just an empty name to a stranger), research shows virtually a 100 percent probability that your name would register. Trouble is, how do you get to arrange that? Repeat the introduction yourself? [Brant]

CHAPTER

2

Your Moods and Mental States

*Remember this, that very little
is needed to make a happy life.*

MARCUS AURELIUS ANTONIUS,
ROMAN EMPEROR (121–80)

WHAT THEY KNOW ABOUT YOUR HAPPINESS

I don't know why, and I choose gingerly not to speculate, but the bare fact is arresting: The learned journals have virtually nothing to tell us on the subject of happiness. Scholars have shown almost no interest in it, compared to the sadder states of mind. (The two-volume *Encyclopedia of Human Behavior: Psychology, Psychiatry, and Mental Health* has no entry for Happiness, nor does the word even appear in its forty-page index. Depression is covered by thirty-six indexed articles and passages.)

Happiness resists definition. The best way to pin down its central characteristic seems to be a double negative: the absence of unhappiness. Perhaps that's the main reason it eludes study and measurement.

But happiness must be something real because it is widely reported to exist, and people say it feels so good. Since "feeling good" is an unscientific report, how is a serious researcher to go about finding out who feels happy, and how and under what circumstances? Answer: Send out a questionnaire.

That's what two psychologists, Philip Shaver of New York University and Jonathan Freedman of Yale, did. To fill that saddest of research gaps, they have completed what surely must be the largest survey on happiness ever. Their questionnaire appeared in *Psychology Today*, and 52,000 readers, ages ranging from fifteen to ninety-five, voluntarily responded. One can quibble that those self-selecting readers do not represent a finely balanced sample of the world's population, and it's anybody's guess as to whether unhappy people volunteer for a questionnaire on happiness in higher or lower proportion than happy people do. To keep the record precise, the self-descriptions of the actual respondents mark them, in average, as younger, more educated, with higher incomes, and more of a liberal bent in politics than the average American.

What, in summary, did Shaver and Freedman find?

First off, happiness distributes itself unevenly. One cluster of respondents claims happiness as a usual state, interrupted only now and then by valleys of sadness or pain. For others, happiness is an oasis in a broad stretch of sorrows, or an island in a stormy sea of battles and bruises.

Respondents also confirmed the adage that whatever happiness is, money doesn't buy it. "Happiness is in the head, not the wallet," the researchers announce. "In fact, happiness has less to do with what you have than with what you want. It comes less often from absolute achievements than from relative ones. Happiness is a matter of setting personal standards, not chasing after other people's."

Not everyone fits that conclusion, of course. "Mostly I prefer the freedom," one young man responded, "that comes with having huge sums of liquid assets." A contrasting reader: "Money has never been a problem for me. I would change lives with anyone who has a decent sex life." And another: "I am now absolutely broke but much happier than I ever was married to a multimillionnaire's son. . . . I am richer now in my love than I ever could be in cash." A successful writer of fiction, feeling burdened by the financial demands of a family, lamented: "Everything I do is done just to get more and more money to pay more and more bills. At one time I could hold other ultimate values. Now I can't. Every time I try to care about a spiritual matter I have to bust my ass earning more money."

If you yearn to compare the success of your personal pursuit against a national "norm," you might start with these happiness statistics:

- Those reporting having known happiness sometime over the last six months: seven out of ten. "But they aren't confident about their feelings, which change from day to day," comment the researchers.
- Those reporting that their level of happiness rises and falls quite often: slightly more than 50 percent.
- Those reporting that they think about happiness daily, or at least weekly: eight out of ten. Also, those who report themselves as most happy are the ones who spend the least time thinking about it. ("Happiness," say Shaver and Freedman, "is like orgasm: if you have to think often about whether you have it, you don't.")
- Those reporting themselves as less happy than most of their acquaintances: three out of ten.
- Those expecting to be happier in the future than they are now: seven out of ten.
- Those optimistic about their personal lives: 83 percent.

And what, according to the survey, are the main components of happiness? That depends on who's choosing. Single women and men name being happy with friends, work, love life, and degree of recognition, in that order. Wives list their satisfaction with love, marriage, their husbands' happiness, and their sex lives. For wives, recognition and "personal growth" tied for fifth place. For husbands, however, personal growth ranked first, followed by love, marriage, work, and their wives' happiness. (For husbands, it appears, recognition does not rank high as a component of happiness.)

For most people one's own physical attractiveness rated low as a source of happiness; for married people, it rated lowest. Happiness with religion rated low for marrieds and singles alike.

The following findings may be reassuring for many: The respondents (who, remember, mostly did report themselves as happy) said they often feel stress, alienation, and psychological problems. How many report "constant worry and anxiety"? One third. How many feel easily tired? One third. Have trouble concentrating? One fourth. Often feel guilty? Almost one fourth. And how many often feel lonely? Fully 40 percent (and they're not limited to single people).

While a satisfying sex life turned up as an important component of happiness, the respondents were divided as to how and where to find it. People with many lovers do not measure as either more or less happy than those who have had only one. Whether those sexual encounters are extramarital or not seems to make no discernible difference. About 40 percent of married respondents (45 percent of the men, 35 percent of the women) have practiced sex outside of marriage, and their reports rank them just as happy, as a group, as the faithful ones.

The happiness of homosexuals ranks neither higher nor lower than that of heterosexuals, provided the homosexuals have accepted their own tendency. Homosexuals and heterosexuals rank about the same on almost every survey question, except that homosexuals report more sexual partners and they give a low value to the importance of marriage and children. (For more of the sex part of the survey, see "Your Erotic Responses," page 102.)

One third of the respondents recalled often feeling guilty in their childhood, and they markedly relate those guilts to their adult feelings of guilt, as well as to insomnia, anxiety, fear, suicidal urges, feelings of worthlessness, and motivation for therapy. Yet "many readers came through bad early and teenage years without a mental scratch, and are perfectly happy as adults."

People who live in large cities are as likely to be happy as those living in the country.

"Atheists and agnostics are just as happy as members of established churches, and people who do not believe in God are just as happy as those who do." The only attitude found important was "the certainty that life has meaning and direction."

The researchers conclude that "four psychological attitudes are essential to happiness:

"Emotional security: disagreeing with the statement 'good things can't last.'

"Lack of cynicism: disagreeing with statements . . . such as expressed by P. T. Barnum's 'There's a sucker born every minute.' The beliefs that life has meaning, that one's guiding values are right.

"Feelings of control over the good things that happen, as opposed to feeling that one is the pawn of events."

Many readers pinned letters to their questionnaires. The comparison-seekers among them typically asked, "Please score my questionnaire and tell me whether I am happy."

The happiest respondents, conclude Shaver and Freedman, "are those who feel in control of their lives, and who compare their progress against their own standards, not those of others."

(That final comment appears to support the discussion in Chapter 6, "Who's In Control Here?," on the advantages of what the chapter defines as an I-Control-Me personality.)

An awful lot of life is lost to depression.

JOSEPH SCHILDKRAUT, PSYCHIATRIST,
HARVARD MEDICAL SCHOOL

WHAT THEY KNOW ABOUT YOUR DEPRESSION

Anyone who has been there has a hard time explaining depression to anyone who has not been there. The innocent nod sympathetically, calling on their recollections of the blahs, of being down in the dumps, and say wise words about stiff upper lips. The afflicted just can't get across that getting doused in a passing thunderstorm is not analagous to tumbling into a bottomless, inescapable black hole. "They've known what it's like to be blue," says someone I know who's been there, "but not to be paralyzed."

True, the blahs can lead one to family upsets, to messing up on the job, and to the neighborhood bar. But real depression is thought to account for 60 percent of suicides. Something like thirty-five million Americans alive today will have been clinically depressed before they die. Of those, about one third will sink into the black hole a second time. For every man who falls, so do two women. At this moment, for every one hundred adults and adolescents around us, six are clinically definable as depressed.

Although some mix of psychotherapy and antidepressant drugs

can help depressed people, it's believed that such help reaches only one in five who need it. One reason is that depressives often don't recognize they have an illness. They just "feel bad."

The National Institute of Mental Health reports that the average age of the depressed has dropped in the past generation from late middle age to the younger spectrum of twenty-five- to forty-four-year-olds. Contrary to a widespread assumption about the aged, people over sixty are least subject to depressive illness.

For the truly depressed who so often don't know how ill they are, what are the criteria? How are they to be told apart from the passing sad? A rule of thumb for diagnosing *major acute* depression is that a patient shows at least four of the following, and for *chronic* depression at least three:

- Inability to experience pleasure
- Sleep disturbances
- Loss of weight
- Loss of appetite
- Loss of energy

A more detailed inventory of symptoms might include:

- Feelings of sadness or hopelessness
- Insomnia, early awakening
- Thoughts of suicide and death
- Restlessness, irritability
- Pronounced guilt or low self-esteem
- Loss of appetite and weight
- Fatigue, loss of energy
- Diminished ability to think or concentrate
- Loss of interest in once-favored activities, particularly sex
- Chronic pains that fail to respond to usual treatment

This doesn't even touch upon the thickly forested territories of the manic depressive and of chemical imbalances that may be treatable with powerful drugs like lithium. To learn much more, the reader need not go into forbidding textbooks. *The Reader's Guide to Periodical Literature* at a public library will lead the reader to well-reported, lucidly written magazine articles on those subjects.

And, of course, a browse of the shelves will yield excellent and readable non-technical books.

LOOK YOURSELF UP

You get depressed around Christmas:

You may get depressed, but it probably has nothing to do with Christmas.

Rochelle Semmel Albin, a psychologist-journalist, scrutinized the myth while serving as a clinical fellow at Harvard Medical School's McLean Hospital. The first suspicions that depressions occurred around holiday seasons had turned up fleetingly in the psychiatric journals in the 1940s, but the idea burst into public view in 1957 through a *New York Times Magazine* article called "Singing Those Christmas Holiday Blues." By 1980, the notion was so entrenched that nobody was inclined to question Jane Brody, the *Times*'s esteemed health writer, when she reported that "for millions" Christmas is "the most depressing time of the year." Psychiatrists, she added, "are busiest then" and "the suicide rate rises." Also in 1980, therapists gathered in Boston for the first conference dedicated to Yuletide depression. "Statistics show," proclaimed a conference brochure, "an increase in suicides and suicide attempts at this time of year." When some nosy reporter in Boston asked to see the statistics, the conference director confidently responded: "We really could not find any, but everyone knows that it happens."

Everyone knows? Reports by the National Center for Health Statistics had shown that between 1950 and 1978, more people killed themselves in April than in any other month. December? The fewest suicides of the year. In the United States, Europe, and Japan, more people are admitted to mental hospitals during summer months than at any other time of the year.

At a state mental hospital in Ohio, George Cerbus and Robert Dallara, two psychologists who studied records of all newly admitted patients in the early 1970s, found no relationship between admissions for depression and the time of year. They also learned that patients already in the hospital reported feeling depressed most often in October, not around Christmas.

Is the "everyone" who "knows that it happens" just dead wrong? Not entirely. Therapists indeed do report persistently that their phones ring more often around Christmas. They do report a seasonal upturn in the blues (or "blahs") that are felt by everybody sometimes, but the blues are a far cry from depression, a serious disorder. As Dr. Anthony Rothschild of Harvard Medical School makes the distinction, "Unhappiness is a part of life. But a person who is depressed clinically can't be cheered up."

Short-term blues commonly result when Christmas heightens either expectations or burdens. Not long ago, the phone rang in the office of Dr. Myrna Weissmann, a Yale psychiatrist. A caller pleaded tearfully that she didn't know how she was going to get through Christmas.

What specifically was the trouble? Dr. Weissmann recalls asking.

The caller's in-laws had just arrived for the holidays.

Can't she get along for awhile with the in-laws?

They're O.K., but they brought ten pounds of shrimp.

Doesn't her family like shrimp?

They love shrimp, said the caller. But gift shopping and wrapping and meal planning and rearranging rooms for guests had already strained her to the limit. Now she was expected to peel, clean, and cook that ten-pound bagful. Something in her just snapped.

That woman felt, yes, put-upon, saddened, overwhelmed, says Dr. Weissmann. But depressed? That's something far different.

Rochelle Albin's investigation of the Christmas-depression myth cast the first shadow of suspicion over many "scientific" findings about human behavior, beyond Christmas and depression. She administered a variety of psychological tests to almost two hundred college students. One test Albin gave the students was a standard measure of depression developed by the National Institute of Mental Health. She tested one group in October and December, another group in March and May. The test confirmed decisively that students felt their worst in December. But what other studies hadn't shown, probably because they didn't ask, was that Albin's student-subjects felt equally awful in May. Clearly, something other than Christmas was "depressing" them.

What do December and May have in common in the life of a student? Right. *Final exams!* One small, disconcerting clue as to how research of "human behavior" can mislead when undergraduate students are appointed stand-ins for the broad human race (as they so often are by researchers because they are so convenient to study).

Albin came up with one more fascinating finding about Christmas and the blues: that people with high feelings of "mastery" over what happens around them (the I-Control-Me folk; see Chapter 6) appear less subject to December blues than those whose test scores on feelings of mastery are average or less (the They-Control-Me's). [Albin; also Saft]

Finally: The records of 180,000 American suicides have recently been examined by a University of California (San Diego) sociologist, who comes up with the news that the suicide rate *declines* before and after Christmas, Thanksgiving, and Memorial Day, as well as shortly in advance of New Year's, Independence, and Labor Days. How about *during* the celebrations? On holidays, including Christmas, the average national count of suicides has been 102 *fewer* than the average of other days of the year. [Phillips, Wills]

You are depressed:

You are twice as likely to live in a city as in a rural area. (On the other hand, if you live in the country, your depression has an increased likelihood of leading you to alcoholism or drug abuse.) That is the finding of a survey, sponsored by the National Institute of Mental Health, of five counties in North Carolina covering 3,921 residents. It may appear on the surface to contradict (but does not) the report in the previous section on Happiness, that people are as likely to be happy living in large cities as in the country. A greater likelihood to be depressed is not the same as a lower likelihood to experience happiness. [Blazer]

You probably can't think as well as the average person who is not depressed—or as well as you did before you were depressed.

This University of California study showed that people measuring as depressed scored significantly lower than average on other tests gauging their ability to think abstractly, their ability to screen out irrelevant but associated information, and their speed of information processing. Furthermore, the more the individual measured as depressed, the lower his or her score on all three tests. (But the authors caution against jumping to conclusions, without further study, as to whether the thought disorder is caused by the depression, or whether a preexisting thought disorder predisposes a person to depression.) [Braff, Sprock, Saccuzzo]

You often have the feeling that people would just as soon not be around you.

And the bad news is that you're probably right. James Coyne, a

University of California (Berkeley) psychologist, gave a standard test of depression to college women. Then, for his experiment, he recruited thirty who scored among the most depressed and, for comparison, paired them with thirty others who were not depressed at all. He further chose sixty more women who were not depressed, randomly pairing them against each other in groups of thirty. All the couples were asked to converse for fifteen minutes about anything they wanted "for the purpose of getting to know one another." Next, the participants responded to a questionnaire about how willing they were to meet their partner again, and how willing they thought their partner would be to see them again. The groups who had depressed partners came out less willing than the others to (1) ask a partner for advice, (2) sit with her on a three-hour bus trip, (3) invite her home, or (4) work with her. The depressed women, in turn, expected such rejections—and, in expecting them, were more accurate than the average nondepressed woman in guessing her partner's feelings. The depressed people, furthermore, "got even" with their rejectors. They rated their nondepressed partners as unpleasant more frequently than pleasant, as well as weak more often than strong, cold more often than warm, and unfriendly more often than friendly. Having the last word, in a sense, the depressed women, more often than the nondepressed women, said they wanted to have nothing else to do with their partners. [Coyne, Strack]

There's a better-than-average chance that your workplace has a hostile social climate, and that you work under a grouchy supervisor.

A University of Southern California psychologist, Rena Repetti, reported to an annual meeting of the American Psychological Association that the way people talk about their work environment is a good predictor of how they will score on a standard test for depression. Repetti surveyed 302 employees at thirty-seven banks, asking them to rate the social climate of their workplace. With significant consistency, when most workers rated it as caring and friendly, individual workers were likely to score on tests as less depressed and anxious, and having higher self-esteem, than individuals working in climates rated by most as hostile.

She also found that a grouchy immediate superior caused more misery than did hostile co-workers, and a supportive boss boosted mental well-being more than friendly colleagues. [Repetti]

If you are a depressed woman, you are significantly more likely than a depressed man to cry. You also are more likely than a man to eat more compared to nondepressed people, as well as to smoke cigarettes, or become irritable. And you're more likely than a depressed man to confront your feelings—and blame yourself for your troubles.

If you are a depressed man, you are significantly more likely than a depressed woman to become aggressive, engage in sexual behavior, spend time alone, and use stimulating and tranquilizing drugs. [Kleinke, Staneski, Mason]

If you are a woman, you tend to dwell on your depressive feelings much more than men, which is why, according to this Stanford University researcher, you have twice the likelihood of serious depression of a man. If you are a man, you appear to have a lower likelihood of depression, she concludes, because you are more adept at distracting yourself, thus shaking off depressive moods. [Nolen-Hoeksema]

If you are a married woman who stays at home, you're three times as likely to be depressed as a woman who goes out to work. The researcher interviewed more than one thousand men and women, ages eighteen to ninety-two. [Aneshensel]

You are preparing to enter a Catholic convent:

Going by a study of several years ago, you probably have "a higher incidence of maladjustment" than the average college woman. In that study, the personalities of women entering convents were measured by a standard test of mental health and psychological abnormality, the Minnesota Multiphasic Personality Inventory.

But hold on. Maybe you're less maladjusted and more of a winner than the college crowd after all. A more recent study using a different measure, the Cattell 16 Personality Factor Questionnaire, which was designed to assess personality traits among normal people, rated postulants at six Catholic convents. They were found to be more conscientious than a comparable group of college students, as well as more self-disciplined, realistic, relaxed, adaptable, and self-assured; also less neurotic and less anxious, and of higher leadership potential. [Rooney]

STRESSES: YOUR FEARS, DAILY HASSLES, AND MAJOR UPSETS

Death of a spouse is 100. A prison sentence is 63, but getting a traffic ticket is only 11. Remember?

Almost everybody has heard of the Holmes-Rahe numerical scale developed by two University of Washington psychologists to measure the impact of personal setbacks on physical health. Thomas Holmes and Richard Rahe interviewed thousands of people, examined their health histories, and then recorded their "life events" over the next year or two. The researchers next came up with "life change units," which put a number value on the probable health impact of a stressful event. Among events assigned high numbers were divorce (73), getting fired (47), and trouble with in-laws (29). Two high-stress events experienced at about the same time, like getting fired the week before a serious injury, or perhaps less coincidentally, the breakup of a marriage and having to change residences, may have a cumulative health impact, Holmes and Rahe suggested.

The scale was so appealing to popular magazines that they began offering their readers easy-to-take pencil and paper "stress tests," with predictions that a score of over 300, or whatever, spelled an 80 percent chance or 50 percent chance of getting sick—and psychologists soon had to warn against hasty conclusions about a direct causal relationship between stressful happenings and illnesses.

The obvious fact, soon supported by new studies, was that nobody could draw a straight line from bad experiences to disease (as we will see in "Who's In Control Here?," Chapter 6). Some people with low stress scores for life events got sick, and others with high stress scores stayed in the pink of health. In fact, some people thrive on challenge and stress, taking them as signals of new opportunities and potential rewards. To these people, described in Chapter 6 as "I-Control-Me" persons, avoidance of stress may seem like a "chickening out" of chances to better their lives.

Now along come Richard S. Lazarus and Anita DeLongis of the University of California at Berkeley, who, with several associates, have amassed evidence that, far more than the major misfortunes of life, "daily hassles . . . may have a greater effect on our moods and our health." They asked one hundred middle-class, middle-aged white men and women to keep written notations for a year of their "hassles." Here were the top ten common hassles of these middle-aged people, listed in order of frequency:

1. Concern about weight
2. Health of a family member
3. Rising prices
4. House maintenance
5. Too much to do
6. Misplacing or losing things
7. Outside or yard maintenance
8. Property, investments, and taxes
9. Crime
10. Physical appearance

LOOK YOURSELF UP

The stresses in your life produce physical symptoms, among them high blood pressure:

One thing you can do to relax—and reduce your blood pressure—is to stare into a fish tank. Two University of Pennsylvania researchers monitored the blood pressure of twenty university employees and students in three activities. Each subject alternated between reading aloud from academic textbooks (a time-tested way of inducing moderate stress), looking at a blank wall for twenty minutes, and gazing for periods ranging from two to twenty minutes into a fish tank that sometimes contained fish and plants and sometimes only plants.

During the textbook readings, as expected, blood-pressure levels rose. When subjects stared at the blank wall, their pressures fell. When they looked into the bubbly tanks, blood pressures fell even further. During periods when tanks contained only plants, however, subjects appeared to lose interest—and their blood pressures would soon begin to rise again. Those staring at fish tended to stay relaxed.

A few of the subjects had chronic high blood pressure. For them, fish-watching was more effective as a relaxer than for the others. [Beck, Katcher]

Your home life is stressed by frequent marital squabbles:

What you may need is not a family therapist, but a second bathroom. A Purdue University study found that couples with more than one bathroom, whether they have kids or not, are less stressed and more content than those in single-john homes. [Inman]

You think you would feel less stressed if only you could be less exposed to noise:

Lots of other people think that too, and they may be right. The U. S. Environmental Protection Agency estimates that more than seventy million Americans reside where noise levels are so high that they interfere with communication and cause stress. More than one third of those questioned in a Census Bureau survey complained about noise, lifting it to their most-mentioned neighborhood problem. According to the National Research Council, twelve million people recently reported they were thinking of moving because of neighborhood noise.

Where does *sound* end and *noise* begin? The sound level of an air conditioner bothers practically nobody. But turn on a vacuum cleaner and you irritate, or at least distract, a high percentage of people. A riveting machine bothers almost everybody, while a jet takeoff generates frequent complaints.

A common definition of noise is *unwanted* sound. After all, people eagerly buy tickets for a symphony orchestra that is far louder than a bothersome vacuum cleaner. A rock band might drown the decibels of a riveter, yet its big beat, insufferable to some, fills rock fans with near-ecstasy.

Annoyance at noise may be governed by feelings or beliefs even more than by the noise itself:

• Sociologists Aubrey McKennell and Paul Borsky conducted studies near London's Heathrow Airport and New York's Kennedy Airport, respectively. People most annoyed by the roar of jets were those who assumed that pilots and aviation officials didn't give a hoot about those forced to hear the noise. Those who believed someone cared were bothered far less. Annoyance was also especially high for those who thought the noise unnecessary, or who believed the roars were harmful to their health, or feared plane crashes, or who were already annoyed by other aspects of their environment.

• At Penn State University, two sociologists, Craig Humphrey and John Krout, found that people reporting high annoyance at noise from a nearby superhighway were most apt to be those who felt the road threatened the value of their property; those least bothered tended to be those who expected the highway to increase their property values. That finding was consistent no matter how far people lived from the highway. The less-annoyed also tended to be those who believed the road enhanced access to jobs, stores, and churches.

Isn't it usually true that the first and more frequent complaints about noise are from the cranky aged, overeducated snobs, or the spoiled rich? Surprisingly, studies in Germany and the United States show that stress resulting from noise is statistically unrelated to age, income, or schooling.

Final wrinkle: Loud noise may reduce your usual impulse to help somebody in trouble. Two psychologists, Kenneth E. Mathews of Seattle City Light and Lance Canon of the University of New Hampshire, had a confederate on a quiet suburban street "accidentally" drop some books from an armload as a passerby approached. About 50 percent of passersby helped pick up the books—when the street was quiet. But when, as part of the experiment, a lawn mower without a muffler was running at full throttle nearby, only 12.5 percent of passersby volunteered help. [Cohen]

You are a full-time housewife:

You feel more stressed about your role than a part-time housewife does, and it's probably because you sense that many people today hold a low regard for homemakers. [Ivancevich, Matteson]

You are a wife and mother holding a job outside the home:

You deserve a prize for inspiring more jumped-at conclusions per square theorist than perhaps any social changer of the century, most of which are trying to explain why you're feeling stressed. You're stressed, they say, because (1) you feel guilty over "abandoning" your children and husband; (2) you feel guilty about not feeling as guilty as you think you ought to feel; (3) you're afraid that if you leave your present work there are not enough jobs around that a women can get; (4) you've found that jobs are plentiful, but it seems they're all as store clerks, secretaries, and scut-workers; (5) those attractive jobs thrown open to you by affirmative action, for which you secretly feel that you lack experience, stir your fears of success; (6) you're overwhelmed by the competing demands of hard-driving bosses and resentful children.

Scarcely any support for those "obvious" explanations of your stress can be found in research. In fact, studies are showing that your job, especially if it's a high-powered job, may be the least stressful component of your life. "The prediction was," says Dr. Grace Baruch, a sociologist at the Wellesley Center for Research on Women, "that when they joined the work force women would have coronaries at the same rate as men. That didn't come true. Why not? Because it turns out that home was never so *un*stressful. The stress the women experienced may even have decreased when they joined the marketplace."

The bad effects of "split roles"—pitting an outside job against the home—also seem to have been exaggerated by "expert" guessers. On the contrary, studies by Dr. Denise Kandel, a Columbia University sociologist, suggest that a woman with several roles—say, as wife, mother, provider, student, and organization leader or contributor—probably functions better than a woman with fewer roles. (Of course, women who carry all those loads, Dr. Kandel allows, may self-select themselves because they had more capacity and a higher level of mental health at the outset.) Dr. Peggy Thoits, a sociologist at Princeton, suggests that the ideal number of roles for apparent well-being may be five. More than that, her research shows, seems to produce overload. On the other hand, only three roles—as wife, mother, and provider—is usually accompanied by a high anxiety level, "much higher than most fathers have." [Darnton]

The greatest source of your stress is not, as many probably think, lack of time, but your feeling that other family members are giving you less than a fair share of help at home. [Ivancevich, Matteson]

If you are a mother with an outside job, you are almost twice as likely as a nonemployed mother to complain of stomach pain. Also there's a 60 percent chance that you have premenstrual or menstrual pain, compared to 39 percent for full-time homemakers. Those are the findings of Dr. Yusoff Dawood, a University of Illinois obstetrician-gynecologist, who surveyed twelve hundred American women.

A pain researcher, Dr. Donald Stanton, director of Michigan State University's Chronic Pain Clinic, says that reducing stress is "one of the mainstays in our treatment of chronic pain," but then adds: "I'm not sure that stress causes pain, but it certainly increases the perception of pain." [Harris]

You are a woman, and you are worried because today's highly stressed woman is losing her life-expectancy advantage over men:

There's cause for concern, all right, but the reason is not increased stress, according to this study. The reason is that women are smoking more, and older men are quitting smoking at double the rate of women. That is the verdict of Gus H. Miller, a statistician, based on his analysis of deaths of Americans after age thirty between 1920 and 1983, as compiled by the National Center for Health Statistics. Miller, director of Studies on Smoking, Inc., a nonprofit group in Pennsylvania, predicts that, while the average woman's life since 1920 has been longer than the average man's, "the life expectancy of men and women will be about the same in the next forty to fifty years," if the present smoking trend continues. [Miller]

You are the husband of a working wife:

The most common source of stress about your role is feeling unable to handle your share of housework and child care. [Ivancevich, Matteson]

You hold a high-pressure job and you wonder if you're cut out to handle its stress:

Your ability to handle stress on the job, almost without regard to your occupation, is most reliably indicated by your getting a high score on a test for self-esteem—unless you're a policeman. If you're a cop, your ability to handle the special stress that goes with your work correlates with only one factor: the state of your marriage. [Ivancevich, Matteson]

A police officer stops you for a driving violation:

As noted in Chapter 1, if the officer is wearing mirrored sunglasses, your feelings of stress, fear, and suspicion rise noticeably. You're likely to rate him less friendly, less courteous, and more aggressive than you would the same cop if you could see his eyes.

If the ticket-wielding officer approaches you wearing a visible holstered gun, your feelings of aggressiveness and anger surge.

You're more likely to talk back aggressively, and if you're armed yourself, the authors of this study warn, the chances are heightened that you'll pull out your own weapon, endangering the cop's life.

These are findings of a study in which eighty-seven male and forty-six female drivers were stopped for cause by Canadian Mounties. Half the time the officer wore sunglasses, sometimes with a gun at the driver's eye level. A female researcher stood behind the officer, recording the emotion on the face of the driver, using a standard rating system. When the policeman went back to his car, the researcher asked each driver a series of questions about the encounter. [Boyanowsky, Griffiths; Canadian study.]

You have been professionally diagnosed as a neurotic:

You are likely to have a higher IQ, more education, a higher employment rate, and 23 percent higher earnings than someone judged as psychologically well. (At least that's so if you are a male. This study didn't cover women.) [Benham, Benham]

You are more likely than someone who's not neurotic to read and believe your horoscope. [Fichten, Sunerton]

You are more likely to feel irritated by surrounding noise than someone who is not neurotic. That's the outcome of this study in Japan that involved 129 education students, mostly women. [Iwata; Japanese study]

If you go off the deep end and wind up in a psychiatric ward, needless to say the hospital staff and your family will probably protect you from R-rated movies that show excessive violence and sex. They'll cushion your nerves with sweet PGs, and even Gs, that star grandmothers and freckled kids and moon-eyed dogs.

Well, they may not know what's good for you. A study has found that those goody-goody movies disturb psychiatric patients more than bang-bang and bam-bam flicks. The study's conclusion speculates that when mental patients see "ordinary, domestic stories of love and everyday family life," their tendency to identify with the film characters makes them "feel frustrated and bitter by the striking contrast with their own life circumstances, limited by hospitalization and mental illness." [Cory]

.   .   .

If you're a patient in a mental hospital, you're far less likely than most others to get cancer. That's especially so if you're diagnosed as a schizophrenic.

Figures collected by a Greek psychiatrist over a period of twenty years at two mental hospitals in Greece found that only 4.9 percent of patients died of cancer compared to 15 percent of the general population. Other figures from mental hospitals in England, Wales, and Scotland showed about the same ratio. However, rates of death caused by cardiovascular disease or diabetes did not differ inside the hospitals versus outside.

In one Greek hospital where 250 people died during the study period, remarkably few—only four—schizophrenics died of cancer. Similarly, in Moscow's Kahsenko Hospital, with a yearly population of twenty-five hundred patients, cancer deaths among schizophrenics run between one and two per thousand, startlingly few.

Why? Nobody knows (yet). [Rassidakis]

You are a child of school age:

Going back for a moment to the impact of noise: If you are a boy in the first to fifth grades, you are more likely than girls to get a better score on a test when the test is given in a noisy room. But if you're a girl, you're more likely to outscore the boys when the room is quiet. That's the result of an Ohio State University study involving 156 boys and girls. [Christie, Glickman]

There's a high chance that your teacher, your school psychologist, and your school nurse will be mistaken in judging what kind of event is likely to stress you, and how stressful it really is. This is true whether you are an American child, a Japanese, or a Filipino.

A group of 197 professionals—97 of them teachers, 39 clinicians, and 61 teachers-to-be—examined a list of twenty experiences a child might find upsetting, and rated them on a scale of one to seven. In addition, they were asked to estimate how children would rate those same events, as well as the proportion of kids who actually experienced each. The results were compared against the ratings by the children themselves, as well as those in comparable studies by the principal researcher involving Japanese and Filipino children.

The professionals were quite accurate in estimating the high importance children attached to "going blind" and "being kept in the same grade next year." They sharply overestimated the importance that children attached to "going to a dentist," and "having a new baby sister or brother." They underestimated the children's ratings of "receiving a poor report card," "being caught stealing something," "hearing my parents quarrel and fight," "being sent to the principal's office," and "being picked last on a team." [Yamamoto, Felsenthal]

You may be subject to an emotional disorder that is spreading among suburban children (according to a report by Swedish psychiatrists at a United Nations conference on human environment): feelings of measurable insecurity unless you are within visual distance of a subway line to the city—which you regard as a "life artery." [*Behavior Today;* Swedish study]

Also, your clean, orderly, perfect suburb, if that's where you live, makes you want to cut loose and scream from suffocation and boredom, a finding that surprised some German researchers.

In the late 1960s, the government of West Germany engaged a raft of avant-garde architects, city planners, recreation experts, and aestheticians, and instructed them to design "scientifically planned communities," mostly to benefit children. Then the government invested heavily in building them. Apartment houses bloomed amidst spacious lawns, shaded walks, fenced-in play areas—open and tranquil space, all for play.

The Ministry of Housing and Urban Development, together with the Institute of Psychology at the University of Erlangen-Nuremburg, set out to survey the feelings of 5,450 children, half of whom lived in those scientifically planned communities and half from just plain schools in just plain natural-growth cities and towns. They did it by having the kids, ages six to fourteen, draw and paint on themes such as "my favorite place to play," "Mommy sends me to do the shopping," and "my way home from school."

The experts were shocked at discovering that what they judged to be the happiest art almost all came from the old towns. Mostly, the pictures showed kids frolicking among trash cans and storm drains and puddles, construction sites, railroad yards, messy streets, and beneath factory smokestacks. From the model communities came gloomy, despairing pictures of concrete-paved, fenced-in prisons of cleanliness, order, and boredom. [Dittrich; West German study]

You are a student taking a long multiple-choice exam:

If you are the anxious type (as measured by a standard personality inventory), you are likely to change your multiple-choice answers significantly more often than someone who is less anxious. Furthermore, if you rate as *both* depressed and cynical, your tendency to change your answers from right ones to wrong ones is much higher than for someone who is not depressed and who has a positive view of mankind. [Range, Anderson, Wesley]

YOUR MOOD REACTIONS TO THE SEASONS, WEATHER, TIME OF DAY, AND LIGHT

LOOK YOURSELF UP

You are inexplicably depressed every year about the same time, usually as the seasons shift to autumn and winter:

You may be afflicted with a syndrome called Seasonal Affective Disorder (SAD). If you have a bad case of SAD, the shorter days of autumn and winter darken your life with sluggishness, pessimism, anxiety, crying jags, withdrawal from sociability, loss of interest in work, play, and sex as well as carbohydrate craving, food binges, weight gain, oversleeping, and thoughts of suicide.

"This is something beyond what someone might feel as winter blahs," emphasizes Dr. Thomas A. Wehr, a psychiatric researcher with the National Institute of Mental Health and a codiscoverer of SAD. "The depression is quite conspicuous [and] interferes with a person's functioning."

Nobody yet knows how many people are afflicted with SAD. In the United States alone, however, the victims are thought to number in the hundreds of thousands. Some evidence suggests that in the far northern latitudes, where winter days are short, the rate of affliction may be worse.

Without delay, let's leap to the good news about SAD. Dr. Wehr and his research partner, Dr. Norman E. Rosenthal, also of NIMH, have struck on a treatment that quickly and effectively liberates victims of SAD from their winter darkness. Not psychotherapy. Not some mood-altering pill. The cure is to turn on the lights. Bright, very bright room lights. Strong white full-spectrum fluorescent lights seem to work best.

Soon after identifying SAD, Drs. Wehr and Rosenthal collected a group of SAD victims who had suffered through nine or ten successive winters of depression. They were mostly women in their thirties. The doctors instructed that every morning before dawn and again at dusk each subject was to sit before a screen that was backed by fluorescent lamps, projecting the illusion of bright sunlight. Within a mere two or three days, the subjects themselves brightened dramatically. That's far quicker than antidepressant pills would work. Then upon termination of the light therapy, the subjects just as promptly fell into their funk again. A few were put back on the lamp therapy to stay with it all winter. Their depression again vanished.

How is one to explain such dramatic results, achieved so simply?

Rosenthal, not entirely surprised, explains: "In most species, the seasonal rhythms governing such things as mating, food intake, hibernation, and migration are cued mainly by the light/dark cycle, which is relatively invariant from year to year." But is there any sound evidence that humans, too, are affected by those deep biological rhythms? Try this: The NIMH team surveyed victims of SAD who collectively had 219 children. They found that those children were twice as likely to be born in May or June as in August or September. Anyone who can count to nine can figure out the peak time of conception: August or September, when all the SAD person's drives are in "go."

The strongest hint of a cause of SAD lies in a secretion of the pineal gland called melatonin. The hormone has been known to affect the timing of seasonal behavior in animals, particularly hibernation and mating. In humans, melatonin was thought to be vestigial, with no known function or effect. Under the influence of light, the pineal gland shuts off the supply of melatonin, like the closing of a valve. Then darkness—or the shortening of days—flips it open again, the melatonin flows, and an animal goes into the low-key mode of winter behaviors. To confirm what seemed to be going on, in one experiment, SAD subjects, who had been energized out of their depression by light therapy, were injected by researchers with melatonin—while still getting their daily lights. Sure enough, the infusion of the hormone sank the patients back into partial depression.

An important additional wrinkle was discovered by Alfred J.

Lewy, a research psychiatrist at the Oregon Health Sciences University. He found that light treatments in the morning lifted the moods of SAD victims practically to the levels of the unafflicted. But light treatments in the evening had virtually no effect. Treatments both morning and evening had some beneficial effect, but not as much as morning light alone.

Lewy thinks that heavy doses of light may help reset the biological clock, thus minimizing the discomforts of jet lag and shift changes, as well as treating other sleep and mood disorders. [Rosenthal, Wehr; also Lewy]

Here's a modern change-of-season mood-changer brought on not by Mother Nature but by technology:

Each autumn, upon changing your clock to Standard Time (thus picking up an extra hour of sleep), you tend to go to bed at your accustomed clock hour and fall asleep as quickly as you usually do. But for most of a week your wake-up mood is improved, and you're likely to report that you slept better than usual. Probably the simple explanation is that the extra hour of sleep made you feel more rested.

But not so in the spring. After changing to Daylight Saving Time (with the loss of one hour for only one night), again your going-to-sleep habits need no adjustment, but you're apt to wake up less happy for the better part of a week.

And, incidentally, if you take a test in arithmetic upon awakening, you do significantly better after those awakenings in the fall than you do in the spring. [Monk, Aplin; British study]

During the week or so following each clock change—to and from Daylight Saving Time—you're more likely than usual to smash your car. During both those weeks auto accidents rise 4 percent over the year-round average. [Hicks]

You're not a sucker for old folk tales, but you've noticed that when the weather changes, regardless of season, your mood—and that of people around you—changes, too:

Stick with that story. Science is behind you.

"Weather-sensitive people"—about one in five, says Dr. Michael A. Persinger, author of *The Weather Matrix and Human Behavior*— "have a volatile autonomic system. Most of these people are what we commonly refer to as high-strung or nervous."

While almost everybody's autonomic nervous system, which controls involuntary actions, reacts to weather change to some degree, either in the direction of producing more irritability or more lethargy, the effects are most emphatic for the "weather sensitive," and the effects will vary according to your psychological makeup. Studies show, for example, that aggressive persons tend to become more so, particularly with the arrival of cold air masses, says Persinger. Depressed people are apt to become more depressed with warm air masses. Those tendencies increase during especially stressful phases of the life cycle, such as adolescence and midlife. You can mark yourself down as weather sensitive if, on days that are rainy, thickly overcast, or gusty, you find that you fly off the handle or need to clench your teeth more than usual, or if you go sharply the other way, feeling sleepy or tired although you're not really lacking for rest. [Persinger]

Over a five-week summer school session, the collective mood of thirty students of Towson State University, average age twenty-seven, significantly dropped whenever the humidity rose. Every weekday morning as the students arrived for their 9 A.M. psychology class, their professor gave them a standard test, the Mood Adjective Check List, in which they marked words that best described their feelings of the moment. They did not know that he was later going to correlate the results with daily records of the National Weather Service. The most consistent correlation was that high air humidity coincided with low ratings for three specific mood states: "Vigor," "Social Affection," and "Elation." The findings, say the researchers, support the old saying, "It's not the heat that gets you, but the humidity." [Sanders, Brizzolara]

You are recovering from surgery in a hospital room that faces a dreary brick wall:

You will require a longer time to recover, ask for more pain relievers, and have more complications than you would in a room that offered a pleasant view of a courtyard. That is the finding of a ten-year study of patients recovering from gallbladder surgery in a hospital in Paoli, Pennsylvania. [Paoli]

Your mood depends a lot on whether the room you're in is chilly or warm or just right:

Of course it does. Almost too obvious to mention, except for this recent discovery:

To change someone's comfort with the temperature of a room, you don't necessarily have to fiddle with the thermostat. You may just have to *talk* about adjusting it.

Researchers asked 105 students in two classrooms to rate their degree of room comfort on a scale ranging from +3 (too hot) to −3 (too cold). About two weeks later, without announcement, the temperature was raised five degrees in one of the classrooms. The forty-seven students in that room were asked once again to rate their comfort. Meanwhile, in the other room the remaining fifty-eight subjects were told the temperature was higher than it had been two weeks earlier, and were asked to rate it again. Actually the temperature in the second room was unchanged.

In both cases, the classes rated their rooms as warmer.

One clear implication: This finding, if word of it gets around, could ruin OPEC. [Stramler, Kleiss, Howell]

> *The whole conviction of my life now rests*
> *upon the belief that loneliness,*
> *far from being a rare and curious phenomenon,*
> *peculiar to myself and to a few other*
> *solitary men, is the central and inevitable fact of human existence.*

THOMAS WOLFE, AMERICAN NOVELIST (1900–38)

LONELINESS

"Loneliness," says Warren Jones, a psychologist at the University of Tulsa, "is the common cold of psychopathology." This month (or any month), a quarter of the American population will feel extremely lonely, estimates the "father of loneliness research," Robert Weiss, of the University of Massachusetts. Studies in other countries confirm that the same is true elsewhere.

Lonely people agree to an uncanny extent in their descriptions of how loneliness feels: like an empty space in the area of the diaphragm or chest, causing mild discomfort to intense pain. The cause of loneliness, answered lonely people in one study, is having no one to whom they can reveal the intimate details of their lives. (For more about this, see "Your Willingness to Reveal Yourself," in the next chapter.)

Weiss describes two different kinds of "lonelies": the *emotionally* lonely person who has many social relationships, but only a few intimate ones, or none; and the *socially* lonely person who has a few close relationships but no general network of friends.

Loneliness is not necessarily harmful. It can be used, says Albert Cain of the University of Michigan, "as a time of redress, resilience and turning toward and strengthening of internal resources." Many spells are temporary or situational: for instance, after a move to another community, or after a divorce, when lonely feelings lasting up to a year are common. But when there is no apparent triggering event and the feelings last two years or more, psychologists call the condition "chronic loneliness."

Weiss disputes a common belief that, after loss of an intimate partner, throwing oneself into social activities or at new acquaintances will erase loneliness. He found that only a new intimate relationship will heal the ache. The good news, however, is that once such a new relationship is established, loneliness will vanish almost instantly, leaving no troubling after-effects.

Psychologists distinguish sharply between loneliness and *aloneness,* a state of chosen solitude. Explorers, solo sailors, and mystics and other religious or meditative people, for instance, comfortably choose solitude. So, too, may forest rangers, fire watchers, trappers, lighthouse tenders, shepherds, people suffering illness, and many who choose not to marry or remarry. Even an unwilled solitude can have positive consequences. Solitary confinement in criminal or political prison can become, for some people, a period of renewal or religious conversion. In some cultures, coming-of-age rituals involve a period of aloneness after which the initiate is thought to have had an important and beneficial experience.

Voluntary loneliness, isolation from others,
is the readiest safeguard against
the unhappiness that may arise
out of human relations.

SIGMUND FREUD (1856–1939)

Our language has wisely sensed the two sides
of being alone. It has created the word "loneliness"
to express the pain of being alone. And it
has created the word "solitude" to express
the glory of being alone.

PAUL TILLICH,
GERMAN-BORN AMERICAN THEOLOGIAN (1886–1965)

LOOK YOURSELF UP

You feel lonely, fairly often and for prolonged periods:

Your loneliness does not mean you're alone a lot. People who measure high in psychological tests for feelings of loneliness—"high
lonelies"—are likely to spend as much time in the company of others
as "low lonelies" do, but their talk is noticeably less intimate.
[McCormack, Kahn]

Not only do you talk and hang out with others as much as low
lonelies, but you're also likely to list as many people among your close
friends as do people who aren't lonely. Still, your perception of
yourself as lonely is probably accurate. Your best friends don't feel
as close to you as they do to other friends. Consequently, your list
of "best friends" tends to comprise people who don't put you on
their list of best friends.

In the study that led to these conclusions, forty-two male and
female students filled out questionnaires on loneliness and were
asked to list their friends. The friends were then asked to participate
by listing *their* friends, thus confirming or refuting the subjects' lists.
[Williams, Solano]

If you are a man who tests as lonely on standard measurement
scales, you are not likely to confess your loneliness to your friends.

Perhaps that is because you have found (as this research has) that if you do admit it, you receive a less sympathetic response than a lonely woman does.

If you are a woman, you may test as less lonely than a lonely man, yet you'll be more likely than he is to admit it and talk about it. That may be because you've learned a woman's loneliness gets a less negative response than a man's. [Borys, Perlman]

You may deepen your loneliness without knowing it by using a conversational style associated with the lonely, which often has the unintended effect of pushing potential friends away.

For example, when talking with someone you don't know, you probably don't make as much eye contact as the average non-lonely person. Also, you're likely to contribute fewer comments about what the other person has just said, you ask fewer questions, and you're more likely to change the subject. You're apt to confuse and discomfort your partner further by not sending signals that you are listening—simple signals like nodding or saying "uh-huh" or "oh, really." Your self-involvement tends also to blind you to the other person's body language, so you miss clues as to how she or he is feeling. For example, you're apt to miss a body-language request to back off a little.

When talking about others you're apt to make hostile or rejecting comments, especially if you are male. The message you send is that you tend not to trust—or even like—other people.

These observations suggest that instead of worrying about your loneliness, perhaps you ought to concentrate on your conversational manner. As a reward for your effort, you might wind up less lonely.

To form these conclusions, the researchers gave forty-eight undergraduates (twenty-four men, twenty-four women) a standard test for loneliness, then paired them for videotaped conversations. Trained raters assessed each for details of "partner attention." In a subsequent study, a group who had been instructed on how to show partner attention tested lower on loneliness and shyness than previously, and showed increased self-esteem. [Jones, Hobbs, Hockenbury]

In conversation with friends and acquaintances, you're likely to reveal far less about yourself than a non-lonely talk partner—and then you tend not to realize how little other people know about you.

You feel freer to open up with strangers, and when you do open up, you talk intimately—often too intimately, too early—to people of your own sex. (If you weren't lonely you could be expected to talk more intimately at first with people of the opposite sex.) If you are a woman, this is especially so. You're not only unwilling, you are *highly* unwilling to talk about yourself to a man. As a lonely man or woman, after you become more acquainted with your talk partner you're inexplicably inclined to switch to topics that are less intimate. The person you are talking to is aware of the change, but you aren't. The presence of the two extremes—running on about intimate matters to a stranger (say, a fellow passenger on a plane) *and* the unwillingness to talk about yourself to people you know, especially to people of the opposite sex, is a strong symptom of marked loneliness.

The study: Seventy-five male and female undergraduates took standard tests for loneliness and willingness to talk about themselves (self-disclosure, as psychologists like to call it). Of students who rated themselves as lonely, twenty-four were paired with twenty-three non-lonelies for conversations which were subsequently rated by both sets of partners. [Solano, Batten, Parrish]

The more confiding and self-revealing you are, the less lonely you are likely to feel. (That conclusion and those that follow in this study are based on analysis of daily records of "social interactions" kept by ninety-six male and female college seniors. The subjects also completed a number of personality scales, including the UCLA Loneliness Scale.)

Regardless of whether you are a man or a woman, you probably feel less lonely when you spend more time with women. Women more often provide the qualities that help stave off loneliness—responsiveness, empathy, and conversational intimacy. But when you find the relatively rare man capable of intimacy and closeness (see Chapter 6 on masculinity, femininity, and androgyny), he may turn out even more valuable than a woman partner in helping combat your loneliness.

If you are a lonely man, the chances are that you spend a lot more social time with other men than with women, but you don't talk very intimately with them. Furthermore, time spent with them doesn't seem to go far in banishing your loneliness. You're probably less close to other men—including your best friends—than most women are to their friends. If you feel you're not too interested in relationships with emotional content, it's all the more probable you make little social contact with women. On the other hand, if you do value conversation about feelings, you are more likely than most men to spend time with women—and you probably find you don't need much of such conversation to prevent loneliness.

If you are a woman who spends a lot of social time with men—and if you describe yourself as lonely—the more time you spend with men, the lonelier you feel.

Whether you are a man or a woman, if you'd like to know a man who can talk intimately, but your circle of friends doesn't include one, perhaps your next best hope is to *coach* a man in the value and techniques of openness. The best way to test his potential, this research suggests, is for *you* to risk the disclosure of intimate information about yourself to him, thus setting a stage that may encourage him to reveal himself.

Finally, you probably feel less lonely when other people take the initiative to make contact with you. That is especially true if you are a man and the contact is initiated by a woman. [Wheeler, Reis, Nezlek]

You are more likely than most to be introverted or shy, and less willing to take social risks. [Peplau, Perlman]

Your loneliness is apt to be accompanied by anxiety, depression, boredom, hostility toward others (especially if you're male), and a tendency to put yourself down. [Jones, Freemon, Goswick; Russell, Peplau, Ferguson]

You are an employed spouse:

If you are the husband, the chances are that you rarely feel lonely. But the probability of your feelings of loneliness increases slightly as the number of your children increases.

If you are the employed wife, you are somewhat more likely to feel lonely than your husband. You are the least likely to feel lonely if you have one or two children living with you—and you have a job. (If you don't have a job, the presence, number, and ages of your children give no apparent clue to whether or not you feel lonely. Employment makes the difference relatively predictable.) [Gove, Geerken]

You are a wife not employed outside the home:

You are much more likely to feel lonely than either wives or husbands who hold jobs. In apparent contradiction of the previous finding, if you have one or two children at home you are even more likely to feel lonely, especially if the children are very young or are old enough to be relatively independent of you. [Gove, Geerken]

You have an adequate circle of friends:

The more people you feel you can confide in or turn to for help in an emergency, the less lonely you are likely to feel. You're even less apt to feel lonely if those friends connect with each other through friendships or family relationships. [Stokes]

But if that network is notably dominated by relatives, so that you tend to be socially isolated from non-relatives, the chances are substantial that you would check out as comparatively unhappy. [Fischer, Phillips]

You are a woman who spends a good deal of time with men:

You tend to have more "regular" menstrual cycles (twenty-nine days, give or take three) than a woman who spends less time with men. ("Spending time" is not to be misconstrued as "keeping company" in a social sense. It means quite literally being in their presence.) The triggering mechanism for regular cycles that this study identifies appears to be something in the perspiration of others.

The researchers collected underarm pads worn by three men and soaked them in alcohol. Then they swabbed the solution on the upper lips of seven women three times a week for at least three months. For comparison, they swabbed plain alcohol on the lips of nine other women. All the experimental and comparison-group women had irregular cycles (fewer than twenty-six days or more than thirty-two days apart); they were unmarried, childless, and did not use birth control pills or IUDs. After the experiment, for those getting the perspiration extract the proportion continuing to have abnormal cycles was reduced. Those swabbed with plain alcohol had no change.

Previous research had shown that women who spend more time with men tend to have more regular cycles than those who don't, but the finding had not yet been explained by the perspiration connection. Other studies have connected more regular cycles with women who have intercourse regularly, or who are masturbated regularly by men. The same effect is not found in women who masturbate alone.

While regularity seems to be affected by the physical presence of men, the specific *timing* of menstrual cycles may shift in response to the frequent presence of other women. Earlier research has shown that women who spend a lot of time together also tend to start having their menstrual cycles synchronously. To further test that finding, the authors of this study recruited women with normal menstrual cycles, divided the group in half, and swabbed the lips of one half with the perspiration extract of donor women, the other half with plain alcohol. By their third cycle, 80 percent of the extract-receiving women began to have periods in sync with the perspiration donors. The women in the plain-alcohol group did not. The researchers say they do not know whether the perspiration had its effects through odor or skin absorption. [Cutler, Preti]

There is but one truly serious philosophical problem,
and that is suicide. Judging whether life
is or is not worth living amounts to answering
the fundamental question of philosophy.

ALBERT CAMUS,
ALGERIA-BORN FRENCH NOVELIST (1913–60)

That life is worth living is the most necessary
of assumptions, and, were it not assumed,
the most impossible of conclusions.

GEORGE SANTAYANA,
SPANISH-BORN AMERICAN ESSAYIST (1863–1952)

THE SPECTER OF SUICIDE
LOOK YOURSELF UP

Someone near and dear to you has given hints of suicide:

By simple acts, you may help dissolve someone's hopelessness just enough to save a life.

"Pain is what the suicidal person seeks to escape," says Dr. Edwin Shneidman of UCLA, a pioneer in suicide research, author of *Definition of Suicide*, co-founder of America's first suicide prevention center, and father of a national network of such centers. "The immediate goal of a therapist, counselor or anyone else dealing with highly suicidal people should be to reduce the pain in every way possible. Help them by intervening with whoever or whatever is causing their distress—lovers, parents, college deans, employers, or social-service agencies. I have found that if you reduce these pressures and lower the level of suffering, even just a little, suicidal people will choose to live.

"Needs for security, achievement, trust and friendship form much of the landscape of our inner lives. . . . Address these psychological needs and the suicide will not occur. . . . The most dangerous word in the dictionary of suicide is 'only.' It implies the options have been constricted to the single one of death. We can see this tunneled and arbitrary logic at work in the Jumper. Suicide is the 'only' solution and jumping is the 'only' method. . . . The goal of the therapist or any potential rescuer is to broaden the suicidal person's perspective."

Shneidman suggests trying to ease the sufferer's pain by:

- "Acting as an ombudsman in the person's life." That may mean enlisting the person's spouse, lover, boss, anyone who can make a *concrete change* that would soften the *immediate* pressure.
- "Don't use phony reassurances or try to cheer them up— they'll see right through that. But suggest that you want to tackle their complaints with them. Suicidal people feel they have no one to turn to for help."
- "Don't accept their either/or logic. Make a list of all their alternatives, including suicide, and discuss each one. The very making of a list may counter the constriction of their thought."
- "Try to find something that will make things a bit better, even if just a tiny bit. This might mean letting them simply ventilate their pent-up feelings. Even a little improvement can save a life." [Shneidman]

You are a candidate for committing suicide:

That does not classify you as depressed, even though the two states are often confused. More than most depressed people, you are overwhelmed by a sense of *hopelessness*. And that is actually a measurable condition.

A standard test called the Beck Depression Inventory includes a group of statements that permit the subject to admit (or reject) feelings of a transcendant sense of despair; among them, "I might as well give up because I can't make things better for myself," and "I never get what I want, so it's foolish to want anything." Those desperate statements, when isolated from the others, score on a "hopelessness scale."

The author of this study monitored, for a period of more than five years, 207 people who had been hospitalized for psychiatric illnesses, and who reported having thought about suicide but who had not attempted it. Within two days of their entering the psychiatric hospital, the researcher tested each patient with the Beck inventory. Of the 207 subjects, fourteen patients eventually killed themselves, usually years after the hospital admission and testing. The striking fact, however, is that of those fourteen victims, fully thirteen had scored high in the hopelessness scale.

So your high score in hopelessness can signal that you are indeed a prime suicide candidate. But it shouldn't be taken as a predictor of your self-imposed doom. Of the 207 patients, eighty-nine scored high in hopelessness. But after five to seven years a great majority, seventy-six of the eighty-nine, were still very much alive. [Beck]

If you are male and elderly (the category that makes you most likely to succeed at suicide), you're three times more apt to kill yourself if you're white than if you're black, Mexican-American, or an American Indian. The reason behind this finding, theorizes Richard H. Seiden, a University of California (Berkeley) researcher, is that "blacks and other minorities are much more likely to be involved in child care, housekeeping, financial contributions to the common budget, food preparation or whatever"—activities that lead the elderly to feeling they are needed and making a contribution, feelings that Seiden describes as antagonistic to suicide. In contrast, many white families "enjoy the economic affluence which allows them to ship their parents off to the dubious virtues of retirement ghettoes, to live out their remaining years feeding pigeons and fighting boredom and loneliness."

Seiden cites data showing that suicide rates are low among communities that value the aging process—in sharp contrast to much higher rates among cultures that place a high value on staying and looking young. Values set by church and extended family, which are more likely to be followed by minorities than whites, emphasize

THE SPECTER OF SUICIDE   99

respect for the elderly, who are believed to have gained special wisdom through their longer experience. Life in the black community further promotes a personal pride that comes with surviving the day-to-day adversities that flow from poverty and racism.

Finally, older white men, according to Seiden, become far more depressed than nonwhites by the reduced employment and finances that often accompany old age. Whites crack under the loss of their power and influence, whereas nonwhite men and women have long accustomed themselves to the lower status brought on by racism and sexism.

Seiden hastens to say that he would hardly advise people to give themselves over to poverty and the miseries of racial discrimination as an antidote to suicide, but rather to study the coping skills developed by minority groups that help them adapt to severe frustration. [Seiden]

The three events that are the most likely to push you over the edge are (1) a marital breakup, (2) losing your job without finding another within twelve weeks, and (3) taking your first sweet breaths of spring.

(1) While divorces are clearly at the root of many suicides, the actual self-destruction may not be performed until long after the decree. Or before the decree: The early period of separation is also a dangerous time.

(2) If you're unemployed, twelve weeks is about the average time for finding a new job. It's also about the time of a noticeable rise in suicides among the continuing jobless—and the longer the unemployment period, the more likely you'll do yourself in.

(3) Whatever the cause, it's more likely you'll kill yourself in the spring than in any other season. Dr. Steven Stack, a Penn State sociologist who compiled this cause-of-suicide study, attributes that to "a gap between the depressed realities of the suicidal population and the wonderland of spring. The suicidal population feels left out and at a distance from the joy. . . ."

Most notable in this study of the causes of suicide, perhaps, is that it finally pins down whether television news reports about suicides inspire others to go and do likewise. They clearly do—yet clearly don't. Dr. Stack matched eight years (1972–80) of national suicide statistics against the airing of suicide reports on evening newscasts by ABC, NBC, and CBS, which he unearthed at the Vanderbilt University Television News Archive. Around the time of a national news segment that reported (or discussed) suicide, yes there was indeed often a discernible bump upward in the occurrence of new suicides. But the *monthly* national rate of some two thousand suicides showed no pattern of variation that could be correlated with the reports. So a TV news report might contribute to the timing of someone doing himself in, but apparently not to the overall rate of occurrence. "The theory that suggestion causes suicide," concludes Dr. Stack, "was not supported by my research study." [Stack]

More on the impact of news reports: When ex–secretary of defense James Forrestal jumped out of a hospital window in 1949, the news was followed by a 4 percent rise in the suicide rate. Later, comedian Freddie Prinze, who killed himself at the height of his popularity, jolted the national rate upward by 8 percent. Marilyn Monroe stirred a 12 percent boost. "It may be," suggests Ira Wasserman, Eastern Michigan University sociologist, "that people identify more closely with entertainment celebrities than with other suicide victims." [Wasserman]

As hopeless and disconnected from the world as you may feel, you're significantly less likely to kill yourself during the heat of a presidential election campaign. A Brown University researcher (who is also an election buff) checked recorded suicides during the home-stretch months—September and October—of fourteen consecutive election years between 1912 and 1972, comparing them against the same months of the preceding and subsequent years. During those campaign climaxes, suicides dropped by 21 percent. Perhaps this underlines the point that just a little connectedness, something extra to care about, no matter how irrelevant to the immediate personal crisis, can make the difference. [Boor]

If you do indeed kill yourself, and if you're male, you are most likely (57 percent likely) to do it with a gun.

If you're a woman, the chances of your using a gun are rapidly rising (up to 39 percent by 1980). But you're far more likely than a man to take poison or pills. [Centers for Disease Control]

You are a teenager:

If you are also male and white, you are much more likely than the rest of the population to commit suicide. Between 1970 and 1980, the suicide rate for men aged fifteen to twenty-four years increased by 50 percent, while the rate for women in that age group increased by less than 5 percent. "It used to be the people who committed suicide were older white men," says Dr. Mark Rosenberg, a Centers for Disease Control specialist on suicide and violence. "Whereas a few years ago, it might have been your grandfather who was ill, widowed, depressed, now it's your son." [Centers for Disease Control].

But that finding—the predominance of white males among youthful suicides—is not as cleancut as it may appear. About 90 percent of all suicide *attempts* are made by adolescent females. More specifically, if you're a young woman, the statistics show you are four times more likely than a male to attempt suicide—but fail. Suicide attempts, speculate the researchers of this study, may be a way for anguished young women to send out an alarm for help, which men may avoid doing until their pain becomes unbearable. [Eron, Huesmann]

The likelihood of your committing suicide is notably higher than normal if your mother or you had a difficult time at your birth, or if she was chronically ill during her pregnancy with you. Of teen suicide victims, compared against a group of living teens, more than half had been exposed at birth to one or more risks: 19 percent had trouble breathing for the first full hour of life or longer, compared with only 4 to 8 percent of the living teens; 21 percent had chronically ill mothers during pregnancy, compared to 0 to 6 percent of the nonsuicides; and 31 percent had mothers who had no prenatal care during the first twenty weeks of their pregnancy, compared with 4 to 12 percent of the control group. [Salk]

Also, your suicide may be ten times more likely than normal if at least one of your parents was chronically depressed during your childhood—regardless of whether or not that parent was suicidal. Of a sampling of teenage psychiatric patients at New York Hospital-Cornell Medical Center in White Plains, New York, 50 percent of suicide attempters had at least one chronically depressed parent, compared to only 5 percent of the nonsuicidal group. [New York-Cornell]

You live near San Francisco and, as your last living act, you decide to leap off a bridge:

You're classy to the end.

You are more than 85 percent likely to choose the Golden Gate Bridge rather than the Bay Bridge. In fact, even if you live east of the San Francisco Bay, there's a 50–50 probability that at the supreme moment of your misery and hopelessness you'll take the trouble to drive the length of the Bay Bridge and all the way across the city to the Golden Gate to end it all in proper style. And nobody, *nobody,* has ever gone the other way to jump off the Bay Bridge (at least, up to the time of this 1983 study).

Why? Each bridge is about as old as the other, both having opened in the 1930s. Both offer a roughly equal dive, about two hundred feet. So what's the explanation? According to suicide researchers Richard Seiden and Mary Spence of the University of California, Berkeley (near the scorned Bay Bridge), the Golden Gate, touted by tour guides and brochures as the world's leading suicide site, simply has glamour and class that is beyond compare. [Seiden, Spence]

YOUR EROTIC RESPONSES

Regardless of what *they* know about us, there's one thing we can guess about *them*—if the sheer quantity of studies tells us anything about the scholars who do them: Behavioral researchers are very curious about sex.

LOOK YOURSELF UP

You feel that your sex life is not as satisfying as most people's. As a result, your general state of happiness is lower than it ought to be:

Join the club—a much bigger club than you think.

Your happiness problem may have less to do with something missing from your sex life than it does with your belief that most other people have a more satisfying time of it. The belief hurts, of course—and you're probably mistaken in it.

A substantial proportion of women—34 percent—and more than

half of all men—55 percent—rate their sex lives as less than satisfactory. Compared to whose? Compared to most other people's. And what do they assume about other people's sex lives? That it's wonderful, of course—or, at least, much more exciting than their own. And how realistic is their comparison? While those 55 percent are less than satisfied themselves, 19 percent of men and 29 percent of women judge that their friends are sexually dissatisfied.

Here's more evidence of widespread misapprehension about the sex lives of friends: Among the 52,000 singles who responded to this huge survey on happiness (for more about it, see the first section in this chapter, "What They Know About Your Happiness"), 99 percent of men and 98 percent of women tend to assume that other singles they know are sexually experienced. Yet, of these unmarried respondents, aged fifteen to ninety-five, actually 22 percent of men and 21 percent of women reported never having had sexual intercourse.

Specific impediments to enjoyment of sex are more commonly reported by women than by men:

- Ten percent of women report pain in intercourse. One in a hundred men do.
- Twenty percent of women complain of slowness or inability to become aroused, and so do 6 percent of men.
- Trouble reaching orgasm: women, 38 percent; men, 8 percent.
- Feeling depressed after intercourse: women, 8 percent; men, 4 percent.

Then there are unhappy experiences, specific to maleness or femaleness, that may harm or destroy sexual pleasure:

- Among men, 5 percent report impotence. Nineteen percent ejaculate prematurely.
- Eight percent of women report they have been victims of rape and 17 percent have aborted. Many women attribute later sexual fears and inhibitions to those experiences.

Finally, according to folklore, men "are interested in only one thing." Yet men who report any of the aforementioned problems are just as likely to measure as generally happy as men who do not. Women who have any of those sexual problems, however, are not only less happy in their sex lives, but likely to be less happy in general. [Shaver, Freedman]

You are a women, middle-aged or older:

You may have endured some confusing times.

If you've been in step with your contemporaries, you probably learned early the conventional expectation of your role in the bedroom: to provide sex, not necessarily to enjoy it. But more recently you've heard from every side that conventional expectations have changed. Conventional expectations? When and how did they change? What are they now? According to whom?

One way to measure year-by-year "progress" in conventional bedroom expectations is through a running survey of the best-selling sex and marriage manuals, which are bought and read predominantly by women. Their importance as a gauge is not so much that they *influence* current attitudes of women and counselors, but that their marketplace acceptance *reflects* what has become "modern"—what a woman is now expected to think, feel, and go for.

Three Indiana University researchers studied forty-nine manuals published in the United States from 1950 to 1980, as well as earlier surveys of manuals from 1830 to 1970.

1869: "As a general rule, a modern woman seldom desires sexual gratification for herself. She submits to her husband, but only to please him; and, but for the desire to maternity, would far rather be relieved from his attentions."

1875–1950: "During the last quarter of the 19th century," say the Indiana researchers, "manuals began to portray sex as intrinsically fulfilling. . . . [then] during the first half of the 20th century . . . as potentially enjoyable for both husband and wife." Still, old assumptions carried over. "First, middle-class women, at whom these manuals were directed, were assumed to have little overt interest in sex. Second, women's sexuality was assumed to be fundamentally different. . . . Third, it was taken for granted that sexual experience in women takes place only within marriage. These three assumptions support a fourth: that women depend on men to awaken their sexual potential."

1965: "Men can enjoy sex, in an animal sort of way, without love. Women can't. . . ."

1970: "It is probably true that the arousal of passion is more closely linked with emotional factors in many women than in many men. . . ."

1971: "A woman's early sexual expression virtually never gives passionate delight, and response often takes years to develop."

1972: "Sex is a much more meaningful, deeper part of life for most women than for men."

1972: That women are sexually dormant and naturally passive "is one of the most destructive myths perpetuated on men and women. The almost wholesale cultural acceptance of the propaganda that men are primarily aggressive and women are primarily passive has forced females to use devious, manipulative ways of expressing their assertions. . . . This is an extremely depreciating process to the female, and thus produces escalating resentment of which she is often not aware because she has been so thoroughly brainwashed."

1973: "Emotionally, a woman's climax, coupled with the joy she receives from giving herself to her husband, completes her." (Note the assumption that her sex partner must be her husband.)

1973: "*It is a very self-centered experience* [italics are the manual's]. . . . Your focus must be solely on *your sexual stimuli* and whatever increases it. . . . To awaken your potential you must assume responsibility for *your own* sexual pleasure and the means of achieving *your own* orgasm. . . . He can give you his penis to enjoy, but the extent to which you enjoy it is *your responsibility.*"

1974: "Sex should be the fullest expression of love we know. In its apogee, there is a fusion of minds and bodies that is truly transcendental."

1974: "Sex is no longer a male-oriented exercise."

1975: "Only [when sex flourishes] . . . will people be able to tap hidden resources of creative energy and love that will ultimately revitalize every aspect of their lives. . . . If men and women are to begin to enjoy sex, they must . . . learn to break free of their neurotic shackles and rid themselves of their inner restraints and conforming disciplines. For sex to flourish it is essential that emotions be free, spontaneous, and without moral or prejudiced attitudes. . . . Years ago . . . a 'good' and moral woman waited for her husband to entice and seduce her. Petting and sexual manuevers were left entirely up to the male's prowess and imagination, or lack thereof. It was a solo act. Today the liberation of sexual ideas has made sex more of a duet. Both partners participate in more or less equal roles, providing themselves and each other similar experiences of heightened pleasure."

1976: "There is an old saying that there are no frigid wives, just inept husbands. Although that sounds rather comforting from the female point of view, it was probably made up by some male who thought he could make any woman come. Nowadays most women like to think that they have something to do with their own orgasms and that they are not dependent on a man for sexual fulfillment."

1977: "And once we become sexually independent and happy, we can apply what we've learned to other areas of our lives as well. . . . Women's sexual power and woman power as a whole are inseparable and complementary. When we learn to take care of ourselves sexually, we become independent in a part of our lives that has always been traditionally dependent on men."

1978: "When you choose to become more positive about being a sexual person, you must take the responsibility for that choice. It is *your choice.*"

[Weinberg, Swensson, Hammersmith; The specific manuals from which these quotations are drawn can be found in the study.]

You are a young (or not so young) woman:

Three major magazines for young women have investigated your sex life—your sexual history, practices, and preferences—if you fit the profile of their typical reader. (If you're aging, at least three major studies have probed into almost everything worth knowing about your sex life, too.)

The first of the magazines to do so (in 1981) was *Cosmopolitan,* whose readers are likely to be youngish and single (or to "think single"); followed by *New Woman* (in 1986), whose readers are apt to run on the professional track; and, most recently, *Redbook* (1987), read primarily by worldly, well-schooled young mothers. A book, *Love, Sex, and Aging* by Edward Brecher, published by *Consumer Reports,* reported the author's large survey that included 1,844 women in their fifties to seventies and some older. The book also surveyed men of that age span. Brecher's conclusions largely confirm earlier findings about sex among the aging by Shere Hite in *The Hite Report* and the landmark *Kinsey Report.* (Men's magazines seem less drawn to asking their readers intimate questions, perhaps because men are less drawn to answering them.) Like most volunteer surveys, all these drew responses from people who were willing to fill out detailed questionnaires on a subject that clearly must interest them. That process, called self-selection, may make the results statistically "unscientific." But the number of responders in all cases is impressive—and their answers are interesting.

Depending upon which of those reader groups you resemble, here is what those surveys say about your probable tendencies:

YOUR FIRST TIME.   Yours may be quite different from that of the woman of not so long ago. In 1953 the Kinsey Report found that only 3 percent of women had had their first sexual intercourse before they were fifteen.

If you are a typical *Cosmopolitan* reader responding in 1981, there's a 21 percent chance you had given up your virginity by age fifteen. If you waited no longer than age twenty, you fall into a large additional 69 percent. That leaves 10 percent. If you're in that small group, there's a 90 percent chance you lost it by twenty-five. Did you have an orgasm your first time? If you didn't, you have a lot of company—90 percent of the responders.

If you are like the typical *New Woman* reader of 1986, you probably began your sex life a bit more cautiously—but only a bit. If you had your "first time" before the age of sixteen, you were in a group of only 19 percent. You would be in the majority, an additional 56 percent, if you started by nineteen, another 21 percent by twenty-four, and 2 percent between twenty-five and twenty-nine. Like the *Cosmo* women, 90 percent of the *New Woman* readers did not experience orgasm their first time.

If you're like the typical *Redbook* responder of 1987, the chances are exactly fifty-fifty that you had your first experience at seventeen or earlier. (Why seventeen, and not sixteen or fifteen as in the other surveys? Simply because that's how *Redbook* asked their question.) Answering a different kind of question, only 6 percent of those still under twenty-five when they answered the questionnaire had been virgins until their wedding night. In contrast, of those over forty when answering, 33 percent had been virgins until they married. Thirty-two percent of all responders had taken six or more lovers before "knowing" their husbands—more than double the percentage in a *Redbook* survey thirteen years earlier.

FREQUENCY OF INTERCOURSE.   Remember the belief that the woman should be the reluctant accommodator of the "needs" of her husband? In utter contradiction of this belief, fully 63 percent of *Cosmo* women said they would like sex more often than they get it. Only 1 percent said they'd prefer it less frequently. Happily, 36 percent felt their frequency was "just right." And just what is that accustomed frequency? Eight percent of *Cosmo* responders make love once a day—or more often; another 36 percent, three to five times a week; 32 percent, once or twice a week; 15 percent, once or twice a month; 9 percent, less than once a month.

Two percent of *New Woman* readers said they would *like* sex twice a day. Ten percent said they'd like it every day—but only once a day; 28 percent, four to six times a week; 37 percent, two or three times a week; 9 percent, once a week.

Redbook readers reported on actual frequency rather than on what they "would like." "Almost" every day, 7 percent; three to five times a week, 24 percent; twice a week, 28 percent; once a week or less, 40 percent. Of the women making love only once a week or less, fully 71 percent said they would like to do so more often.

Of the older married women in the Brecher study, 28 percent reported making love more than once a week. Seventy-seven percent were happy with their frequency; 18 percent said it was not enough; 5 percent would be happier with less.

FOREPLAY. If *Cosmo* readers could have sex exactly as they wanted, 14 percent would choose a full hour or more of foreplay; 48 percent, up to a half hour; 36 percent, fifteen minutes. Two percent would take five minutes or less.

New Woman readers said in impressive majority (72 percent) that sometimes they just want cuddling and sex play without following through to intercourse. Nineteen percent can willingly go along with play and no climax when that's what their partners want, but 8 percent disapprove of uncompleted play.

CONJUGAL POSITIONS. Only *Cosmopolitan* asked, and learned that 61 percent of its responders prefer the missionary position. Twenty-six percent of the women like best being atop their partners; 8 percent, side by side; 8 percent, the woman positioned for the male's entry from behind her.

ORGASMS. Of *Cosmopolitan* responders, 20 percent consistently have an orgasm as part of lovemaking; 50 percent, usually; 20 percent, sometimes; and 10 percent, seldom or never. Two out of three of the women have multiple orgasms occasionally; an additional 10 percent, always; 23 percent, never.

Of *Redbook* readers, 22 percent say they reach orgasm every time. Sixty-one percent reach it "almost" every time; 5 percent, never. Fifty percent "often" have multiple orgasms.

In the Brecher study, of the older women who said they are happily married, 93 percent usually come to orgasm. Of women listing themselves as unhappily married, only 7 percent usually have orgasm.

ORAL SEX. Eighty-four percent of *Cosmopolitan* readers receive cunnilingus "regularly." An identical percentage perform fellatio on their partners.

Similarly, 84 percent of *New Woman* women report fellatio. Sixty-four percent say they like it. Nine percent don't. Cunnilingus: 72 percent, with 65 percent enjoying it, 5 percent wishing it weren't offered. *(Cosmo* didn't ask about its readers' likes and dislikes.)

Forty-five percent of *Redbook* women receive cunnilingus at least half of their lovemaking times. Of them, 84 percent say they enjoy it. Fifty percent give fellatio at least half the times.

While oral sex appears more popular with young magazine-reading women than with Brecher's older subjects, it is not a new fashion. Brecher found that 43 percent of the older women "have performed" fellatio, with three quarters of them saying they liked doing so. Forty-nine percent experienced cunnilingus, 82 percent of them with pleasure.

MASTURBATION. If you read *Cosmopolitan*, you're considerably more likely to masturbate than if you read *New Woman* (the only other magazine that asked). Eighty-nine percent of *Cosmo* responders have masturbated at some time. Moreover, 37 percent of that great majority now do so several times a month; 25 percent several times a week; 3 percent daily; and 35 percent "rarely." Twenty-six percent use a vibrator.

New Woman readers were asked different questions, impeding direct comparison, but appeared less active than *Cosmo* readers: 18 percent of *New Woman* readers masturbate "frequently," 48 percent "sometimes," 21 percent "rarely," and 13 percent never. But a higher percentage of *New Woman* responders—43 percent—have used vibrators and other sex toys.

Asked if they "approve" of masturbation by older people, 62 percent of the older women in the Brecher study said they do, and 53 percent said that they themselves masturbate.

EROTIC MOVIES AT HOME: Twenty-two percent of *Cosmopolitan* responders said that X-rated videotapes stimulate them.

New Woman readers were asked if such videotapes interfere with their pleasure when shown as stimulants by their partners. Of those who see them during sex play, 59 percent said the movies never interfere, 13 percent said "sometimes" or "rarely"; 1 percent saying they frequently interfere.

The Brecher study found that 37 percent of the older women had dipped into erotic literature, and that 81 percent liked it. [*Sex Over Forty*]

If you resemble the 327 women in a study involving members of Mensa—to qualify, members must have IQs in the top 2 percent of the population—there's a 39 percent chance that you fantasize actively during sexual activity. Your most probably fantasy image is of a man other than your sex partner of the moment. Other fantasies, in order of probability, are of participating in group sex, recreating scenes from pornographic books or films, having sex with animals, watching others having sex, exhibiting yourself, being a prostitute, involvement with blacks (if you're white), lesbianism, masochism, and rape. [DeMartino]

You have been looking at nudes depicted in Playboy, Playgirl, *and* Penthouse:

After perusing the pictures, regardless of whether you are a woman or a man, you are likely to rate your own mate less attractive sexually than you did a while before you looked, and to report yourself feeling less in love with him or her. [Arizona State]

You're going to see a romantic or sexy movie:

If you are a woman in college, it's fairly likely (39 percent) that such a movie sometimes inspires you to sexual activity. The activity is most likely to be intercourse (more than 50 percent of inspired times), oral-genital engagement (25 percent), or masturbation (20 percent). What kind of movie might do it? In the early 1980s when this survey was taken, the movies most likely to have induced you to sexual activity were *An Officer and a Gentleman* and *Endless Love.*

If you are a man in college, it's very likely—64 percent, more than half again as likely as college women—that movies sometimes inspire you to sex. The forms of sex, by probability, are exactly the same as a woman's: intercourse, more than 50 percent of the time; oral-genital activity, 25 percent; masturbation, 20 percent. The early-1980s movie most likely to lure you to those activities would have been *10.*

To arrive at those answers, the researchers, over a period of a year, asked several classes of undergraduates to fill out a questionnaire about how major movies, selected from a list of 603 titles, affected their own sexual practices. [Wilson, Liedtke]

You have just seen a highly explicit erotic movie:

For decades, an inconclusive debate has raged over whether sex on the screen incites men to violence against women.

According to an Iowa State University study, if you are a man, a movie containing explicit eroticism probably heightens your aggressive feelings, especially if you were already angry when the movie began. Furthermore, the movie is likely to make you feel just as aggressive toward men as toward women. If the movie was only mildly erotic, however, it is more likely to soothe you, making you feel less aggressive, even if you were angry before seeing it. [Donnerstein, Barrett.]

Whether you are a woman or man, whether you're married or single, according to this study you are more likely to be turned on by movie scenes of sex between strangers who, you are led to believe, have just met by happenstance, than you are by the very same scenes when you think the couple are husband and wife, or a prostitute and her customer.

To determine this, sixty-two psychology students, and thirty-six married couples recruited by a newspaper ad, were divided into small groups and shown silent films that the researchers "advertised" as "X-rated from Denmark." Scenes depicted sexual encounters, including intercourse. The characters in the encounters were described interchangeably among the viewing groups as a married couple, a prostitute and her client, or a couple who had just met at a dance. After each film was described, the subjects were asked to report their reactions, in specific terms of erection or vaginal flow. The "strangers" consistently got the most reaction. [Fisher, Byrne.]

Three women sociologists at the University of Wisconsin stumbled into a subject for a study as a result of showing two sexually explicit films to an introductory class in human sexuality. The professors showed a film called *Soma Touch,* depicting male masturbation. While the lights were out, a scattering of male students were observed slipping out, but no women. At the next class meeting, the professors showed another film called *Susan,* depicting female masturbation. About halfway through the film, a "column of young women" began to leave, but not men.

These reactions suggested a more formal study of male and female reactions to male and female masturbation and homosexuality. First, the professors showed the same films, *Soma Touch* and *Susan*, to another class of fifty-eight students and collected reactions according to two scales. On one, the Byrne-Sheffield Feeling Scale, students chose words that best described their reactions to the films over a wide range: *excited, entertained, sexually aroused, curious, not bored, disgusted, nauseated, angry, depressed.* On Griffitt's Physiological Arousal Scale, subjects indicated specific reactions on a scale from zero to six: for men, "no erection" (0) to "ejaculation" (6); for women, "no genital sensations at all" (0) to "orgasm" (6). The subjects were also asked, "Overall, to what extent were you physically excited or physically aroused during the movie?" and were told to indicate answers ranging from "not at all physically excited" (1) to "very physically excited" (5). Next, to another introductory class in human sexuality, this one much larger (556 men and women), the professors showed, over a period of two weeks, a series of films selected for measuring a broader spectrum of turn-ons and turn-offs: *Vir Amat,* depicting male homosexuals at play, and *Holding* with female homosexuals; *Auto-American Dreams,* with males masturbating, and *Shirley,* with female masturbation. Then *Rich and Judy,* starring two young, attractive heterosexuals, as well as *A Ripple in Time,* depicting heterosexual play of a fifty-year-old woman and a sixty-three-year-old man.

The results of the first pair of films, *Soma Touch* and *Susan*: "Both men and women were sexually aroused by watching the sexual activities of the opposite sex; both were somewhat repulsed by watching the sexual activity of their own sex. . . . Men's and women's reactions to the masturbation movies were mirror images."

As for reactions to homosexuality: "Men found female homosexuality extremely arousing; they found male homosexuality extremely unarousing. The women had a comparable reaction, but it was far less intense." [Hatfield, Sprecher, Traupmann]

Practically none of the above applies to you. Most of those artificial erotic stimulants, like hot bedroom scenes in movies, bore you, and certainly don't sexually stimulate you. If asked by a researcher, you acknowledge that sex, including thoughts about it, makes you feel at least slightly ashamed, unclean, and somewhat uncomfortable (which might be called feelings of guilt about sex). All in all, you don't think sex itself is very important, nor as much fun as others make it out to be:

You may not know yourself—or your actual, measurable sexual responses—as well as you think you do.

If you are a woman, according to a recent pioneering study by Dr. Patricia J. Morokoff of the Uniformed Services University of the Health Sciences, Bethesda, Md., and if you score high in sex guilt (in answers to multifaceted questions on a standard sex-guilt inventory compiled by D. L. Mosher), you probably report less arousal than most women at seeing an erotic videotape. For the first time in such a study, however, Dr. Morokoff hooked up the women to a relatively new technology, vaginal photoplethysmography, which uses special sensors to monitor increased blood flow to the genital regions during sexual excitement. This device has become accepted, after numerous studies, to be a valid and reliable physiological measure of sexual arousal in women. For the first time, the technology enables a woman's subjective report of sexual arousal to be compared with her physiological responses.

In Dr. Morokoff's experiment, sixty-two women subjects were given a test to measure negative attitudes about sex and "sex guilt." Then they were randomly divided, half of them to view an erotic videotape, the other half to watch a nonerotic one. Afterwards, all the women were asked to give themselves over to a sexual fantasy and to write it out. Finally, they were asked to rate the level of their sexual arousal. All the time, they were continuously being measured by the vaginal photoplethysmograph.

Sure enough, women who had scored high in "sex guilt" reported less arousal than women low in sex guilt. But the *physiological* measures of the arousal of these high sex-guilt women, despite their denial of feeling, was significantly greater than that of the low sex-guilt women. The women who expressed the highest degree of guilt about sex declined to watch the videotapes and submit to the measurements of physiological arousal, but did consent to respond to questionnaires about their sexual experience and attitudes. They generally reported substantially less experience than the others. [Morokoff]

You are repelled by the practice of "swinging" (swapping sex partners) and you can scarcely imagine having any sexual, moral, or social attitude in common with a swinger:

In fact, you probably view swingers as so alien that "practically everything about [them] becomes odd or immoral." That was the assumption that Richard J. Jenks, a sociologist of Indiana University Southeast, decided to put to a test. First he rounded up 134 men and women (mostly white college students) who said they disapproved of swinging, and asked them through a questionnaire to describe their image of swingers: their average age, income, and other demographic details, and an estimation of the swingers' use of drugs. Also, the subjects were asked to report their own attitudes toward prostitution, homosexuality, and a variety of controversial social issues—and to estimate the probable attitudes of swingers on the same issues.

Then Jenks located 342 professed swingers, at a swingers' convention and among readers of a swingers' magazine—and gave them a parallel questionnaire about themselves.

If you are typical of the nonswingers queried by the study, you have the impression that "a large percentage" of swingers are nonwhite. Of the swingers responding to Jenks, 93 percent were white. They were also predominantly middle class and fairly well educated.

If you're typical, you probably substantially overestimate the swingers' use of alcohol, marijuana, and "hard drugs." Also you're inclined to overrate their moral acceptance of prostitution, homosexuality, and premarital sex. On other major social issues, swingers and nonswingers showed *no major differences* in attitude, except for one: Swingers approve of swinging, and nonswingers don't. [Jenks]

You are a man who patronizes a massage parlor:

If you are typical of 183 patrons of an Illinois massage parlor interviewed for this study, you are thirty-five years old and white, with some college education and a lower- or middle-class job. You have relatively high self-esteem, go to church on Sunday, and do not live in the same town as the massage parlor. You consider yourself sexually and personally adjusted, a liberal, sympathetic to the women's rights movement, and the massage brings you to orgasm. [Simpson, Schill]

CHAPTER
3

The Secret Life of Your Mind

YOUR MOST PRIVATE THOUGHTS

Human behaviorists learn a lot about how we behave simply by watching us. Opinion pollsters learn about our opinions mostly by phoning us. But how is anyone to find out what we secretly *think* during our most private moments? One can only devise questions, ask them in a way calculated not to make us defensive—then hope we reply with something like the truth. Creating the right questions is a difficult art, but that has not deterred the curiosity of human-naturists bent on poking into the dark corners of our most guarded selves.

LOOK YOURSELF UP

You are willing to go to great lengths to avoid making decisions:

This researcher, a Princeton philosopher, gives that common tendency a name, *decidophobia*. He observes that you probably have chosen one or more of ten basic strategies to avoid decisions. Each of those strategies is based on *one big decision* that automatically "takes care of" many future choices. "Most popular of all, one that often spells total relief," he says, is marriage—"a little like a prefrontal lobotomy." Other strategic ways out of further decision-making are religion, meaningless drifting, a commitment (like joining a movement or cause), allegiance to a school of thought, absolute interpretations or explanations such as literal interpretations of the Bible, and Manichaeanism (an ancient doctrine of warring principles of good and evil, such as God versus Satan, the spirit versus the flesh). The latter two philosophical stances help keep thought simple, thus helping to avoid the decisions inherent in dealing with daily life as a complex of contradictions and unpredictables. [Kaufmann]

You are a teenager:

The fears that most haunt your life are probably not what your elders would suspect. This survey reveals the happenings you secretly most fear, at least if you are typical of the twenty-seven teenagers (thirteen to eighteen years old) who live in the low-income Crotona Park tenement section of the Bronx, according to this 1983 study. (Note the special category of teenagers surveyed. No comparison study has been made of teenagers in general.)

If you're a boy, your worst fears, in order of prominence, are:

- Going to jail
- Not being promoted in school
- Impregnating a girl
- Being rejected by a girl you're interested in

If you're a girl, your worst fears are:

- Your parents dying
- Getting pregnant
- Failing in school

What makes teenage boys most uncomfortable is being around older male homosexuals.

The worst discomfort for girls is talking to one or both parents about sex. Also, girls frequently express discomfort at being around friends who smoke marijuana or take other drugs.

Both boys and girls fear the death of their parents more than they fear their own.

For highest dislikes, girls most often name waking up in the morning. Boys dislike not having enough money. [Beale, Baskin]

You are an outstanding success in your profession:

Soon after your success became apparent, if you're like fully 70 percent of highly successful people, you secretly feared that you were a fraud, a fake, an impostor—and you couldn't shake off a dread that you would be exposed.

Think that's peculiar? Try this: No matter how long you've been at or near the top, there's a 40 percent probability that the fear *still* haunts you.

"Despite their high test scores, advanced degrees, honors, awards, or promotions," says Dr. Joan Harvey, a psychologist at the University of Pennsylvania Medical School, "victims of the impostor phenomenon persist in believing they are less qualified than their peers, and suffer from the fear of being found out." If you're facing a new challenge, she says, the feeling is normal and it usually recedes as tasks of the new status are mastered. For example, according to a previous study, first-year graduate students commonly feel they got where they are by fakery or luck, but later learn to feel more deserving. Similarly, Dr. Harvey has widely encountered the what-am-I-doing-here feeling among young psychiatric residents and hospital physicians during their first year or so of working without supervision.

Dr. Harvey's major finding, however, emphasizes not those beginners but the successful people, often famous ones, who feel like frauds throughout their careers. The more those beleaguered high achievers accomplish, the more they secretly perceive each new success as a lucky accident, or due only to exhausting effort rather than special competence, or even the result of good looks and charm rather than ability. Thus the success itself, always perceived as something in *contrast* to natural ability, reinforces and deepens the self-doubt, rather than contributing to self-confidence. Yet Dr. Harvey's research shows that these self-doubters usually don't lack general self-esteem. Instead they imagine their lack of ability—and their "fraud"—only in the very professional activity that gives them their success.

Those who are first-generation professionals are especially susceptible to feeling so. "When people perceive themselves as having risen above their roots," Dr. Harvey told a *New York Times* interviewer, ". . . unconsciously they equate success with betraying their loyalties to their families."

Among kinds of people especially prone to fall into the "impostor" trap, according to Dr. Harvey, are these:

• Workaholics, who usually so dread a failure that they make a do-or-die crisis of every task. Then they say, "See all the work that took? I almost had to kill myself to do it right." They rarely give themselves a chance to learn whether a normal effort using their innate ability would have carried the day.

• Extreme worriers, who are driven by vivid images of failure. Since they usually succeed, they are always reinforcing their vision of an essential partnership between worry and success.

• Charmers, so doubtful of their true competence that they constantly stroke and flatter their superiors. Then, of course, when the accustomed success is at hand, they can "blame" it on their wily social skills. [Harvey]

Often you simply walk around thinking about nothing in particular—or so you think:

If you are stopped in the street by a researcher who asks what you've been thinking about in the last five minutes . . .

> . . . you are twice as likely to say you were thinking about religion than thinking about sex.
> . . . you are six times more likely to report thoughts of sex if you are young than if you are older.
> . . . you are twice as likely to report thinking about death if you are an older person than if you are a young adult. [Cameron.]

. . . and if the researcher encounters you on a fancy shopping street, you are more likely to say you were thinking about the immediate scene than any other topic. Next most likely topics: work, then love.

. . . and if you're encountered on a lower-class shopping street, you're more likely to report thinking about money, material concerns, future plans, and love, in that order.

. . . and if you're a woman at either of those locations, you're more likely than a man to report thinking about work. [Shaw, Francois, Filler, Sciarillo]

For the first of the above studies [Cameron], 3,416 people in five cities were asked what had passed through their minds in the previous five minutes.

For the second study [Shaw], 187 people on two New York streets were asked to write down the thoughts they had just been having. One locale was at the city's swankiest corner, 57th Street and Fifth Avenue; the other, a less toney area (Union Square).

Can one really rely on those people giving truthful answers to such intimate questions simply because a total stranger claims to be taking a survey? Perhaps not. That's why each of the above statements is carefully labeled as what people *say* or *report.* And for each location (and its class implications), that may be as revealing as the "truth."

You think you think often about your health:

You certainly do (think so). According to this survey of 25,000 magazine readers, ages fourteen to eighty-seven, two thirds of them women, fully 42 percent of the volunteer respondents said that they think about their health more often than any other subject they can think of—including love, work, and money.

In addition to how much you think about health, if you're young you're likely to *feel* less healthy than most older people do.

If you are an adult who had a traumatic experience of sexual abuse before you were seventeen, you probably feel less healthy than most other adults. What's more, you are apt to be incapacitated by illness more often and longer than most others.

If you are a man who played on a high school or college varsity team, you probably feel—and are—among the healthiest adults. This correlation does not hold up for women.

There's a fair chance (one in five) that you feel you're going to live beyond the age of one hundred. If you're not one of those ultimate optimists, there's an additional one-in-five chance that you feel you're going to live beyond eighty-six.

If you are a woman, it's quite likely (two chances out of three) that at some time you have told a friend or relative that you'd rather be left to die than be kept alive unnaturally by a machine. If you're a man, there's a fifty-fifty chance you've expressed that wish. [*Psychology Today*]

Speaking of private thoughts, there are some thoughts you wish people would keep private:

One of them is anything to do with menstruation.

About one out of three Americans believes the female cycle is an unfit topic of conversation at the office or in social situations. About two thirds believe that a woman at work or in social situations should avoid mentioning that she is having her period. Similarly, she shouldn't mention having cramps or permit her supply of tampons or napkins to be seen by others.

Eight percent of this survey sample—composed of 1,034 people representing all ages from fourteen up, both women and men, and including all ethnic, education, and economic components of the population, as per "The Tampax Report," conducted for the tampon manufacturer—said they believed that women who are menstruating should avoid contact with all others.

"There is a strong feeling that [menstrual health] should be taught," says Vera Milow, vice president, educational affairs, for Tampax Inc., "but everyone feels they should let someone else do the teaching. Mothers often postpone telling their daughters. Schools write it into the curriculum, but many teachers avoid dealing with it in depth."

Although the evidence is that mothers put off talking about menstruation, 64 percent of women said they were first told about it by their mothers. That is changing, however. Women under twenty-two are more likely than their elders to have learned about it from teachers. Only one in a hundred says she learned about it from a health professional. In contrast, men are most likely (31 percent) to have learned about menstruation from friends, which presumably can be translated to "in the street"; 21 percent learned in school about the cyclical secrets of women, and about an equal number from their mothers.

Whatever happened to the once powerful opposition to sex education in the schools? Only 9 percent of those surveyed opposed teaching the facts about menstruation in schools. But 25 percent made it clear the subject should not be taken up in coeducational classrooms.

The taboo is declining—but it persists. Among women over thirty-five, a surprising 39 percent say that they did not know what was happening to them the first time they menstruated. Even of women under thirty-five, fully 19 percent didn't know. More than two out of five—43 percent—said they felt frightened, confused, panicky, or ill.

How about the emotion-laden topic of whether women become more emotional around the time of their period? An unexpected finding was that men and women are very close in their consensus that, yes, women do become more emotional: 85 percent of women say so, as do 89 percent of men. [Tampax]

You have just finished using a public restroom:

And, of course, your first thought is to wash your hands, right?

It certainly is—if another person is present who might see you. But it's highly unlikely you think you have to wash if nobody else is there.

A Brigham Young University psychologist had a confederate observe thirty-nine women's-room users. (No comparable survey has been done for men.) For twenty of those washroom visitors, the confederate made her presence obvious by combing her hair, or whatever. Upon exiting from a stall, eighteen of those twenty users dutifully washed their hands. For the remaining nineteen, the confederate concealed herself in a stall, hung an "out of order" sign on its door, and propped up her feet out of sight. Then she counted a handwashing each time she heard the water faucet turned on. Handwashings by those nineteen restroom users (who thought they were alone) plummeted to three. [Pedersen]

If you are a high school student in a big city, you're likely to find more than seven times as much graffiti on the walls if you use the women's room than if you use the men's. This striking finding comes from a survey of two male and two female restrooms at each of four sizeable schools in Cincinnati, selected for their contrasting socioeconomic and ethnic populations. (Since some of those schools frequently washed restroom walls to erase illicit markings, the researchers arranged for a halt to washings for a three-week period leading up to the day of collecting graffiti.)

And what do the students write about? Researchers categorized markings into sixteen groups, among them, racial insults, sexual insults, sexual humor, a sexual request, sexual or scatological words, romantic, political, drugs, religion, and morals, with these results:

Inscriptions by young women were predominantly romantic ("Mary loves John"), but what they scratched on their walls varied substantially with the social makeup of their school. The "classier" the school, the more likely its women made erotic inscriptions rather than romantic ones.

Male graffiti, on the other hand, were 86 percent sexual and erotic, regardless of class.

Schools that were broadest in their racial mix as well as in the income and education levels of parents produced more than twice as much graffiti as schools that were more homogeneous—say, mostly poor and black, or rich and white. Finally, when mostly white and mostly black schools are compared, race is shown to have little or no influence on either the quantity of graffiti or its content. [Wales, Brewer]

And what happens when you get to a nearby college? A "content analysis" at the University of Cincinnati of graffiti in men's and women's restrooms in academic departments reveals that a "majority of women's inscriptions" offered advice about love, life, marriage, and happiness. Men were more likely to inscribe erotic sayings or to comment on politics and "competition concerns." [Loewenstine, Ponticos, Paludi]

You read book reviews:

You are likely to perceive a critic who writes a negative book review as more intelligent, competent, and expert than someone who writes a positive review—that is, if you resemble the Brandeis University undergraduates who took part in this study, At the same time, you are likely to judge the negative reviewer as significantly less likable than the positive reviewer. [Amabile]

YOUR PRIVATE THOUGHTS
ABOUT AGING

You're an adult and someone asks how old you think of yourself as being:

You probably give an age five to seven years younger than you actually are. That is, until you approach and pass retirement age; then the disparity may stretch to your thinking of yourself as much as fifteen years younger than you actually are. [Cadwell Davis]

You're an adult and someone asks how old you feel:

You're likely to answer that you feel between thirty and thirty-five. If you do say you feel older than you actually are, you're probably under thirty, or, a little less likely, over sixty. [Cadwell Davis]

You are retired and feel older than your real age:

You are more likely to be a man than a woman. [Cadwell Davis]

You are a woman and have frequent fantasies about being much younger than you are:

You probably also feel high levels of stress, especially when you detect marked symptoms of your aging. [Rossi]

You sometimes worry about what your life will be like when you're seventy:

Stop worrying. Just look at how it was (or will be, or is) when you were thirty. You'll probably behave—and feel—essentially the same. This was determined through a study of 142 middle-class residents of San Francisco in 1928, who were then located and resurveyed in 1968–69. Of those aged people resurveyed, the sickest were generally those who, at age thirty, worried and talked most about their health. Among elderly women, the most depressed, fearful, self-doubting, and least active were those who, at age thirty, were depressed, fearful, self-doubting, and inactive. The happiest, most active men and women at seventy were those who were happy and active at thirty. [Maas, Kuypers]

You sometimes fear that getting old means you'll fade into a sameness with other old people:

You're probably mistaken. Advancing age is more likely to bring on a more complex and distinctive personality rather than one of "sameness." [Maas, Kuypers]

You are over sixty-five and you feel poor:

You're very likely kidding yourself. Researchers believe the main reason you feel poor is that your income is probably slightly lower than it was during your peak earning years, and you feel uneasy about the pinch. The average income for people over sixty-five, however, is 92 percent of the average for the entire population, equal to the average income of people between twenty-five to forty-four. (Those young people are actually poorer than you are because they're paying off home mortgages and raising families.) [Davis, van den Oever]

You are a widow whose grown children have left home:

If your earlier life centered on your family, it's probable that you have felt a very low level of life satisfaction—and possibly prolonged depression. In contrast, if you have maintained a career and kept up your social contacts, the loss of your husband and children depressed you for a much shorter time. [Maas, Kuypers]

You are elderly and trying to decide where to live:

Your least likely voluntary choice is the high-rise multiple dwelling unit restricted to the aged. [Maas, Kuypers]

You are elderly and your grown children visit you:

You start wishing they'd go home sooner if you are widowed than if you're still married. [Davidson, Cotter]

You're elderly and not very happy, and you think the reason is that your children neglect you:

You're probably mistaken. The only factor that appears to correlate with a sense of well-being in older people is the number of friends they have, not the attentiveness of sons and daughters. According to several studies, this is true whether the elderly people are married or widowed. [Davidson, Cotter]

Truly be what you would be thought to be.

FRENCH PROVERB

Oh wad some power the giftie gie us
To see oursels as others see us!

ROBERT BURNS (1756–96),
"TO A LOUSE"

YOUR SENSE OF SELF

W. H. Auden once confessed that his private image of himself was "very different from the image which I try to create in the minds of others, in order that they may love me."

Auden surely realized perfectly well that his "secret" was and is the same as just about everybody's. "In a sense," says Steven Penrod, the University of Wisconsin social psychologist, "we are like actors on a stage, playing different roles to different audiences."

William James, as early as 1890, probed into our secret tricks for persuading the world to see us as we wish to be seen. He described the image of "self" as extending beyond one's physical body to include a person's possessions, reputation, family, and social ties. He divided the "self" into three:

1. A material self: the physical person.
2. A social self—the identity that is perceived by others. A person, wrote James, "has as many social selves as there are individuals who recognize him and carry an image of him in their mind": the self that may go to school, or teach in one; the one that goes dancing, or heads a family; the one

that is offspring of parents, or who is parent to offspring, and many more. In each of these roles the social self changes.
3. A spiritual self: the inner core of identity, including the person's goals, ambitions, and beliefs.

Another scholar, R. H. Turner, has said that if we are to understand ourselves and others, we need to divide the idea of "self" still another way. He drew a strong line between *self-image* and *self-concept.* The self-image, as Auden's confession suggests, changes opportunistically, one frequently traded for another. We can even have several self-images at the same time. Turner's idea of self-concept, however, is a person's picture of "the real me." It is our deepest sense of who we are, and remains relatively stable. Roger W. Brown, in his book, *Social Psychology,* calls the self-concept a "theory of one's life."

In 1922, C. H. Cooley meshed James's idea of the *social self* with Turner's *self-concept* to make another historic insight. He redefined self-concept as a reflection of how each of us *believes* others perceive us. That *belief,* whether accurate or not, he said, largely influences who we think we are. Cooley created the idea of "the looking-glass self," which he said is shaped by three elements:

1. How we think we appear to other people
2. How we think other people judge that appearance
3. How we feel about what we think that judgment is

Then G. H. Mead took what seemed the final step in 1934, in his book, *Mind, Self, and Society.* He asserted that as we become aware of other people's perceptions of us, our "looking-glass self," or self-concept, becomes a framed, permanent self-portrait. We tend to become what *we* think *they* think we are.

Virtually all of the foregoing was stated still another way by Tom Wolfe, in a *New York Times* interview shortly after publication of his novel about the complexities of life in New York, *The Bonfire of the Vanities:* "My conviction is that external circumstances, particularly in a city—I think everywhere, but particularly in a city—determine so much of the individual psychology of a person, and it's folly to try to understand individual psychology without understanding the complete social context of a person. The self is our ties to other people. And I try to bring that out in the novel."

Those fascinating perceptions, to be sure, cannot be verified directly by much research evidence. They are intuitive theories advanced by eminent intuitors. A few researchers have tried "scientifically" to verify bits and pieces of the theories, and have gone a way toward doing so. But only a little way, and unconvincingly. That doesn't mean the theories aren't sound, but simply that they resist statistical measurement. Therefore they must for the time being remain more in the realm of art than of science. Psychology being the humanistic study that it is, perhaps there's some comfort to be found in that.

While we all may worry about how our behavior comes across to others, Mark Snyder of the University of Minnesota has pinned down specific and widely different styles of anxiety and sensitivity that seem to contribute heavily to making each of us who we are. What we actually do to *observe* and, more importantly, to *control* how we "come off" to those around us, Snyder has named *self-monitoring*.

In 1972, Snyder published what some call his "Who Am I?" test—a seemingly simple Self-Monitoring Scale, composed of twenty-five statements, to each of which a subject answers true or false. Between 1972 and 1981, more than ten thousand people took it. The test identifies what he calls "high self-monitors" and "low self-monitors." Then Snyder and others tested how "high self-monitors" and "low self-monitors" are likely to compare—predictably—in a surprisingly wide variety of behaviors and attitudes, as the studies below show.

Before reading further, you may wish to take Snyder's "Who Am I?" test. Decide whether each of the statements that follow is *more true than false* for you (mark those statements "T"), or *more false than true* (mark those statements "F"). The way to score your result immediately follows the list of questions.

Please note: The simplicity of the questions stirs me to remind the reader that this is not one of those instant self-analysis tests that serious people love to disdain in the popular magazines. It is a yardstick of personality developed by an eminent psychologist and accepted as such by his colleagues, as the studies that follow will show.

1. I find it hard to imitate the behavior of other people.
2. My behavior is usually an expression of my true inner feelings, attitudes and beliefs.
3. At parties and social gatherings, I do not attempt to do and say things that others will like.
4. I can only argue for ideas that I already have.

5. I can make impromptu speeches, even on topics about which I have almost no information.
6. I guess I put on a show to impress or entertain people.
7. When I am uncertain how to act in a social situation, I look to the behavior of others for cues.
8. I would probably make a good actor.
9. I rarely need the advice of my friends to choose movies, books, or music.
10. I sometimes appear to others to be experiencing deeper emotions than I actually am.
11. I laugh more when I watch a comedy with others than when alone.
12. In a group of people I am rarely the center of attention.
13. In different situations and with different people, I often act like very different persons.
14. I am not particularly good at making other people like me.
15. Even if I am not enjoying myself, I often pretend to be having a good time.
16. I am not always the person I appear to be.
17. I would not change my opinions (or the way I do things) in order to please someone else or win their favor.
18. I have considered being an entertainer.
19. In order to get along and be liked, I tend to be what people expect me to be rather than anything else.
20. I have never been good at games like charades, or at improvisational acting.
21. I have trouble changing my behavior to suit different people and different situations.
22. At a party I let others keep the jokes and stories going.
23. I feel a bit awkward in company and do not show up quite as well as I should.
24. I can look anyone in the eye and tell a lie with a straight face (if it's for a good cause).
25. I may deceive people by being friendly when I really dislike them.

To rate yourself, count one point for each False response to statements 1, 2, 3, 4, 9, 12, 14, 17, 20, 21, 22, and 23. Then count one point for each True response to statements 5, 6, 7, 8, 10, 11, 13, 15, 16, 18, 19, 24, and 25. The higher your score, the higher you rate as a high self-monitor. You can consider yourself a high self-monitor if you acquire a score of seventeen or more; lows are those who get no more than eight points.

High self-monitors, Dr. Snyder summarizes, are pragmatic, sometimes chameleon-like actors in social groups. In contrast, he says, "low self-monitors typically refuse to be in situations that force them to be something they're not." They strive to maintain consistency between their inner and outer selves.

"High self-monitors paint portraits of themselves in terms of the roles they play. They give answers like 'I am a student,' 'I am a post office employee,' 'I am first violin in a chamber group.' The low self-monitors make greater use of adjectives to describe their traits: 'I am friendly,' 'I am reliable,' 'I am even-tempered.' "

The difference, observes psychologist Daniel Goleman, "seems to have a profound influence not only on [a person's] social successes and skills, but also on the quality of his intimate relationships. For example, research suggests that those who are most adept at making a good impression, paradoxically, tend to have less stable and satisfying intimate relationships, suffering in both the quality of their friendships and the stability of their romantic ties.

"On the other hand, those that tend toward the other extreme, those who do not bend at all to fit in, have problems of their own, the research suggests. While their sense of self is far stronger than the person skilled at making impressions, they can suffer from the social costs of their rigidity."

High self-monitors do especially well in certain professions, Snyder has found: "Professional actors, as well as many of the more mercurial trial lawyers, are among the best at it. So too are many successful sales people, diplomats and politicians.

"Those who are at the extreme [high] in self-monitoring are sociopaths, con artists who will say and do whatever gets them what they want at the moment. On the other hand, those who are extremely low in self-monitoring are, like obsessives, utterly stubborn in their adherence to the sense of being right no matter what. If a situation doesn't mesh with that sense, they are totally unwilling to change to fit in. They act as they feel they should, no matter what others make of it."

Which is it "best" to be? For people in the range of moderation, there is no apparent choice. Neither high nor low self-monitors are especially susceptible to psychological problems, Snyder suggests, except at either extreme.

LOOK YOURSELF UP

When you enter a social group or situation, you markedly alter your behavior—even the way you think about yourself—in order to fit into that group:

You probably test high as a *self-monitor*. You tend to be driven by a near-compulsion (and a pronounced ability) to blend swiftly into a social group or situation. People with a notable tendency like yours comprise about 40 percent of the population. (In contrast, a "low self-monitor" acts about the same—almost stubbornly—no matter who the company, as though not yielding an inch on a set of values or opinions or an accustomed manner.)

At one time, psychologists tended to view highly self-aware people as fragile souls, "social chameleons" seeking to prop themselves up through seducing the approval of others. But since Mark Snyder's introduction of the concept of self-monitoring, that viewpoint has changed. There is now a growing recognition that high self-monitors like you have a finely tuned capacity to be truly empathic, thus making social life easier and more rewarding for others as well as for yourself. [Snyder]

When you are with other people, as a high self-monitor you have a strong tendency to appear friendly, outgoing, and extroverted. You probe for what you and a new acquaintance may have in common, as though exploring the potential for friendship. You usually are first to talk and you take the conversational lead. Your partner is likely to feel your greater need to talk, and will probably let you do so. But you are so versatile that you can become the quieter, more passive partner when you think that that will make things go better. After all the intensive conversation, you probably don't remember as much of what someone tells you about him/herself as most others would— unless you expect to deal with that person in the future. You quickly sense how to talk the other person's language, not only in vocabulary, but emotionally. And you have a knack for talking about yourself with the other person's language and level of intimacy. If this special talent is pointed out by your partner, you probably explain it away by talking about the situation you find yourself in, not in terms of your personality. (If you're a low self-monitor, you are more inclined to account for what you do in terms of your personality—"I'm the kind of person who . . ."—or your values—"I'm the kind who believes. . . .") You seem to have one eye on how your pleasure in a relationship tomorrow might be affected by how you present yourself today. (Low self-monitors don't seem to care much about tomorrow's consequences of today's straightforward behavior.) [Shaffer, who cites studies by Davis; Ickes, Barnes; Berscheid et al]

You are better able than most people to detect a liar or a fake. In a social group, you are highly sensitive to how other people act, and what you can say or do to influence their actions or attitudes. After sensing from their behavior how to conduct yourself, you have a superior ability for judging how well you are doing. [Ickes]

If you are obese you are more likely to test high on self-monitoring than someone who is not. Psychologists aren't sure if that's because your weight makes you more sensitive to the possibility of social rejection, or if you are simply more sensitive as well as fatter. [Ickes]

You have a more than usual likelihood of being a skillful impromptu speaker, even on topics you know little about. [Sobol]

For all your outgoing manner, you set up subtle barriers that make it difficult for others to get to know you well. You often try to lead people you dislike to think you feel friendly toward them.

You tend more than most to respond to advertising that appeals to one's image rather than stressing a product's quality.

You may have begun demonstrating your tendency to change who you are for different situations when you were as young as age seven.

When you feel that your social behavior hasn't measured up to the way you want to be, you tend to get depressed. (What depresses low self-monitors, on the other hand, is feeling they have betrayed their own values by changing how they act to please others.)

You like to have a wide range of friends, each liked for a single trait or shared interest: an expert tennis friend for tennis (and to share with other tennis friends), a music friend for musical parties or for going to concerts.

In your romantic relationships, you are cautious about becoming emotionally intimate. You tend to avoid commitment, and you're probably more willing than your partner to end a relationship. During sex, you are more likely than most to fantasize about people other than your partner. (In all these ways, low self-monitors tend toward the opposite.) [Snyder; Goleman]

. . .

You tend to be more accurate than most in identifying persons you have seen previously (which would probably make you more reliable as an eyewitness, say, to a crime, or as a security guard, or in a job where there is an advantage in making people feel flattered by being recognized). This was determined in a field experiment involving eighty-six store clerks, both male and female, in convenience stores. They were asked to try to identify "customers" (confederates) who had been in the stores two hours earlier. Then those clerks were asked to take the Self-Monitoring Scale test. To a large degree, high self-monitoring and high recognition went hand in hand. [Hosch, Platz]

If you are a man choosing a woman for a date, as a high self-monitor you are likely to pay more attention and put greater weight on the woman's looks than do low self-monitor men. (In contrast, low self-monitors pay more attention than you do to interior personal attributes in sizing up women as potential dates.) [Snyder, Berscheid, Glick]

Like most people, you somewhat reshape your personality and evaluate yourself according to how you think others think of you. But surely, some "others" are more important to your self-concept than other "others." And you wonder which "others"—say, among friends, parents, and teachers—have counted most:

If you are a woman, the greatest impact on how you felt about yourself during your formative high school years was produced by what you thought was thought by *friends* (more than by parents or teachers).

If you are a man, the greatest impact was produced by what you thought was thought by *parents* (more than by friends or teachers).

This was determined by tests and interviews with 1,367 high school seniors. [Hoelter]

All personal secrets have the effect of sin or guilt.

CARL JUNG,
SWISS PSYCHOLOGIST (1875–1961)

Everything secret degenerates; nothing is safe that
does not bear discussion and publicity.

LORD ACTON,
ENGLISH HISTORIAN (1834–1902)

YOUR WILLINGNESS TO REVEAL YOURSELF

Surely you've met one of those troublesome types who, without so much as the ring of a bell, flings open the doors and windows of the soul to display more about his or her inner life than you want to know. No matter how that kind of revelation sometimes bugs you, there's one thing to be said for it. Erich Fromm, the psychologist who wrote the esteemed book *The Art of Loving,* has said that when two people start breaking down barriers by disclosing their private selves to each other, they are setting the stage for romantic love.

But when romance is not on the agenda, say researchers, here is what self-disclosure may be disclosing:

A person who discloses his or her "real self" to at least one "significant" other person has an important "prerequisite for a healthy personality." Those who "open up" to a *few* significant others and a "medium" amount to a few more also are sending an important signal of "positive mental health." But those who reveal either an unseemly lot *or* precious little about themselves to almost everybody are probably very lonely or, less specifically, "poorly adjusted."

A "normal" level of self-disclosure is especially hard to read because what may be too high for one social scene may be too low for another. Your roommate may expect, as the normal signs of friendship, a level of detail about your dating life that, if disclosed to your boss, might make her or him squirm.

All of us, the researchers agree, need quite constantly to have someone to whom we can disclose ourselves, or we pay a significant price in loneliness. A corollary is that when the level of our disclosure is held below the "expected" level for a social situation, we feel lonely. The reverse also appears true: During periods of loneliness or isolation, either social or physical, we are likely to feel the greatest impulse to confide in strangers. (For more on this, see Chapter 2, "Loneliness.")

LOOK YOURSELF UP

You're quicker than most people to talk intimately about yourself to a stranger or a new acquaintance:

You are more likely than most to be seen as "poorly adjusted."

You probably need to escape from loneliness.

You are more likely to be a woman than a man.

You are more likely than most to describe your mother as cold, distrustful, and selfish. (If you describe your parents as close, warm, friendly, and accepting, you appear to have less need to disclose to other people, including your friends.)

You are more likely to be a later- or the last-born in your family than the firstborn.

You are more likely to be American than German or Mexican. (Compared to other national groups, Americans disclose a great deal about themselves and make friends easily, but do not often develop highly intimate relationships, says the researcher.)

If you are a man, you are more likely to be Jewish than a Baptist, Methodist, or Catholic.

You are more likely to be white and middle class than either black or white and working class.

When you are talking intimately, the closer to your conversational partner that you sit or stand, the longer you are likely to continue talking.

The more certain you are that you'll never have to see or deal with your listener again, the more you are likely to disclose about yourself. [Cozby, in a review of other studies]

You are about average in your willingness to talk about yourself to people you know:

If you are a woman, you are likely to reveal more about yourself than if you're a man.

If you are white, you are likely to reveal more about yourself than if you're black.

If you are a man, you are likely to tell more about yourself to your mother than to anyone else. Next comes your father; next after him, your male friends; and next after them, your female friends.

Of all topics, you are least hesitant to talk about your tastes and interests, your attitudes and opinions, and your work. You are most reluctant to talk about money, matters of personality, and your body.

Those tendencies are generally the same whether you are married or single, except that if you're single you are likely to reveal more than a married person to your parents and same-sex friends. If you are married, you won't be surprised to learn that you're more likely to "tell all" to your spouse than to anyone else; in fact, you'll probably tell your spouse more than a single person will tell *anyone* else, including his or her mother.

This study involved forty liberal-arts college and nursing-school students, evenly distributed by race and sex. [Jourard, Lasakow]

You are approached by a total stranger who asks to interview you for a study on "how people describe themselves":

If you are a man, and if the interviewer is also male, you are less likely to agree to participate than if the interviewer is a woman. If you do agree, and even if the interviewer tries to melt the distance between you by revealing personal information about himself or herself, you tend to reveal comparatively little.

If the interviewer, whether a man or a woman, is attractive, you tend to reveal more about yourself on topics of higher intimacy than you would to a less attractive interviewer. If the interviewer is a woman and notably attractive, you tend to reveal most of all.

If you are a woman, you are also more likely to refuse a male interviewer than a female interviewer. But if you do consent, you'll probably reveal more about yourself than a man would to either interviewer. And, inconsistent as it may seem, you'll probably reveal more to a male interviewer than to a female. If the interviewer is a woman, you're likely to reveal more if she is unattractive than if she is pretty. Also, you are less likely than a man to reveal your name.

Whether you are a woman or man, the more highly schooled you are, the less likely you are to reveal your name. If you are a young adult, you are considerably more likely than an older person to reveal your name. And no matter who you are, you are more likely to reveal your name to a female interviewer than to a male.

(To put some of the findings that follow in perspective, you need to know that for this study ten students approached passengers at Boston's Logan Airport asking them to participate in a "class research project" on "how people describe themselves" or on hand-writing analysis. Of 534 people asked, 360 males and females agreed to participate.)

Whether you are a man or a woman, you are likely to reveal more about yourself if you are from out of town than if you are at your hometown airport. If you are a man who flies once a month or more, the more you travel the less you reveal about yourself. If you are a woman who flies once a month or more, in contrast to male frequent flyers you're apt to reveal *more* about yourself than if you travel less often. [Rubin]

You tend not to reveal much about yourself to other people:

You probably think of yourself as fairly consistent, one who is pretty much the same person from one situation to the next. [Shaffer, Smith, Tomarelli]

If you are a firstborn, as the preceding group of studies points out, you tend to be less self-revealing than your later-born sisters and brothers. But it should not be assumed that you need people less than later-borns. In fact, you may need people more, but you are probably not as good as your brothers and sisters at getting close to others.

When you are at work, you're especially likely not to reveal much when you speak either to a subordinate or an equal. Oddly enough, however, reticent as you are to reveal yourself, you tend to disclose more to your superiors than to your peers and subordinates.

When a person talking to you tells you far more than strangers customarily do, you tend to judge that person as someone in trouble—and you're probably right. As a result, in that conversation you probably disclose even less about yourself than you normally would.

In conversation generally, the more intimate the subject, the less you're inclined to disclose of yourself. [Cozby, review of studies]

The more intimate the topic gets, the less likely you are to hold eye contact. [Amerikaner]

You have just made a new acquaintance who interests you, and who you think might become a friend:

Each time you meet, the topics you discuss are likely to become steadily more intimate, compared to the last meeting. Each of you manages to respond to the other's bit of self-information at about the same rate of increasing intimacy. If you are the person who finds it easier to talk intimately, you take the lead as "pacesetter." If you're the one who finds intimacy more difficult, your partner will lead the way, and you take on a symmetrical role as "reciprocater." In that case, your relative silence may also at times control the progress of intimacy by simply inhibiting your partner.

This was concluded from a study of ninety-six students in a first-year psychology class who were paired in same-sex couples and asked to try to learn as much as possible about each other during one-minute conversational turns on twelve topics. They selected their topics from a long list that list included choices of both high and low intimacy, as rated by a second group. [Davis]

Both of you are likely to sense quite accurately who is revealing more and who less, and to sense the progress of mutual disclosure. The reciprocity as the level of self-revelation rises is critical to the unfolding of the friendship. If that early reciprocity becomes unbalanced, the person who is revealing more may begin to doubt the trustworthiness of the less revealing one. Simultaneously, the quieter person, feeling crowded by the other's rate of self-information, begins to dislike the more revealing one. By refusing to match the other's rate and level of self-revelation in early conversations, we signal our clear disinterest in continuing a relationship.

Later, when mutual respect, trust, and comfortable friendship have been established, the pressure to reciprocate is relaxed. Friends then move beyond stereotyped rules. Their conversations can be less or more intimate as the moment warrants. One partner may listen quietly and simply show concern, or may respond by divulging personal information if that seems right. In that way, older relationships may flourish while seeming unreciprocal over long periods of time. [Derlega, Wilson, Chaikin, drawing from a group of previous studies.]

Once the "dance of reciprocity" begins, you can expect the level of intimacy to increase until one of you begins to feel anxiety about too much intimacy.

You can best signal your interest in a closer relationship by disclosing medium amounts of personal information about yourself. Too little signals disinterest. Too much signals that you lack discretion.

You can best create an impression that you are open, interesting, and worth getting to know by revealing something intimate about yourself, but not too early in an initial conversation. The same information revealed early induces an impression that you are immature and maladjusted, "phoney and insecure."

You feel the greatest impulse to match levels of intimate talk when you are developing deeper trust and heading toward a close friendship. After you become close friends, as the previous group of studies found, you no longer need to keep matching levels of intimate disclosure with friends, lovers, or spouses. For this study, twenty-eight male students were exposed to experimenters who "revealed" at three different time spots within a ten-minute interview that their girlfriends were pregnant. Subjects rated the early revealers significantly less likable than those who revealed late in the interview. [Wortman; Altman; Won-Doornink]

The person with whom you risk opening the "dance" of mutual self-disclosure probably does not wield a great deal of power, compared to your own. [Cozby]

THE KINDNESS OF (AND TO) STRANGERS

At Harvard University, psychologist David McClelland began a class by asking each student to produce a small saliva sample. Then, as though not related to that request, he showed the students a film of Mother Teresa doing her good works among the sick and poor of Calcutta. Immediately afterwards, he asked the students for another sample. Testing showed that the second sample contained a significant increase in immunoglobulin A, an antibody that helps subdue respiratory infection.

Perhaps the conclusion ought to be: Go to the movies and you won't catch cold. But McClelland's suggestion (not yet convincing to many scientists) is perhaps more startling: Doing good can help keep you well.

In Tecumseh, Michigan, a ten-year study divided 2,700 people into those who gave volunteer service and those who did not. Among men studied, those who did no volunteer work died at two and a half times the rate of those who donated services to others. Some skeptics believe that people who volunteer are happier and healthier to begin with, but many volunteers—and researchers—insist that doing good is a *cause* of feeling well. Dr. Dean Ornish, a heart specialist at the University of California Medical School in San Francisco, prescribes the helping of others as a medicine for reducing self-involvement and hostility, which appear to raise cholesterol levels and induce angina.

LOOK YOURSELF UP

As a parent, you hope your children will grow up unselfish, generous, and attentive to the needs of others:

Nobody can influence them more than you can.

Eighty fifth-graders, evenly divided between boys and girls, were asked to rank one another's generosity and caring for others. Also, each child's mother and father were separately interviewed. The children rated most "altruistic," to use the researcher's term, correlated significantly with behavior of their parents. Among girls, generosity appeared significantly related to altruistic attitudes of their mothers, and even more so by similar attitudes of their fathers. Girls also were clearly led to caring about others when their fathers couched their scoldings and discipline for undesirable behavior by directing the child's attention to the harmful consequences inflicted on another, and asking the child to imagine the victim's feelings. Boys seemed led to altruism by their fathers' example more than by their mothers', by their mothers' calling attention to the harm inflicted on victims (more than by their fathers'), and by the affection regularly shown by their mothers. [Hoffman]

Sometimes you overflow with the spirit of the Good Samaritan—and sometimes you don't:

Two professors at Princeton think they have discovered why. John M. Darley, a psychologist, and C. Daniel Batson, a theologian, reconstructed the biblical tale of the Good Samaritan in modern dress. In the Gospel according to Luke, Jesus tells of a priest and a Levite who cross a road to avoid a man in pain pleading for help, while a Samaritan stops to give aid. The Princetonians set up their experiment not between Jerusalem and Jericho, but between Princeton's Green Hall and Green Hall Annex just off Washington Road. They fibbed to forty volunteers, who were all male Protestants and all students at the Princeton Theological Seminary, that they were studying the job placement of seminarians and asked each volunteer to prepare a talk for a recording. Half were instructed to prepare a text on job opportunities; the other half on the Good Samaritan parable. Then one by one, each was handed a sketch of how to exit Green Hall, turning right at the front door, turning right down an alley, then taking the first left to the Annex, where they were to record their talk. One group of the volunteers, who were dispatched at fifteen-minute intervals, were advised to take their time because they were early for the recording. Another group were dispatched with the instruction, "It's time to go now." A final group were told to hurry because they were already late for the recording.

In the alley along their way, each seminarian passed a young man lying in a doorway coughing and groaning as though in pain. The "victim," of course, had been put there as a confederate of professors Darley and Batson. Of the forty seminarians, sixteen stopped to help the groaner. Twenty-four plunged onward as though not seeing him. One even stepped over the "victim" to open a wrong doorway after misreading his instructions. The results apparently had little relationship to the altruistic attitudes of the seminarian, but appeared controlled simply by whether or not the student was in a hurry. Of those in "low hurry," 63 percent stopped to inquire how they could help the "victim." Of those in an "intermediate hurry," 45 percent stopped. In a "high hurry," only 10 percent stopped. (In all cases, the "victim" declined help, saying he had just taken medicine given him by a doctor and that he was resting. After all, the "victim" had to be ready for the next seminarian who was due in fifteen minutes.)

One other finding: Whether the volunteer was on his way to record a speech on job opportunities or on the Good Samaritan didn't seem to make a whit of difference.

"Common interpretations of the parable," said Dr. Batson to Israel Shenker of *The New York Times*, "seem to emphasize personality types and our results do not. One can imagine the priest and Levite, prominent public figures, hurrying along with little black books full of meetings and appointments, glancing furtively at their sundials as they go. In contrast, the Samaritan, a man of much lower public status, would likely have fewer and less important people counting on him to be at a set place and a set time." [Darley, Batson]

The more you sacrifice to accomplish a goal, the more you're likely to say the goal is justification for your sacrifice. But only up to a point.

Two Canadian psychologists kept checking with forty-seven participants, all ten to fifteen years old, who had committed themselves to a marathon march to benefit a charity. The longer they marched the greater the number of marchers named the charity as the justification for their ordeal—through the first twenty-seven miles of the march. At only one place was there a noticeable drop in the number of citings of the charity. That was at the thirty-five-mile finish line. [Barefoot, Strickland, Guild, Turnbull]

When a solicitor comes to your door asking for money for a charity your likelihood of being generous varies with the age of the solicitors, how they're dressed, and whether they work alone or in pairs.

Two Ohio State researchers sent thirty-two female volunteers collecting door to door for the Leukemia Society of America. Sixteen of the solicitors were members of the League of Women Voters, wore dresses, and averaged thirty-eight years of age. The rest were students (average age nineteen) wearing jeans. In each group, half the canvassers approached homes in pairs, the others alone. The older collectors got contributions 58 percent of the time, averaging 90 cents. The younger ones succeeded only 46 percent of the time, averaging 60 cents. Teams obtained money on 58 percent of their calls with an average gift of 88 cents; solo collectors, 46 percent, 62 cents. Thirty-two homedwellers asked for envelopes for sending contributions "later." None of them did so. [Jackson]

You tend to trust strangers until they give you a clear-cut reason not to:

You are less likely than low-trusters to tell lies, and there is some evidence that you are also less likely to cheat and steal. That is the finding of a University of Connecticut researcher who did a broad survey of previous studies on trustfulness. The survey also concluded that you are more likely to give others a second chance and that, more than low-trusters, you tend to respect the rights of others. You are less likely to be in conflict with yourself, unhappy, or maladjusted. Both low-trusting and high-trusting people like you more and seek you out as a friend more often than they do people who they sense are low-trusters.

Do high-trusters tend to be suckers—naive, easily fooled, gullible? No, says Julian B. Rotter, the researcher (who also developed the Locus of Control Scale described in "Who's in Control Here?," page 254). He says it can be shown over a series of previous studies that high-trusters are not suckered any more often than low-trusters. [Rotter]

YOUR IQ, YOUR MEMORY, AND YOUR CREATIVITY

At a two-day conference of five hundred Eastern educators in Washington, D.C., the accustomed scholarly calm of the conferees suddenly fell to pieces. The speaker was Dr. Henry S. Dyer, an author of the College Entrance Examination Board tests and vice president of the Educational Testing Service. He declared that intelligence quotients—"IQs"—the most commonly used comparison of the worth of one individual's mind over another, are "psychological and statistical monstrosities . . . probably the most convenient devices ever invented to lead people into misinterpretation" of children's learning abilities.

The terrible harm that children can suffer—and often do—from unintelligent interpretation of intelligence testing has been illustrated in California. The state's Department of Education was disturbed by the large number of Mexican-American children shunted into classes for the mentally retarded because of low IQs. The state decided to retest a sampling of "hopelessly uneducable" students, most of whom were children of migratory workers. The tests the children had taken were in English; they were retested in Spanish. Of forty-seven children in the sample, thirty-seven were no longer classified as "mentally retarded." What made the difference was *not* translation of language alone, but also certain translations that acknowledged the children's life experience. For example, one of the questions asked was, "In what kind of store do we buy sugar?" In recognition of local custom, in the retest a child was given credit for answering "liquor store." After the discovery that most of these children had nothing at all wrong with their minds, they were transferred to regular school classes. Some researchers and educators, however, wonder what injuries these young minds may have suffered as a result of serving an unjust sentence—some for as long as three years—in the stultifying atmosphere of special rooms for the retarded.

"What have we come to?" challenged Dr. Robert M. Coles, a Harvard research psychiatrist, at another educators' conference. "What is the magic these numbers, these scores, have over our common sense? I think IQ testing is an incredibly naive and simple-minded way of looking at human beings . . . of evaluating what a child shall learn, in what classroom at what school, which 'track' a child goes into, and what kind of education he is going to get."

Deprived and seemingly dull children are not the only victims. The simple IQ number often conceals hidden problems and potentials of bright-eyed, striving children from high-literacy homes. Many high-IQ children who do not do well in school, for all sorts of psychological reasons that the tests do not explain, are labeled "underachievers"—putting the onus on them, not on the school that failed to reach them. Meanwhile, other children with modest "intelligence" accomplish extraordinary things. Not long ago in England, at Cambridge University, 148 science instructors were surveyed to compare their school IQs—which are taken for the sole purpose of predicting their academic success—against their actual accomplishments. The IQs of some of these dons were in the unimpressive neighborhood of 110. The man estimated by his departmental colleagues as the best scientist among them turned out to have the lowest IQ. In the words of one British psychologist, Liam Hudson, "The field of intelligence measurement is still in its pre-Copernican state."

How can a test measure intelligence, a common question goes, when nobody has come up with a widely accepted definition of what intelligence is? What *is* an IQ? So far, the only widely accepted answer is: An IQ is a score in whatever it is that an IQ test measures.

If Robert Coles wonders what we've come to, we might all wonder how we got there. Where did intelligence testing come from—and what was it designed to accomplish?

In the ancient days of 1905, the public schools of France hired a celebrated psychologist of the day, Alfred Binet, to invent a test that would serve a simple purpose. They wanted to be able to determine within an hour or two whether a child six or seven years old was bright enough to fit into France's notably rigid style of schooling or whether he ought to be left by the wayside and put into a special class for the dull-witted.

Binet asked teachers to send him children they considered "bright" and those they considered "dull." By making an inventory of the mental characteristics that teachers favored, before long he figured out ways to test whether a child had them in adequate supply. Since a child's success was to depend upon meeting the demands of an unbending system rather than whether the system bent to the child, it's no wonder that educators found it "efficient" to identify the "right kind" of child as early as possible.

The Binet test for a six-year-old was translated for Americans in 1916 by Lewis H. Terman, and has since been revised slightly on two occasions and renamed Stanford-Binet. It is surely a straightforward way of testing whether a child starting school has acquired certain commonplace knowledge and skills: vocabulary, number concepts, and the ability to make analogies, to tell things apart ("What is the difference between a bird and a dog?"), and to solve simple puzzles ("What is wrong with this picture?")

But remember, the only thing Binet was out to do was to separate those children who couldn't make it in a certain kind of school from those who could—in a nation where virtually all schoolchildren shared a homogeneous culture and where one school was much like another. A child either passed or failed Binet's test.

The trouble—if one wants to call it that—began when the Binet test was Americanized. Terman added to his translation of Binet the concept of the "intelligence quotient"—a numerical way to assess the mind. After giving his test to many children, he determined what an *average* child ought to score at the particular age, labeling that ability as a "mental age." An IQ is a child's mental age divided by his actual age and multiplied by 100. Thus it is called a "quotient," not a simple score. By this definition the average child has an IQ of 100. So Terman believed he now had an effective device for grading the minds of *all* children along a comparative scale, saying that this one is "smarter" than that one by so many points, instead of Binet's simpler goal of saying this one is apt enough for a certain kind of school and that one is not.

Although Terman sternly warned that an IQ is only an approximation, and that 100 really means somewhere between 90 and 110, school psychologists and teachers frequently forget the warning. Some schools blithely and mechanically route a child with 81 into a regular class and another with 79 to a room for the hopeless, a child with 131 to a class for the "gifted" but not his schoolmate with 129.

The Americanization of Binet's test did not end with the invention of the numerical IQ. A year after Terman invented it—in 1917—the United States entered World War I and needed a quick, cheap way to screen the training potential of drafted doughboys. There was neither time nor personpower to sit a psychologist down with every draftee, as was done with each schoolchild in Binet's and Terman's testing. So Terman and others designed a new kind of test, offering multiple-choice answers to the same kinds of questions, that could be given to large numbers of young men at a sitting. These paper-and-pencil group tests were not expected to be as reliable as the results gained in face-to-face testing, but they served the rough purposes of the Army's personpower needs.

The quickness and cheapness of paper-and-pencil tests soon proved as attractive to officials of fast-growing, crowded public schools as they were to the Army. By 1929 group tests—and the notion of intelligence as a single mental entity describable by a single number—was firmly fixed in America, and *only* in America. Almost all schoolchildren were being group-tested, their quotients accepted as labels of their intelligence.

The single numerical score troubled many psychologists, starting with Charles Spearman, who had been analyzing test results since 1906. He was the first to establish that two people with the same IQ might be vastly different in mental ability. One might be very good at science, arithmetic, and spatial designs but poor in language; the other person, quite the opposite. A section-by-section look at almost any IQ test shows that its preponderant weight lies with measuring language skills.

Jean Piaget, the distinguished Swiss observer and theoretician of child development, came to the conclusion that the essence of intelligence lies in a person's *reasoning* capacities, not in mastery of words and sentences. While a skilled use of language seems to require development of one certain kind of intelligence, said Piaget, it is not the essence of intelligence.

Piaget's view is quite different from the view that took over the American schools during the first half of this century, when "intelligence" tests attained their present status. Schools have been temples of words and language. There is little in the traditional grade school curriculum that goes far in developing an ability to reason, especially in an individual way. Just as the first Binet test defined school aptitude as those traits liked best by teachers, so modern 'intelligence" tests still place the greatest weight on what teachers value most—skills of language.

Some time ago Dr. Herman A. Witkin, a professor of psychiatry at Princeton, examined the IQs of boys at Letchworth Village, a New York State institution for the "hopelessly" retarded, breaking down the test scores to compare subtests of their verbal abilities as against their mathematical and reasoning abilities. These boys had attained total scores of 60 to 80, thus excluding them from normal school experience, mostly because of their verbal subtests. Many of these "stupid" boys did better on their mathematical and reasoning subtests than some regular-school children with higher-than-average IQs. Yet they were condemned for life by an old system of school values that prizes words more highly than the ability to reason.

Another psychologist, Ernest A. Haggard of the University of Chicago, studied the personalities of high IQ children who excelled in word skills. Among high achievers in spelling and grammar—the kind who most often are pleasing to teachers—he found a surprising incidence of children he described as intellectually passive, obedient in carrying out rules and striving to gain acceptance by conforming to parental standards and expectations. Haggard identified another group, high achievers in reading whether or not they spelled or punctuated well. This group showed up in personality tests as more independent.

In contrast to both groups, Haggard found that high achievers in arithmetic viewed their environment "with curiosity and felt capable of mastering any problem they might encounter . . . [They] were emotionally controlled and flexible. . . . In their relations with authority figures and peers, they were more assertive, independent and self-confident than were children in the other subgroups."

A small number of psychologists have pried open a whole new field affecting millions of school-age children. Their concern is not with identifying mental abilities, but with *disabilities*. Take a nine-year-old, Jimmy, who speaks impressively, can fix a bicycle like an expert, but stumbles over simple reading. He confuses *b* with *d*, *was* with *saw*. Jimmy is obviously intelligent; yet on a printed, multiple-choice test he gets a low score, which conceals both his disability and his brightness. Researchers have given Jimmy's trouble a label—*dyslexia*—but do not yet have much knowledge of how to help him. Still more interesting, perhaps, is a substantial number of children who fail to master such basic spatial concepts as up and down and left and right, yet are so fluent in words and the manipulation of sentences that their IQ scores often are impressively high.

But the purpose of the IQ, its defenders point out, is not to diagnose the ills of a special child who may need a special school. It is to measure the school aptitude of "normal" children. How well does it do that? According to Robert L. Thorndike, of Teachers College at Columbia University, author of a leading textbook on psychological testing, its reliability in predicting grades in elementary school is "substantial." It is less reliable for predicting them in high school and still less for college. However, for predicting school grades at all levels, says Thorndike, there is a considerably more reliable guide: previous school grades.

Lewis Terman, the "translator" of the IQ into American life, also is known for another historic contribution—our knowledge of the super-intelligent. Having grown up in a small Indiana farming town, the Stanford psychologist had noticed repeatedly that most of the brightest children in his hometown had gone on to become leaders. He wondered what else a high IQ foretold about a child's later life.

In 1921 he identified 1,528 children (857 boys, 671 girls) in the California public schools with IQs between 135 and 200, representing the top 1 percent of the school population. Specifically he felt he could disprove widespread myths about superbright children, including the belief that they were almost surely headed for mental or physical illness, eccentricity, or social maladjustment.

"There was a myth that said, 'Early ripe, early rot,' " said Robert Sears of Stanford, who took over the research after Terman's death in 1956, in an interview with Carole Rafferty of *The New York Times*. "If you were very bright as a kid—a genius—you were supposed to become crazy."

Terman's ambitious goal was to follow those children all through their lives, periodically charting their reported satisfactions, hopes, successes, and disappointments; their religion and politics, their marriages, illnesses, emotional development, family history, careers, and children. Now in its eighth decade—and probably its last, since few of its subjects are expected to survive it—the Terman Study of the Gifted is the longest psychological study ever conducted. The average age of remaining subjects—who were to become known as "Termites"—is now past eighty, and the focus of the study is now on their aging.

When the Terman subjects were in their fifties, the data overturned many misconceptions. They were earning four times as much as the average American. Many married mothers among the studied said that if they could start all over again they would choose to have a career.

The names of "Termites" have never been released, but Professor Sears, himself a Terman-study subject, said the group includes a prominent motion picture director of the 1950s, three child movie stars of the 1920s, a nuclear scientist, two dozen "top level" medical research scientists, eight appellate-court judges, a successful science fiction writer, and a female metallurgist. Two subjects had at some time in their lives received welfare payments—and none had won a Nobel prize.

LOOK YOURSELF UP

You are the parent of an especially bright child:

If you are the father of the unusually intelligent child, you are likely to be more intelligent, more independent, more aloof, more assertive, and more tense than most men in the general population. That is the conclusion of this study of sixty-two parents of gifted children who completed a standard personality measure called the *16 Personality Factor Questionnaire.*

If you are the mother of the gifted child, according to the same survey, you, too, tend to be more intelligent and more independent than most women, but also more conscientious and persistent, and you take a more calculated, controlled approach to life.

As a couple, you probably measure as more intelligent than most couples, more likely to stand by your own ideas, more assertive, more independent, more self-controlled, and more persistent than the general population. [Fell, Dahlstrom, Winter]

Your child is more likely to be a pessimist than most of his classmates. But, according to this study of 110 intellectually gifted fifth- and sixth-graders in a southern city, your gifted child is also more apt than most to foresee problems and to invent more solutions for them.

Two educational psychologists asked the children to predict whether "our lives will be better or worse in fifty years," and to give reasons for their opinions. More than half the gifted students foresaw futures of crime, inflation, and shortages of food and natural resources, compared to similar pessimism by only 28 percent of the nongifted children. Next the children were asked to agree or disagree with twenty predictions, such as, "By the year 2000, jobs will be available for people who want to work." Again, gifted students tilted to the pessimistic side, most notably on the subjects of pollution, crime, and the quality of schools. Finally, the children were asked what might be the possible consequences of a variety of possible futures, for example, "What if everyone born lived to be exactly 100 years old?" One "average" child responded, "The population [will] get worse," leaving it at that. The gifted children were much more likely to suggest possible solutions, one of them replying, "Because there will be more old people, we will need more retirement homes."

In one important way, the gifted children resembled most adults as recorded in many polls and surveys: While pessimistic about the generalized future, they tended to be optimistic about their own futures. [George, Gallagher]

Your IQ is so high, it rates you as a "supergenius":

Whereas a score of 140 on the Stanford-Binet Intelligence Test is generally considered the threshold of genius, you are near the pinnacle of the pyramid because you have 180 or more. If forty points can make the difference between the "norm" of 100 and the "genius" score of 140, what does that additional forty-or-more points make of you?

That's the question asked by a researcher who delved into the long-term records of the original 1,528 eleven-year-olds begun in 1921 at Stanford University by Lewis Terman. Sixty years later, in 1981, David Feldman of Tufts University examined the life records of the twenty-six highest-scoring survivors of the original Terman group (those scoring 180 or above), and compared them against twenty-six run-of-the mill geniuses in the 140–150 class. What he found is that you can hardly tell the supergeniuses from the plain ones. In the fields of marriage, family, and domestic relations, the life records show no discernible difference. As for professional achievement, a majority of both groups earned advanced degrees. Both groups show a small sprinkling of achievers ranked by Feldman as "distinguished," and *all* the rest of the men (not enough of women survivors for comparison) have enjoyed "relatively successful" careers. Feldman concludes that, while the IQ is generally accepted as a reliable foreshadower of success in school, it is only a "crude predictor" of career or life achievement. [Feldman]

Extending Feldman's findings on achievement, James R. Flynn, a New Zealand political scientist, reviewed IQ data from fourteen countries, including Great Britain, Japan, France, the Netherlands, Canada, and the United States. His first surprising discovery was that IQ scores show "massive" increases from one generation to the next. In a single generation (thirty years), the gain averaged the equivalent of fifteen IQ points. While no firm explanation can be made, a probable reason is that schooling, and therefore mental training, is more universal.

That discovery led Flynn to ask about the consequences of such a gain. If the traditional view of IQ is correct, Flynn proposed, "a generation with a massive gain should radically outperform its predecessors." But nothing of the sort could be discerned. The Netherlands, for example, produces today almost sixty times the number of "geniuses" (IQ over 150) as it did in 1952. Yet Flynn cites a recent study showing no dramatic increase there in scientific discovery. In fact, the number of patents granted each year had declined by one third. Flynn therefore minimizes the meaning of generational differences in intelligence in the higher brackets. [Flynn]

You are an unusually successful executive:

Your IQ is probably moderately high or better, but is not the factor that separates you from other executives who have not done as well as you. What does seem to account for your success is a style of approaching problems and of decision-making—a subtle combination of thinking and behavior that is notable for its complexity, but is unrelated to IQ. That complexity, according to the research of Seigfried Streufert of the Pennsylvania State University College of Medicine, includes your ability to plan strategically while not locking yourself into one course of events; a capacity for handling large amounts of decision-making information without feeling drowned by it all; and being able to maintain your balance amidst rapidly changing events without losing sight of how those events affect one another. To be sure, most executives don't think in these complex ways. They see problems discreetly, as though isolated from one another, and often hold to a single primary goal, such as showing a profit. But those executives usually are not the ones who rise to the top. [Streufert]

You are nearsighted:

Have your thick glasses caused you to be taunted as a "smartie"?

Your taunters are apt to be right. Two opthalmologists tested 157,748 Israeli military recruits, ages seventeen to nineteen, and discovered a significant correlation between nearsightedness and high IQ. They reported in the American Medical Association's

Archives of Ophthalmology that, of recruits with IQs of at least 128 (average IQ is 100), 27.3 percent were nearsighted. That compares with a general rate of 15.8 percent of the recruits who were myopic in both eyes (unable to see clearly at medium-to-long distances). Of those with an IQ of 80 or below, myopia afflicted only 8 percent.

Comparable findings came out of a study of eighteen-year-old draftees in Denmark. That study was done by researchers at Copenhagen University and the Danish Institute of Myopia Research. [Rosner, Belkin, Israeli study; Teasdale, Danish study]

You are a woman and you do not know your IQ score:

If you're asked to guess your IQ, you'll almost certainly underestimate it. Many men also do so, but significantly less often than women do, and they underestimate their scores by lesser margins.

You are twice as likely as a man to attribute to a stranger a higher IQ than you claim for yourself.

You are almost certain to attribute a higher IQ to your father than to your mother—and men are likely to do the same with an equally high degree of certainty. Furthermore, both you and virtually all men assume that your father has a higher IQ than you assume for yourself.

The researcher suggests that the American woman's extremely high tendency (*invariable* tendency, the study startlingly shows) to downrate her own intelligence "must be added to the American female's already lengthy list" of perceived deficiencies dumped on her by herself as well as by society. He quotes *Invitation to Sociology* by P. L. Berger: "The most terrible thing that prejudice can do to the human being is to make him tend to become what the prejudiced image of him says that he is." (Perhaps it's harsh to observe that Berger, by using the male pronoun to include all, unwittingly adds to the prejudice he denounces.)

These conclusions were drawn from unusually extensive studies— eleven separate ones, conducted in Louisiana and Tennessee between 1973 and 1976, covering 881 males and 1,021 females, all white. Of them, 479 were high school students, 1,311 were college students, and 112 nonstudent adults. As part of a larger survey, subjects were asked, "By comparison with the national average IQ score of 100, what do you estimate your IQ score would be?" [Hogan]

You are a homosexual:

You are likely to have a higher IQ than a heterosexual who otherwise shares your station in life—unless you are in a category of having been imprisoned for your homosexual behavior. That is the conclusion of a survey of fourteen studies comparing homosexuals against similarly-stationed presumed heterosexuals and the intelligence scores of both groups. Typical homosexual groups and their presumed heterosexual counterparts were: 50 homosexuals contacted through friends versus 50 married people; 35 homosexual student activists versus 35 first-year university students; 85 homosexuals and transsexuals seeking treatment versus 85 married men with normal sperm seeking treatment for sterility in marriage; 100 prisoners convicted of homosexual acts versus 100 prisoners convicted of non-homosexual acts, and numerous other comparison groups. The survey concludes: "Most studies found the more homosexual subject groups' scores to be higher than those of the more heterosexual controls, and *all exceptions* to this trend are concentrated in one subgroup: prisoners." [Weinrich]

You know an attractive, urbane, classily dressed, charming, even seductive woman who is in psychotherapy—and her treatment is getting her nowhere:

That's not all. Her therapist may have discerned clear symptoms of hysteria, anxiety, depression, schizophrenia, or personality disorder. The doctor may have given her antidepressant drugs, tranquilizers, or electroconvulsive therapy, and she shows no more response to those than she does to the conventional "talking" psychotherapy. What has the doctor left out?

Where the doctor may have failed, which might explain all the rest, is in not giving her an IQ test (which psychotherapists almost never give their patients). That is the conclusion of two Australian therapists, Norman Gold, a psychiatrist, and Julie Shaw, a psychologist, both at Malvern Clinic, a large suburban psychiatric clinic near Melbourne. Gold and Shaw identified sixteen women marked by the above combinations of features—the trappings of success and self-expression valued in upper-class suburbia, yet persistence in what the two clinicians call "therapeutic failure." A strong hunch led the two doctors to give IQ tests to the sixteen nonresponders, and discovered that their scores ranged from 69 to 88. These intellectually dysfunctional women "got by socially," suggest the researchers, because of their physical attributes, grooming, and "right" behaviors. The low intelligence of the women, say Gold and Shaw, "was an unrecognized primary factor in misdiagnosis and inappropriate treatment."

What can be done for them? Their most important need, Gold and Shaw suggest, is help in setting realistic goals, and in guiding their families in realistic expectations and support. [Gold, Shaw]

You know that there's a lot of evidence that intelligence is at least in part transmitted genetically. You further know that some racial groups in the American patchwork score lower average IQs than other racial groups—and you feel troubled by the possible implications of this evidence:

Obviously, a counterbalance to the genetic side of the race evidence would be evidence on the environmental—or life-training—side. And here is an arresting chunk of such evidence:

Richard Lynn, a social psychologist, has presented extensive data in the *British Journal of Social and Clinical Psychology* to show significant differences in average IQ among different regions of the British Isles, where racial inheritances are not a definable factor. The mean IQ is highest in London and Southeast England, and tends to drop with distance from this region of the measured population. Distance from London is not the only factor. Average IQs also correlate highly with average per capita income, rate of unemployment, rate of infant mortality, degree of urbanization, and with school achievement. "The regional differences in the mean population IQ," Lynn concludes, "appear to be due to historical differences which are measured back to 1751 and to selective migration from the provinces into the London area." [Lynn; British study]

YOUR MEMORY

Your sixtieth birthday is behind you, and you feel your mental skills slipping away:

It might be truer to say that you are slipping away from your mental skills. A Pennsylvania State University authority on aging, K. Warner Schaie, led a twenty-eight-year study of four thousand people, and concluded that adults lose their sharpness as a result of long-term relative disuse of their minds—but that mental skills can be restored and resharpened.

"After a while," says Dr. Schaie, who conducted his study with Sherry L. Willis, "the pressure isn't on you anymore to engage in mental exercises. It's very much like physical skills: Once you stop using them they get rusty."

Schaie demonstrated his case by setting up tutorial sessions for aging people in whom he had diagnosed weak areas of mental performance—and these areas of deterioration differ from person to person. The sessions resulted in pronounced improvement for about two thirds of the people who had slid back in spatial conception, problem-solving, numerical, and verbal skills. Perhaps more impressive, 40 percent restored themselves to the test-score levels they had recorded fourteen years earlier. Naturally, victims of Alzheimer's disease or other degenerative disorders are excluded from these conclusions.

Women seem to decline more rapidly than do men, Schaie has tentatively observed. That appears to be the result of a greater tendency of aging women to fall into mental inactivity, because in his group tutorial sessions, women seem to benefit most by the retraining of mental skills.

"There is virtually no decline of people's mental abilities into their 60s," Schaie says. "That has important policy implications for age discrimination. Perhaps we should invest more resources in continued education in the last third of a person's work life."

The Schaie-Willis findings are consistent with others that have shown that some mental abilities, notably the making of sound judgments, continue to improve well after age sixty, even as other skills decline through disuse. [Schaie, Willis]

You worry that your memory is failing—or doesn't work right:

Almost everybody thinks so, and almost everybody exaggerates the problem.

"Most people think their memories are much worse than you find they actually are when you go out and observe them," says a psychologist at Emory University, Ulric Neisser, who actually has gone out to observe them, working with a Hamilton College psychologist, Douglas Herrmann. For one thing, they studied two hundred people to determine what most people worry about forgetting most often. The most common lapses:

- Meeting someone socially and, mere minutes later, not remembering the person's name;
- Waking up with a pervasive aura of a dream, but unable to recall a single detail about it;
- Making a conscious mental note to drive home a point in the conversation, then, in the course of talking, forgetting to do it.

Less frequent lapses, but sometimes just as bothersome, are departing from somewhere without taking something you know you'll need, and going blank as to what date it is and having to ask someone.

The popular notion of gradual and continuous memory loss is contradicted by the findings of Harry Bahrick, a psychologist at Ohio Wesleyan University. "If you retain knowledge for five years," Dr. Bahrick has concluded, "it seems you'll remember it for another twenty-five." Bahrick studied one thousand people who had studied Spanish in high school or college. Of course, they lost mastery of much of what they had learned, but most of what they lost was forgotten in the first three to five years after finishing their courses. Over the next twenty-five years, they forgot little.

One kind of memory seems to withstand hardily the passing of years. Dr. Bahrick found that people recognize both the names and the faces of 90 percent of their high school classmates thirty-five years after their graduation. Fifty years after graduation, they identified classmates' names and faces with accuracy ranging between 70 and 80 percent. Former professors, seventy-five years old, remembered their former students with about the same accuracy as those tested at age thirty-six.

Certain kinds of memory improve with age, mainly because maturity teaches the reliance on memory aids. John Harris of Cambridge University studied how well people remembered to keep an appointment for making a telephone call at a certain time. He found that college students were fourteen times more likely to forget the commitment than sixty-five- to seventy-five-year-olds. He found young people "cocky" about their memories, which may be what does them in. "There is a tendency," Harris says, "for those who trust their memories and make comments such as 'I've got an internal alarm' to be more likely to miss an appointment."

People of orderly habits and physical surroundings probably have less memory trouble than those who live more scattered lives. "We structure our surroundings, in large part, so that it acts as a memory aid," says Donald Norman, a psychologist at the University of California at San Diego, who specializes in memory. "People make a sort of natural map of their world by putting things in places that fit their habits. When there is no fit between where things are and what you need them for, then memory is more likely to fail."

Norman sees implications of that "natural map" for product designers and inventors in a world of increasingly complex technology: "One of the basic rules of good design is that a user should immediately recognize and remember how to use an article, whether a blender or a computer. I have a fancy European car with 112 different controls, counting all the different radio knobs, the windows, and so on. I picked it up at the factory, and a guy sat beside me and showed me everything just once. That was enough. That's good design. But I still can't remember how to use my phone for all the things it can do, like call forwarding. There's nothing in its design to remind me." [Goleman]

Your memory loss may be real, and caused by one of the most common prescription drugs—Valium (generic name: diazepam; 23 million prescriptions written in 1985). This tranquilizer, often also used as a sleeping pill and/or muscle relaxant, has been found to affect memory in a special way. It doesn't seem to interfere with recalling the Spanish you learned in high school, nor with remembering to remember that today is Tuesday, and on Tuesdays you call Mother at noon. But it does seem to block out or interfere with remembering what you learned or experienced shortly before taking the drug, or while under its influence.

Steven Mewaldt of Marshall University, who directed a series of studies, reports that diazepam's memory-blocking action cannot be attributed to the drug-takers becoming too "laid back" to take the trouble to memorize. Certain wrinkles in his testing methods eliminated that possibility. Mewaldt has collected evidence that diazepam interferes with a neurotransmitter, called GABA, thought to be at the biochemical heart of memory formation.

"If people are taking diazepam as a sleeping aid," says Dr. Mewaldt, "[the memory-blocking effect] will probably be gone by the time they wake up in the morning. But if they are taking it during their daily activities, that presents more of a concern. . . . I have had students admit to taking diazepam in order to calm down so they can study for an exam. That's certainly counterproductive." [Mewaldt]

You know you have a reliable memory and you trust it:

There's an excellent chance that you're kidding yourself.

"Most people would be quite surprised at how malleable their memory is—even those memories they feel most certain about," asserts David C. Rubin, a Duke University psychologist and memory researcher who edited *Autobiographical Memory* for Cambridge University Press. "It seems to be that reminiscence flows more freely about the period in life that comes to define you: the time of your first date, marriage, job, child. It's not that life is duller from 40 to 55 than from 20 to 35, but that the patterns are more stable, and so less memorable."

People who have passed middle age, Rubin's research shows, tend to recall more incidents from their youth and early adult years than from their more recent past. Memories tend to be selective in even more significant ways. This is illustrated in another study, conducted by Lee Robbins, a sociologist in the department of psychiatry at Washington University in St. Louis. Robbins delved into records of the early home-life of 310 adults who had childhoods so troubled they were treated in a child guidance clinic. Thirty years after their childhood treatment, these adults were tracked down by researchers who found that the well-adjusted among them had fewer memories of their painful childhoods than did those still afflicted by emotional problems. Those who have become adjusted now "like to look back on life as though it were always that way," says Robbins. His study has appeared in the *American Journal of Orthopsychiatry.*

Selective memory can work both ways, Robbins points out. Pain, for example, tends to enliven our memories about pain. A study showed that people with arthritis are more likely than their unaffected brothers or sisters to remember details of a parent's suffering from the disease. Perhaps even more striking as evidence of selectivity, Gordon Bowers and others at Stanford University discovered that depressed people more easily recall sad occurrences in their lives than happy people do—and happy people more easily recall happy events.

A psychotherapist, Dr. Robbins points out, "relies heavily on the ability of people to tell about their past. But their answers are likely to be highly colored by their current view of themselves. And the vaguer the question—for instance, how happy was your child-hood?—the more open to inaccuracy the answer will be."

A professor of psychiatry at Cornell Medical School, Theodore Shapiro, adds, "Although there is much forgetting that is simply forgetting, a rule of thumb is that the more psychodynamically important a memory is, the more prone it is to warping or forgetting altogether." [Goleman]

YOUR CREATIVITY

Creativity is one of the hallowed words of our era, but no one is quite sure how to define it. Parents crave it for their children. Teachers speak adoringly of pupils who have it, yet those children are often first to be sent to the principal's office for not following the rules. Often creativity is defined by what it is not. And since the early 1950s, when creativity first became the subject of research, it has become increasingly clear that what it is not, is intelligence—or, at least, not the same skills of mind that are measured by IQ tests.

People who score high in tests designed to measure creativity usually score high as well in IQ tests. The reverse is not true, how-ever. A high IQ is no hint whatever of a high score in a creativity test.

Creativity, says Robert M. Goldenson in *The Encyclopedia of Human Behavior*, is "a form of directed thinking applied to the discovery of new solutions to problems, new techniques and devices, or new artistic expressions." He refers to a "closed system" of every-day thinking that is "largely devoted to problems that can be solved by assembling readily available information and applying established rules." That kind of common analytical thinking can help us repair a lawn mower, organize a file system, or plan a membership cam-paign. But sometimes we need "open system" thinking, which has no known rules: for creating an invention or a design or a story, even a practical joke; or, perhaps most difficult of all, for creating a new theory. Nobody quite knows the elements of the genius that led Charles Darwin, after years of collection of data, to explode with the conception of evolution based on survival of the fittest. All the world admires and reveres Beethoven and Shakespeare, but we know little of how they "thought up" what they did.

Darwin's "explosion" does not mean his conceptions just arose as though from nowhere. "To be creative," says Howard Gruber, author of *Darwin on Man: A Psychological Study of Scientific Creativity* and biographer of Jean Piaget, "you need to know a lot, and cultivate special skills. Darwin studied barnacles for eight years and came to know more about them than anyone else. Leonardo drew a thousand hands. . . . The most stable generalization about the creative life is that you work hard, probably for a long time. Of course, what would be hard for others becomes easy for you. Freeman Dyson, the physicist, describes how as an adolescent he discovered the calculus and spent the whole summer working like a madman, solving every problem in a big calculus textbook. . . . For the creative person, the greatest fun is the work. I think you have to take notice when Darwin says he read Malthus 'for amusement.' "

Perhaps the best way to attempt a clear focus on the misty subject of creativity is to describe what modern tests of creativity try to test. One such measure, J. P. Guilford's Southern California Tests of Divergent Production, is divided into these subtests:

WORD FLUENCY.   In one sample item, the subject is asked to write in an allotted time as many words as she or he can containing, say, an *s* or *w*, or beginning with a certain prefix, or rhyming with *book*. Scores on this section have been found to correlate quite reliably with achievement in art and science courses.

IDEATIONAL FLUENCY.   The subject must name all the things that come to mind under certain class headings, such as solids that will not burn; or list as many things as come to mind for possible uses of a common object, like a ruler or a spatula.

ASSOCIATIONAL FLUENCY.   The subject is asked to list in a specified time words that resemble in meaning a given word, such as "excellent"; or provide an adjective to complete an image, such as "as—— as a firecracker."

EXPRESSIONAL FLUENCY.   The subject is given a four-letter series and is told to invent as many sentences as possible using them as initial letters of words. Example: M-A-T-S (Mothers are too serious).

FLEXIBILITY.   Among the puzzles used here are Hidden Pictures (finding concealed faces); Hidden Figures (finding a circle, oblong, or figure-8 in a more complex pattern); Match Problems (removing a number of match sticks to leave a specified design of squares or triangle).

ORIGINALITY.   One item is a Free Association Test, in which the subject is to respond with the first word that is stirred to mind by a stimulus word. The responses are scored on the basis of uncommonness. A study has shown that scientists, engineers, artists, musicians, and writers tend to give more unexpected associations than executives, politicians, teachers, or salespeople. A second part is the Consequences Test. For example, when asked "What would happen if every telephone went dead at the same time?" the subject is to list as many different consequences as possible.

What garlic is to salad, insanity is to art.

AUGUSTUS SAINT-GAUDENS,
AMERICAN SCULPTOR (1848–1907)

You are a creative artist:

If people approach you as though you're slightly off your rocker, there's a better-than-average chance they're right.

To confirm centuries of suspicion that creative artistry is linked to madness, Nancy C. Andreasen of the University of Iowa College of Medicine interviewed thirty distinguished writers who, over a fifteen-year period, served on the faculty of the University of Iowa Writer's Workshop, a highly esteemed graduate program. (She also interviewed thirty professionals in hospital administration, law, and social work of comparable age, sex, and education as a control comparison.) Fully 80 percent of the writers reported that at some time in their lives they had had at least one episode of either severe depression or manic depression—the latter including either a pronounced mania with evidences of euphoria, increased energy, and poor judgment, or a milder "hypomania." None of the subjects had a history of schizophrenia, marked by severe thought disorders, but 30 percent of them had been diagnosed as alcoholic. Two of the writers committed suicide during the fifteen years of the study. Among the nonwriting comparison group, 30 percent had experienced depression or manic depression (compared to the writers' 80 percent), and only 7 percent were alcoholic; like the writers, none were schizophrenic.

In 1983, while visiting Oxford University, Kay Jamison, a professor of psychiatry at the University of California at Los Angeles, also came up with persuasive results in a study of forty-seven leading British writers and artists. All were Royal Academicians, and the poets among them all had received the Queen's Gold Medal. Jamison found an "overwhelming correlation" between manic depression and creativity. Fully 38 percent of them had gone so far as to seek treatment for depression or manic depression—about thirty times the rate of the general population. The most likely subgroup to have suffered severe mood disorders or dramatic mood swings, Jamison found, were the poets.

In still a third study, not yet completed, two psychiatrists, Kareen and Hagop Akiskal, both of the University of Tennessee in Memphis and the University of Paris, have examined twenty French writers, painters, sculptors, and musicians. Nearly 70 percent of the group have "some type of affective disorder," Hagop Akiskal reports, the most common being moderate to mild manic depression or mood swings. A disorder more severe, he believes, would probably block the artist's effectiveness and disrupt a career.

Approaching the question from a different direction, the Akiskals also recently studied 750 psychiatric patients in Memphis, and found that those diagnosed as mild manic depressives or mood swingers were more likely to be creative artists than were those with other mental disorders. They also found, however, that mild manic depression and mood swings also occur more often among people successful in business and leadership positions than among the broad run of patients, although not as often as among creative artists. [Andreasen; Jamison; Akiskal, Akiskal]

Your endowment with the magical (or, more precisely, undefined) powers of creativity has little to do with intelligence, talent, or acquired expertise, confirms David N. Perkins, codirector of Harvard University's Project Zero study of cognitive skills in the sciences and humanities. Among traits that Perkins has found are shared by creative people is a drive to "uncover the aesthetic"—or what cellist Janos Starker has called the obsessive desire for reducing chaos and finding beauty. Another creative trait, says Perkins, is a sense of detachment that allows the creator to test and judge ideas despite the rush of creative energies. Linus Pauling, the two-time Nobel laureate, once told a student that the key trick in coming up with successful ideas is to think up a great many of them and simply get rid of the bad ones.

You apparently have as strong an interest in discovering and formulating unusual problems as in solving them in unusual ways, Perkins believes. You have an extraordinary capacity for metaphor, for producing unexpected connections, and for challenging traditional assumptions. You are a risk-taker, willing to function on the edge of your competence, says Perkins. Finally, he says, as a creative individual, you are driven by "intrinsic" motivations, like curiosity, need for beauty, craving for understanding and order, that do not move most people. You are not stirred, as most are, by the lures of money, grades, awards, or job promotion. Says Pauling about the same point: "At an early age I had a strong curiosity about the nature of the world. I don't think I was ambitious."

Perkins has further concluded that if you are creative, you were probably made so by your life experiences, not by your genes. Conventional schooling does not foster creative traits, he concludes. Students are rarely given the freedom to define their own problems to be solved and are even less often encouraged to uncover new ones.

When artistic people like Janos Starker use the word "beauty" and when scientific creators use the words "aesthetic" or "elegance" they appear to be talking about somewhat the same thing. In science, says National Academy of Sciences president Frank Press, the aesthetic solution is often the correct solution. A drive for aesthetic simplicity created the periodic table, replacing an almost useless "potpourri of tortured arrangement of elements." [Perkins]

You are a trained social worker:

You score lower in creativity than any other category of college majors in a comparison group, if you are typical of the fifty-four social work students in this midwestern university study who took the Torrance Tests of Creative Thinking, the standard measure of creativity.

Even more discouraging, perhaps, the further you advanced through your four-year course of study, the lower your creativity score dipped. Don't take that finding too personally, however. Four years earlier than this study, in 1970, R. Eisenman, a psychologist, reported a similar decline in creativity among student nurses at two different professional schools. Worst of all, the recognized authority on creativity, E. P. Torrance, developer of the Torrance tests, demonstrated as early as 1965 that the longer a student stays in school—*regardless of his or her course of study*—the deeper that student's creativity score sinks. The Baylor University author of this study concludes that these social work students (and perhaps most college students) "appear to be socialized into a noncreative orientation." [Johnson]

You are a graduate student:

Regardless of your field of study, you tend to score lower than artists or the intellectually gifted in tests of five dimensions of mental functioning. A team of three researchers measured two groups of talented people—artists and those who rated as intellectually gifted—for five different kinds of mental functioning: intellectual, imaginational, emotional, sensual, and "psychomotor" (such physical expressions of excitement as pressure of speech and nervous movement). They also measured graduate students in a range of academic fields for the same kinds of mental functioning. As a group, the graduate students scored significantly lower in all five dimensions. [Piechowski, Silverman, Falk]

You jog and/or exercise regularly:

Perhaps you often taunt non-exercisers with claims that your workouts not only make you feel better, but that they make your mind work better. You don't mean to taunt, you say, but are just trying to tell the truth.

Well, you probably *are* telling the truth. Two psychologists, in New York City and Florida, tested the creativity of forty-two college students in a health and exercise class that included jogging. Actually, they tested the students twice, once at the start of the semester and again at its end. The tested students ran for twenty minutes twice each week. A comparison group attended lectures only, but didn't run. The standard creativity tests asked them, for example, to come up with novel uses for common objects, and to imagine a variety of results if the world were covered by a foot of water. Runners won hands down—in two ways. They scored higher than their nonrunning counterparts. But perhaps more impressive, they improved their own score significantly from the first test (before they ran regularly) and their second. Exercise sessions in school, conclude the researchers, "are not frills, but should be central to our learning and educational processes." [Gondola, Tuckman]

CHAPTER
4

Crime, Violence, and Aggression

YOUR RESPONSES TO CRIME AND VIOLENCE

One of the powerful influences on the quality of life in most Western nations since the 1960s has been crime—awareness of its constant presence, fear of it. The apprehension is both real and imaginary. To say it is imaginary is not to diminish it. Fear of being robbed, mugged, raped, or murdered is an assault on a person's tranquility and personal rights comparable to a physical assault itself.

How realistic are the fears of most people that a criminal might leap from ambush and attack? The studies that follow show that in some ways most people exaggerate the threat; in some ways, they are too complacent; and in still other ways they are remarkably realistic.

Most of those studies measure our apprehensions of what we might call short-term threats: Am I likely to be mugged in my own neighborhood if I go out tonight? Can I protect myself from physical harm if I surrender my purse or wallet without a peep? If I am being threatened with rape right now, can I scare off my attacker by screaming or kicking him in the groin?

Until recently, nobody knew your chances of becoming a victim of a crime at *some time* in your life. Now the U. S. Department of Justice has concluded a large-scale study to answer that question, using figures compiled by the National Crime Survey over a ten-year period, 1975 through 1984. The conclusions are more reliable than most crime statistics, which are usually derived from the number of crimes reported to the police. The police themselves know that many, perhaps most, crimes go unreported. For the National Crime Survey, researchers tracked an impressive sample of 101,000 people aged twelve and over in 49,000 households. Those people were interviewed twice a year for the full decade of the survey.

Before learning the answer, would you like to guess the percentage of probability that at some time between your twelfth birthday and the time you die you will have been the target of an actual or attempted assault, robbery, rape, or murder?

The answer, which may startle all but the most committed pessimists, is 83 percent. If you are male, the likelihood rises to 89 percent; female, it declines to 73 percent. The most likely victims are black males, at 92 percent; least likely, white females, at 71 percent.

Perhaps it's a consolation that only one American out of 133 dies by murder, less than 1 percent. One out of twelve women, however, or about 8 percent, at some time endure an attempted or actual rape.

There's a 30 percent chance that you will have been the victim of a robbery or an attempted robbery sometime in your life. If you're male, the chances rise to 37 percent; if you're a black male, to 51 percent.

You can be fairly sure that at some time a physical assault will be made, or at least attempted, on you. It happens to 74 percent of us—and to 82 percent of males. Perhaps worse, there is a 40 percent chance that you will have been robbed or assaulted with a resulting injury.

Statistically most certain of all, you are 99 percent sure to have been the target of an attempted or successful theft (not involving a physical threat to your person).

The older you are, the less likely you will be the victim of a crime during the remainder of your life. If you are twenty, you are 72 percent likely to be robbed, assaulted, or raped in the future, although the probability of personal theft remains at 98 percent. If you are forty, a violent crime against you in the future is 36 percent likely; an assault resulting in injury, only 11 percent; personal theft, still hanging over you heavily at 82 percent. If you are sixty, the probability of a future violent crime against you drops to 14 percent; of robbery or assault with injury, 4 percent; personal theft, 43 percent.

LOOK YOURSELF UP

You are walking down a lonely city street at night:

The way you walk may invite—or repel—an assault by a mugger.

Dr. Betty Grayson of Hofstra University secretly videotaped sixty persons walking a high-crime street in New York City. She then met with twelve prisoners convicted of assault upon strangers, showed them the tapes and asked them to rate the walkers on a scale of one ("a very easy ripoff") to ten ("too big a situation, too heavy, would avoid it"). To corroborate the ratings, she repeated the procedure with a second group of twelve muggers.

Next, she subjected the tapes to Labanalysis, a system for identifying twenty-one different body movements to study nonverbal communication. From these twenty-one, Dr. Grayson isolated five movements as significantly more common among persons rated by muggers as highly vulnerable. The characteristics are:

- A stride abnormally long or short for the person's body size and leg length.
- A walk that swings arm and leg on the same side in unison, instead of opposite-side leg-and-arm swings.
- Rising and lowering on the whole foot rather than a smooth heel-to-toe roll.
- A "gestural" walk (moving hand and/or foot as though disconnected from body movement) instead of a "postural" walk (integrating the whole body in a single, graceful effort.)
- A seeming independence of the top and bottom halves of the body. For example, holding the upper half tightly, while freely swinging the lower half.

A question that the study did not attempt to answer: Could potential victims—especially the elderly—be taught to alter their body styles sufficiently to discourage assault? [Grayson]

You are reminded constantly by newspapers and TV of the prevalence of violent crime:

You probably imagine violent crime to be more prevalent than it actually is. Thus your fears exaggerate your actual danger. [Lichtenstein, Slovic, Fischhoff, Layman, Combs]

Under some circumstances a news report of a violent crime may make you feel reassured instead of alarmed. It's most likely to reassure you when the victim is described as someone markedly unlike yourself, or was chosen for some special reason that would not fit you, or if you feel you would not have acted as the victim did. To determine that, the researcher classified thirty-six newspapers in twenty-six cities according to the proportion of their crime reports that involved local crimes, sensational crimes, and random crimes. A random sample of 335 readers of those newspapers were then questioned by telephone about their fear of crime. In a second part of the study, eighty college students read reports of crimes (local or nonlocal, random or premeditated) and then commented on their level of fear of crime. The students showed the same fear-of-crime patterns as the newspaper readers. [Heath]

You probably overestimate the likelihood of unusual or spectacular disasters, like murder, hotel fires, polio, or Legionnaire's disease. But you're apt to underestimate the frequency of less dramatic, single-victim disasters, such as suicide or drowning. When it's all averaged out, however, you're likely to estimate rates of risk almost as well as the pros with their actuarial charts. [Slovic, Fischhoff, Lichtenstein]

When you read a newspaper report of a particularly shocking crime, your resulting agitation is apt to raise (for no fact-based reason) your generalized fears of assault, rape, hijacking, nuclear war, highway accidents, poisoning, lightning, hurricane, and leukemia— as well as any other form of life-endangering disaster. [Johnson, Tversky]

You feel less safe in a large city than in a small one:

Your fears are based on good information. In a city of over a million, you're twenty times more likely to be robbed than in a city of 10,000 to 25,000. Fully one third of the nation's robberies in 1982 were perpetrated in our six largest cities, even though those cities have only 8 percent of the population. Eighteen percent of the nation's robberies took place in New York City alone. [Cook]

You become more apprehensive of crime when the moon is full:

Trust your feelings. Under a full moon, crime goes up 19 percent. [Jarmon]

You get similarly apprehensive in hottest summer, dead of winter, and on holidays and weekends:

Right again. The crime rate goes up at those times too (see previous item). And that's not all. Even pollution gives you extra cause to look over your shoulder: A study in Newark, New Jersey, has found that for all months of the year except December, the rate of assault rises and falls with the measure of oxidants in the air. [Jarmon]

To protect yourself and your family, you keep a loaded handgun or rifle in your home:

The weapon is about forty-three times more likely to kill you or a family member than it is to protect you against an intruder.

Two physicians—Arthur Kellermann, M.D., of the University of Tennessee, and Donald Reay, M.D., of the King County Medical Examiner's Office, Seattle—examined police records of deaths by gun between 1978 and 1983 in Seattle and surrounding communities. Guns had killed 743 people, and of them 398 of the deaths occurred in the home where the weapon was kept.

Of those 398, self-protection was the recorded reason for only 9 of them.

Of the remaining 389, fully 333 were suicides. (Suicide experts have long argued that an important encouragement of suicide is ready availability of the means.) An additional 41 were listed as criminal homicides (but not by an intruder), and 12 as accidental deaths. Three additional deaths by self-inflicted gunshot wounds were of undetermined motivation. [Kellermann, Reay]

You are suddenly threatened by a robber:

The chances that he'll kill you are less than one in a hundred. Those chances are further reduced if you clearly accept that your attacker is in charge and if you give him what he wants without a show of reluctance. If you want to reduce the chance he'll take any of your possessions, you can do so by fighting back, yelling, or trying to run away. But if you do any of those, you'll increase the chances that he'll shoot, knife, or beat you. [Cook]

You are a woman threatened with rape:

You are most likely to prevent the rape if you yell and hit back. "Rapists often think the rape will be easy because the woman won't resist, or they think the woman wants to be raped," concluded Pauline Bart, a professor of sociology in psychiatry at the University of Illinois at Chicago, who conducted a three-year study along with Patricia H. O'Brien, a doctoral candidate. They interviewed ninety-four women, fifty-one of whom successfully avoided rape and forty-three who failed to prevent the assault.

Women trained in self-defense and who exercised regularly were more likely to avoid rape.

Most women who failed to forestall the rape sustained serious injuries, mental as well as physical. Those who resisted, by yelling, fleeing, or physically fighting back, reported minimal injury even when the attacker had a weapon.

The questionnaire produced another surprising conclusion: Most of the women who successfully turned back the rapists were the oldest daughters of their families who had grown up with major household responsibilities. Most described themselves as having to fight their own battles. [Bart, O'Brien]

You may be able to prevent it—if you're willing to endure a beating. A National Institute of Justice study shows that women who resist "are more likely to be battered in a non-sexual way, but less likely to be raped." [Block, Skogan]

You are threatened by a robber or rapist:

There's a good chance that the weapon he uses to subdue you exists only in your imagination. In 40 percent of robberies and more than 50 percent of sexual assaults and rapes, the attacker has no weapon. [Block, Skogan]

You are a woman who has been beaten by your husband or your lover:

That makes you a victim of the most common form of violence experienced by women. Each year, 1.8 million American women are beaten by their male partners, according to Richard J. Gelles, a sociologist and domestic violence specialist who is dean of the College of Arts and Sciences of the University of Rhode Island.

The desire may have crossed your mind to consult your doctor about the beatings and their consequences, but your doctor has probably failed to question you about the signs of your injuries, and you were probably too embarrassed or too fearful to open the subject. You may not know it, but part of the reason the doctor didn't probe is that no state requires a doctor to report cases of domestic violence to the police. "Even when they do," Dr. Gelles told 3,500 members of the American College of Obstetricians and Gynecologists at their thirty-third annual meeting, "doctors often ask questions that are too general, because they're afraid of the patient's response. Although wife-beating occurs in every socioeconomic class, the most likely victims are young pregnant women who can't or won't fight back."

Also at high risk are women who have two or more children and few friends or relatives, women unhappy with their standard of living, women whose husbands work part-time, and women who were victims or witnesses of violence in their own families when they were children, according to studies collected by Dr. Gelles. [Gelles]

You are a Quaker child:

Contrary as this may be to the Quaker image of pacifism, nonviolence, and the "peaceable kingdom," your father is more likely to commit acts of violence against you, and your brothers and sisters are more likely to be severely violent with one another than their counterparts would be in the average American family.

These surprising conclusions came from a survey of 288 Quakers (130 male, 158 female), members of seventeen congregations in Michigan, Ohio, Pennsylvania, and West Virginia, comprising a regional grouping called the Lake Erie Yearly Meeting. The two researchers who conducted this study with the approval of the Friends Organization warn that the results should be interpreted cautiously. For one thing, 78 percent of the respondents were not raised in Friends families, and may have brought with them the patterns they learned in the general population. For another, it is possible that the Quaker commitment to truthfulness may have brought forth more honest answers than the comparison survey of the national population. [Brutz, Ingoldsby]

You have witnessed a violent crime:

The chances that you can describe or identify the perpetrator correctly are only one in four. If there's more than one perpetrator, the chances are even lower. When you are "positive" of your identification of the perpetrator, the probability that you are correct is no higher than that of a witness who isn't sure. Trial lawyers and several high-court rulings, however, continue to uphold the myth that if you witness a dramatic crime, your awareness is sharpened and your testimony is reliable. [Clifford, Hollin]

The more details of the crime scene you accurately recall, the *less* likely you are to recognize the face of the correct suspect in a police lineup. Yet juries consistently accept accuracy of on-scene physical detail by a witness as evidence that his/her identification of a perpetrator "must be right." [Wells, Leippe]

If a lawyer questions you in advance and rehearses you for your court appearance, your testimony will not be more accurate than that of others who haven't been briefed. You'll just be more sure of your answers, particularly if your answers are wrong. [Wells, Ferguson, Lindsay]

You are a member of a jury in a rape trial:

Even though you want to judge the facts fairly, you're likely to be swayed to a marked degree by personal attractiveness in deciding whose word to believe among conflicting accusers and accused. For example, you're more likely to vote to convict an unattractive man than an attractive one, based on the same facts. In trials of men accused of rape, jurors convicted 57 percent of defendants rated attractive. Among men rated unattractive, juries convicted 82 percent. Furthermore, you're likely to vote to give a convicted man a longer sentence when the female victim is attractive than when she is not. [Jacobson]

But if you are a woman member of the jury, you are likely to want to mete out a longer jail sentence for the same rape than a man would. [Feldman-Summers, Lindner]

If the testimony, appearance, and behavior of the rape victim lead you and your fellow jurors to question her respectability, you become more likely to hold her responsible for the rape and you are less likely to feel that the crime had a serious effect on her. [Feldman-Summers, Lindner]

If the victim of the alleged rape is emotionally expressive, you and your fellow jurors are more likely to believe her testimony than if she is emotionally controlled. Furthermore, you and the rest of the jury are likely to feel that the emotionally controlled victim had less aversion for the rape, and you are apt to like her less. [Calhoun, Cann, Selby, Magee]

If the victim, on the witness stand, refuses to discuss her sexual experience, you and your fellow jurors are likely to perceive her as sexually active. If the judge prohibits testimony about her previous sexual activity, you are likely to hold her less responsible for the rape than if she admits sexual activity or gives no information. [Cann, Calhoun, Selby]

If you are a female juror, you are less likely than a male juror to believe the testimony of an accused man, and are more likely to vote for his conviction. But, in apparent contradiction of the Feldman-Summers and Lindner findings above, you are also likely to vote for a shorter sentence than male members of the jury. [Thornton]

If you are a male juror, and if the testimony brings out that there was a close personal relationship between a rape accuser and the alleged rapist, you become more likely to believe that the woman was responsible for the incident. If you are a woman juror, however, and you hear that testimony, you become less likely to believe she was responsible.

If the victim of the alleged rape comes off to the jury as sexy, and if you are a male juror, you tend to lose belief in the woman's credibility and you become more inclined to believe she was responsible for the rape. If you are a woman juror, however, your reactions are just the opposite. [Wyer, Bodenhausen, Gorman]

YOUR TENDENCY TO CRIME, VIOLENCE, AND AGGRESSION

Starting about the time of the rise of social work as a profession early in the twentieth century, certain explanations of the causes of crime were widely accepted as correct: People who robbed and raped and murdered did so because they grew up in poverty, or in broken homes, or had lost their jobs, or were angry as victims of discrimination. More recently, some crime has been explained by psychological illnesses and distortions. Why people do bad things is a perennial subject of research, and the more that good questions are asked and researched, the more puzzling becomes the search for explanations.

Especially puzzling have been the causes of a sharp rise in street crime, particularly in cities—American cities first, then cities worldwide—during the mid-1960s. Before then, an evening stroll in Central Park was a treat, a relatively safe one. Police traveled the subways only to get to and from work. In quiet city neighborhoods and in small towns, people left their doors unlocked.

Then came the Baby Boom. And the Vietnam war. And student unrest. And youngsters who instructed each other, "Never trust anyone over thirty."

And with it all came crime in the streets.

Did the coming of one have anything to do with the coming of the others? Correlation is not the same as cause, although they are often confused.

In 1985, the National Institute of Justice, the Justice Department's principal research agency, put out a report on crime, and its director, James K. Stewart, said, "The researchers were amazed at the findings." What amazed them in particular was the finding that more than 50 percent of all the men and women arrested in New York City and Washington, D.C., for serious crimes were found to be using one or more illegal drugs. For the institute's study, fourteen thousand defendants were given urinalysis tests, and over 25 percent were found to have used more than one drug close to the time of the arrest. In New York, the most popular drug among those arrested was cocaine; in Washington, phencyclidine, or PCP. Marijuana and alcohol were not checked in the study. Counting the acknowledged occasional users who had not used drugs recently, nearly two thirds of people arrested in Washington were users—twice the number that experts had predicted before the study.

> *America has a bizarre interest in violence. This heritage*
> *of violence has been passed down lovingly to the*
> *present generation. And if a man has tried to solve*
> *most of his problems since age six by punching someone,*
> *he is not likely at age twenty-five to begin negotiating*
> *for acceptance or solutions.*
>
> ROBERT T. ARMSTRONG,
> A FORTY-SIX-YEAR-OLD SERVING A SEVEN-YEAR SENTENCE
> IN TENNESSEE FOR CHECK FORGERY

LOOK YOURSELF UP

You were an aggressive child who pushed and shoved other kids around and took their belongings; in short, a bully:

If you are a man, you've got about a 25 percent chance of having a criminal record by the time you reach thirty. Your crimes may range from trespassing to assault with a weapon. You also tend to abuse your wife, and you are something of a menace on the road, honking your horn and swerving around other cars in traffic, and driving while drunk.

If you are a woman, you probably punish your children severely, and there's a good chance you've got a lower-paying job than a nonaggressive woman.

Your aggressiveness did not (or does not) get you what you want. It just made you a social outcast, interfered with your learning, and made your teachers loathe you as a troublemaker.

Researchers traced the development of 875 third-graders through adulthood in Columbia County, New York. They interviewed more than half the subjects at ages nineteen and thirty, and also talked to their spouses and children. One of the sobering things the researchers discovered was that aggressive behavior patterns are set before age eight. [Eron, Huesmann]

You tended (and perhaps still tend) to interpret, say, an innocent bumping as an intentional attack, and react with hostility. "Bullies see threats where none exists," says Kenneth Dodge, a Vanderbilt University psychologist. "They take these imagined threats as provocations to strike back. . . . Bullies see the world with a paranoid's eye. They feel justified in retaliating for what are actually imaginary harms." This patterned misinterpretation becomes a fixture of personality by around age seven, according to Dodge's research. [Dodge]

You are a murderer, waiting on death row:

There's a high probability (more than 80 percent) that sometime since your childhood you suffered a severe head injury. It may have come at the hands of your parents or other relatives, because there's almost as high a probability (about 66 percent) that they beat you as a child. If you weren't beaten, there is a good chance you witnessed extreme violence in your family. You are almost 100 percent certain to have frequent memory lapses and sudden episodes of déjà vu. The chances are almost 50 percent that you experience blackouts and losses of consciousness and that your EEG is abnormal. Despite your high ability to keep up a normal appearance, you are almost 100 percent likely to burst out in brief psychotic behaviors, ranging from suicide threats to illogical thinking, bizarre ideas, visual and auditory hallucinations, and extreme mood swings. [Lewis]

You are more likely to have killed your victim on a weekend or holiday than any other day. You probably had been drinking shortly before you did it, but you are probably not an alcoholic. The chances are also fairly high that your victim also had been drinking, and the two of you may have been drinking together. [Lunde]

Your willingness to murder may have been influenced, at least in part, by your cultural environment. This is borne out by a finding that the highest murder rates in the United States are in the South, and the lowest in the Northeast. The murder rate among blacks is eight and a half times higher than among whites. Yet those who hastily attribute that difference in rate purely to race or income level are overlooking the influence of the culture where the killer was reared, which appears to be most important of all. Regardless of where they were living at the time of the crime, blacks raised in the North had the lowest murder rates and blacks raised in the South had the highest. [Lunde]

If you killed in Boston, where this study was done among 243 accused murderers, ages fourteen to sixty-seven, the chances are nine out of ten that you are a male, and they are high that your victim was an acquaintance, friend, or relative. Your most likely reason for killing was monetary gain. [Rizzo]

You are a member of the Gebusi, a small tribe living in a New Guinea rain forest:

By Western expectations, your lifestyle offers all the elements of tranquility and harmony. Much of your daily activity revolves around *kog-wa-yay*, "good company," good talk, and zesty humor. Your society of about 450 has no political structure, therefore no authority. The strong among you do not jockey for power. Decisions about the community are made by consensus in "longhouse" meetings. Abundantly grown bananas and the occasionally hunted wild pigs are routinely shared by all. Warfare, violence, and anger are not acceptable behavior, by tradition.

Yet your fellow Gebusi murder one another at one of the highest rates ever recorded—forty times greater than the 1980 homicide rate of the United States. Between 1940 and 1982, nearly one third of adult deaths were by murder. Four out of five of them were killings of someone branded as a sorcerer, or performer of evil magic, for having allegedly caused the death of another Gebusi through disease. Infections and parasites are ever-present among the Gebusi, and to give one's disease to another is considered an act of sorcery. The killings of accused sorcerers are carried out by men only, "including some who were among the least assertive and aggressive even by Gebusi standards," says the researcher. "The character of homicide appears to change in simple societies that have no pecking order or dominance hierarchy among adult men," says Bruce M. Knauft of Emory University, who documented the Gebusi homicide rate during almost two years of field work. "Especially in these societies, there may be a pattern of social life that is generally peaceful and tranquil but is punctuated by aggression which, when it does occur, is unrestrained and frequently homicidal." [Knauft]

You have committed rape:

You are clearly more able, by actual measure, to perceive signals of positive reactions from women, as you are virtually blind to signals when a woman is not interested. For this study, psychologist David Lipton showed a series of videotapes to eleven convicted rapists, and, for comparison, to eleven other violent offenders and eleven nonviolent criminals. The tapes showed a man and woman having a conversation, either on a first date or in a more intimate scene. One person in the taped scene always expresses positive feelings, while the other displays one of five feelings: very positive, extremely negative, or somewhere in between. The inmates were asked to describe the feelings they saw.

All the criminals proved relatively insensitive to signals of feeling shown by either men or women. But the rapists had the most trouble in reacting to conversations that simulated a first date. Feelings expressed during first-date moments are often negative, Lipton points out, and the convicted rapists were practically blind to the negative cues, especially by women. "It's as if rapists wear a filter," says Lipton. "They always seem to pick up on the positive and ignore the negative." Lipton concludes that if a woman overtly insulted a rapist, he would still have a difficult time understanding that she was trying to say "no." The study, Lipton says, is the first to show that rapists are marked by specific deficits in social skills. [Lipton]

The chances are better than even (59 percent) that as a young boy you were sexually molested by an older woman. Moreover, according to this study of eighty-three men in a medium-security penitentiary, all convicted of raping women at least seventeen years of age, there's a one-in-seven chance that you were separately molested by two or more women. For more than three quarters of the victimized boys, the molesting woman did so more than once. The acts took place when the boys were between the ages of four and sixteen.

Of the forty-nine victims, most were led to intercourse (sixty instances, of which thirty-four involved both cunnilingus and fellatio). Five of their women molesters induced the boys to perform only cunnilingus, four of them masturbated the boy, two performed fellatio and accepted cunnilingus, one performed fellatio, and one led the boy to mutual masturbation. Almost half of the molesters (twenty-three) were older neighbors, twenty-two were friends of the family, seven were baby sitters, five were aunts, four were teachers of the boys, four were strangers, two were the boys' mothers, two were their grandmothers, and one each was a sister, a foster mother, a co-worker, and a probation officer. (Judging by the researchers' imprecisely described arithmetic, apparently some molesters fitted into more than one of those categories.)

"The heterosexual molestation findings are surprising," say the researchers, "not only because incidence is high but because of the nature of the acts and the relationships between child and older female." A previous major study by A. N. Groth, author of *Men Who Rape: The Psychology of the Offender*, reported a far lower incidence of molestation of male children who later grew up to be rapists. [Petrovich, Templer]

You are a college student who goes out on dates:

The chances are better than 50 percent that you have committed at least one physically violent act against a person you are dating. That is so whether you are a man or a woman. If you are a man, you are slightly more likely than a woman to report being a *victim* of such an act, if this survey of 504 college students is representative.

If you are like the subjects who either committed the acts or were victims of them, the chances are better than 50 percent that you have both committed violence against your date and received it. If you are the woman abuser, when you become violent, you are most likely to slap, kick, hit, bite, or throw something. If you are the man abuser, you are primarily likely to push or shove, although you may throw something, slap your partner, or try to hit her with something.

Violence is not a usual part of your life, because the chances are relatively low that you have experienced it except with your date—and you and your date did not first engage in violence until your relationship had grown beyond the casual dating stage, perhaps after you began living together. You are likely to feel (or, at least, to report) that the violence was mild and isolated, and did not have an important impact on the relationship.

If you are the abusing male, you tend to be young, from a family of low income, traditional in your attitudes toward women, and abused as a child. If you are the woman abuser, you probably score low in a measure called the Social Desirability Scale, which measures your tendency to describe yourself in favorable or socially desirable ways, even when such statements may not be true; also, you were probably abused as a child. [Sigelman, Berry, Wiles]

You have been convicted as a sex offender:

You can probably be "cured" if a judge sentences you to seeing a psychiatrist. But you'll do just as well seeing a probation officer. A five-year study shows that under both forms of "treatment," 70 percent of ex-offenders avoided re-arrest for up to three years. You're most likely to succeed if you're sent by the judge into group therapy *and* if you're among the strenuous complainers about having to go to "group." [Peters]

You are a schizophrenic in a mental institution and you have a choice of watching either Rambo *or* Love Story:

If you're looking for long-term peace of mind, opt for *Rambo*. Contrary to research linking violent movies with aggressive behavior, the researchers found that schizophrenics become more aggressive after viewing nonviolent movies (comedies, adventures, love stories) than violent ones with scenes of cruelty, fighting, and murder. In 1978, the researchers showed forty-three violent and thirty-eight nonviolent films to about three hundred patients in the Veterans Administration Medical Center. Within twenty-four hours after seeing a violent movie, patients caused twenty-six disturbances, including fighting, breaking windows, and attempting suicide. Within the same period after a nonviolent movie, patients caused fifty-seven disturbances. The researchers propose that people in institutions are more upset by representations of ordinary life than they are by those of chaos. [Johnston, Lundy]

You would like to avoid getting a criminal record:

Stay in the house when the temperature starts to rise. The hotter it gets, the more likely you are to commit aggressive crimes (rape and murder)—as opposed to nonaggressive crimes (robbery and arson). The researchers have also linked aggressive crimes with the day of the week. Seems you're more likely to commit such crimes on Sunday and Monday than any other day. [Anderson]

You are a prison inmate:

Nobody is likely to be surprised if you and forty-nine other inmates, chosen at random, take an attitude test and measure high in hostility, alienation, impulsiveness, and antisocial drives. But there was considerable surprise when Allan Berman, a University of Rhode Island psychologist, reported to a convention of the Eastern Psychological Association that he gave the same tests to one hundred men about to be hired as correction officers. The soon-to-be jailers came out as high as the jailed—except for a measurement called the "hysteria scale." On that, the guards came out *higher.* Among officer appointees tested, the younger they were, the more intense their measurable hostility. And what kind of work did these younger men plan to do? Mostly, they chose work with juveniles. [*Behavior Today*]

You are a felon who has been released on probation instead of being sent to prison:

You'll probably be arrested again.

In a forty-month study commissioned by the National Institute of Justice, researchers looked at 1,672 felony cases in California. They found that 65 percent of released felons were arrested again; 51 percent were convicted of new crimes; and 34 percent ended up in prisons. Repeat offenders tended to commit burglary, robbery, and theft, and about one third of those convicted were put on probation yet again. [Petersilia]

You are an athlete playing in a game against another team:

If the crowd of spectators is densely packed, you'll perform worse than you would if the crowd were more dispersed.

If your team has already played the other team earlier in the season, you'll play more aggressively this time.

If you are playing against a team within your own division, you'll be more aggressive than you would if you were playing against a team from another division.

If you are playing an important game, better hope it's on the other guy's turf; visiting teams in the study performed better during important games than home teams. And if you are on the visiting team, to further boost your chances of winning, pray for a puny crowd; the smaller the crowd, the more aggressively and better you play. [Russell]

You are a male who sometimes feels a need for a good Donnybrook:

That may be *just* what you need to make you feel better. In the first two years that followed its 1970 outbreak of political rioting, Northern Ireland's rate of depressive disorders among men markedly diminished. Also, its rate of suicide among males dropped by 50 percent. The researcher's speculative conclusion: Rioting may be good for a man's mental health. [Lyon]

Sometimes you get an urge to break a window:

You'll enjoy it more if the window doesn't break on the first try. The highest pleasure comes with success on the third or fourth try, particularly if you can't predict when the window will shatter. (The authors of this study of "aesthetic enjoyment" at destroying things express a worry that when we create "vandal-proof" surfaces in public places we may encourage destruction by increasing the vandals' pleasure at succeeding.) [Allen, Greenberger]

CHEATING AND COMMITTING PETTY CRIME

LOOK YOURSELF UP

You occasionally cheat and sometimes feel guilty about it:

You're not the only one. But are you essentially honest or basically a rationalizing crook?

The magazine *Psychology Today* invited its readers to fill out a long confessional questionnaire on lying, cheating, and rule-stretching—and, as though itching to unburden themselves, 24,100 readers responded. Here are some results of that mass self-purging:

- More respondents admitted cheating on their spouses (45 percent) than on their tax returns (38 percent) or expense accounts (28 percent). Of the marriage cheaters, 84 percent felt guilty. But only 59 percent felt guilty about their tax shortcuts. Also a little nervous: Although only 38 percent owned up to cheating on taxes, 54 percent said that if their tax returns were audited, they would expect to owe the government money. (Only 10 percent thought they would owe $500 or more.)

- One out of three respondents admitted having deceived a best friend about something important in the past year. The feeling of guilt was widespread: 96 percent. But 73 percent of the lapsers said they had done so only once or twice.
- About four out of ten respondents had driven while drunk or high on drugs.
- Almost four in ten (38 percent) had purposely failed to declare an item to a customs agent.
- Almost half said that if their car scratched another in a parking lot, they would drive away without leaving a note. Eighty-nine percent, however, said that doing so would be immoral.
- If a store clerk gave too much change, 26 percent would pocket the excess.
- Sixty-eight percent took home office supplies or other materials in the past year.
- More than one respondent in three (37 percent) made personal long-distance calls at work during the past year.
- Almost half (47 percent) took sick days from work during the past year, although not particularly ill.
- Sixty-seven percent said they cheated on school examinations or assignments when they thought they could get away with it.
- Those who admitted cutting into line or failing to wait for their turn in a public place came to a mere 19 percent.
- An optional question asked readers to name their most troubling moral dilemma. About one third of the answerers, by far the most numerous, named something sex-related, usually an extramarital affair.
- Almost all—93 percent—came clean about speeding: that at some time they had done it. But less than half that number—43 percent—admitted breaking the speed limits "almost every day."
- People rating themselves as religious were least likely to report deceiving friends, cheating in marriage, chiseling on expense accounts, or even ignoring no-parking signs.

Some respondents proved adept at self-justification. One of them, the head of a state agency, admitted using the office phone for personal long-distance calls, making personal Xeroxes, "and I usually clip a few extra dollars out of most travel vouchers. On the other hand I work a phenomenal number of hours per week. I often spend my own money for office functions. . . . I would be dazzled if anyone could find a better bargain in an employee. Yet I would probably emerge as a mild cheat on your scale." [Hassett]

But if your occasional cheating has to do with federal income taxes, you probably measure it on a different "guilt yardstick." That is shown in a variety of surveys collected in a book, *Minds, Markets, and Money,* by Shlomo Maital, a leading Israeli economist who spent three years at Princeton studying American taxpayers, taxes, and productivity:

• The IRS itself surveyed a sample of Americans on the comparative guilt they would feel about various kinds of tax evasion. Almost two in three (62 percent) said they wouldn't worry much about failing to report a bartered service as earnings. Another 53 percent said they would cover up gambling earnings with a more or less free conscience; 49 percent padded business travel expenses. Perhaps the most rubbery consciences among them are of the 42 percent who say they would remain unbothered by simply understating regular income.

• Two political scientists at East Carolina University, Young-Dahl Song and Tinsley Yarbrough, found that their survey respondents ranked tax evasion just a hairline more reproachable than stealing a bicycle.

• Economist Michael W. Spicer and psychologist Sven B. Lundstedt determined in a study that "the more tax evaders a taxpayer knows, the more likely he is to evade taxes himself."

• That's bad news, because a recent Gallup–U.S. Chamber of Commerce poll recorded two thirds of its respondents as believing that tax evasion ("people not paying the taxes the law says they are supposed to pay") is widespread. Even more respondents, five in six, thought that many are guilty of tax *avoidance* ("finding *legal* ways to take advantage of the tax laws to pay less than they fairly should").

• A Gallup poll has shown that a majority of Americans feel that:
   —they pay more than their fair share of taxes;
   —new services provided by government in the past decade weren't worth the additional money spent on them;
   —20 percent or more of government spending is wasted;
   —government spending causes inflation. [Maital]

You sometimes lie, but not to people who you think would catch you:

Your judgments of them are probably wrong. This experiment compared law enforcement officers against college students in a lie-detecting contest. The officers and students listened to tapes of sixteen people, each of whom had been recorded telling two lies and two truths. The professionals scored no better than the untrained college students in picking out the liars or their lies. The only difference between the groups was their degree of confidence. As the test progressed, the most experienced cops rated themselves as progressively more sure of their answers. The truth was that their accuracy did not improve. [DePaulo, Pfeifer]

You are an adult shoplifter:

Chances are you're a high school graduate with a middle-level income, and, when you're caught, you probably have enough money in cash, checks, and credit cards with you to pay for the items you've lifted.

According to the Greater Washington, D.C., Board of Trade, 45 percent of accused Washington shoplifters had middle-level incomes; 28 percent had high-level incomes; and 27 percent had low-level incomes. As for educational level, 40 percent of the thieves were high school graduates; 12 percent were high school dropouts; 27 percent had some college background; and 21 percent were college graduates. [Curtis]

If you are a shoplifter in Texas, according to this "local profile," you are probably female, Mexican-American, anxious, depressed, and self-doubting. But if you are a male, you tend to act more impulsively than a woman in your shoplifting style. She considers her merchandise more carefully, as a good shopper does. [Ray, Solomon, Doncaster, Mellina]

You are a woman:

Perhaps you've been made uneasy by publicity indicating that crimes committed by women are, more and more, resembling those committed by men, and that the reason for the shift can be traced to the women's movement that emerged in the mid-1960s.

Not so, says a Penn State sociologist. After examining annual data collected by the FBI since 1965, Darrell J. Steffensmeier finds that the only important change in women's criminality can be observed in an increase in arrests in two categories: shoplifting and fraud, crimes women have long been committing. In fact, if larceny of those types were downgraded from its present status as a serious crime to a nonserious one, attention-getting claims of dramatic changes in crime by women, Steffensmeier points out, "are easily invalidated." Therefore, he says, the emergence of the "new female criminal" because of the women's movement is pure myth. [Steffensmeier]

CHAPTER
5 _____

Your
Relationships

YOUR DATING

Dating is more than a search for the "right" other. It is also a search for oneself; more precisely, for the worth of oneself.

That was observed early on—in 1937—by a sociologist named Willard Waller in a still-famous study of students at Penn State University, called "The Rating and Dating Complex." Dating, he concluded, determines one's prestige on campus. To rate high, a man needed to belong to one of the better fraternities, have access to a car, have spending money, be prominent in student activities, be well-dressed, have smooth manners, a "good line," and dance well. A woman had to have good clothes, a "smooth" line, dancing skill, and be known as a popular date. (This is another example of college professors studying easily available college students, then projecting their findings across the whole population. In the field of dating, perhaps that shortcut is more justifiable than in other activities.)

A few years later, Henry A. Bowman postulated that a person's prestige ranking arises from a subtle combination of the frequency of dating and the ratings of the persons he or she dates. In 1945, Ernest W. Burgess and Harvey J. Locke wrote about dating as a competitive *game*. One wins the game by dating more high-ranking persons of the opposite sex than the other players. By their view, playing the game is an end in itself. It need not lead to a continuing relationship or marriage to be successful. A dater's rating, Burgess and Locke said, is computed from a combination of physical attractiveness, personality characteristics, participation in university activities, and membership in prestigious organizations.

Dating is an educational process, added Robert F. Winch in 1968. It teaches "proper deportment" and "social graces." It also teaches what kind of partner provides each person with the most gratifying relationship. Usually, one such relationship will deepen and lead a person through the steps of courtship toward marriage.

LOOK YOURSELF UP

You are looking for someone to date:

Whether you are a man or a woman, whether you belong to an organization of divorced people or to an organization of never-married people or to no singles organization at all, the older you are, the more you are likely to feel relatively happy, productive, generally satisfied with your job, your family life, and with yourself—just about everything except your social life. What you feel you lack, and are searching for, are ways to meet members of the other sex and to develop relationships with them. These are the general findings of a survey of 138 single adults in Youngstown, Ohio, a medium-sized city.

If you are a woman, whether divorced or never married, you are highly likely to be having financial difficulties, especially if you have children. You are most likely to be employed in traditionally female-dominated work where pay scales are low.

If you are a man, you are more likely than the single woman to feel held back by your inability to communicate about your emotions. You are apt not to know of social support systems available to you that compare with those known to women.

Whether you are a man or a woman, if you have never been married you probably feel more stresses about relating to others than divorced people do, chiefly because you are less experienced socially. (The author of the study urges that organizations of the never-married initiate the kinds of small discussion groups that are common in organizations of the divorced, in which subjects like dating and sex are raised and can be aired—if for no other reason than to permit people to get used to talking about them.) A substantial number of the never-marrieds in the survey reported observing that their divorced friends were significantly more perceptive than most never-marrieds about the behavior of themselves and others. Never-marrieds, these never-marrieds generalized, "are afraid to expose their true feelings."

Noting that fully one third of the U.S. adult population is unmarried, a proportion that would seem to demand a greater amount of serious research than it has received, the author urges that there is "a great need for places where men and women can meet each other. These places should be nonthreatening and humane and should provide a sufficiently large number of contacts so that stagnation does not occur. The places, events, or institutions also must be nonexploitative. The potential for exploitation is great when people are lonely and vulnerable." [Danziger]

Whether you admit it to yourself or not, you are looking for someone just about as attractive as you are. That is a consistent finding in a number of studies of college students.

But what if you are *not* a student? What if you are considerably beyond college age? What then are you more likely to look for? Personality? Kindness? Education level? Occupation? Age?

Answer: None of those. You too are looking for someone just about as attractive as you are. Furthermore, that "attractiveness match" is also the best predictor of whether a relationship will progress. This study was conducted among sixty-seven subject couples (mean age, thirty-five) who were members of a dating service. They were asked what steps they had taken toward forming a dating relationship. Sample reactions ranged from refusal to give one's surname or phone number (the most negative reaction) to agreement to a second date (most positive). The *only significant correla-*

tion with positive reactions was matched attractiveness, as judged by an independent panel. [Folkes]

If you *are* a college student, you may set out to have a good time at a college "mixer" dance. You probably won't have a good time.

A well-known courtship researcher, Pepper Schwartz, and a colleague, Janet Lever, conducted deep interviews with ninety-six male and female undergrads who attended five "mixer" dances at Yale. The students generally rated those affairs as far from "enjoyable opportunities for meeting students of the opposite sex." They often saw them as "conflict-ridden situations that produce tension and anxiety." The only people who enjoy these affairs, said one typical respondent, are really pretty women and exceptional dancers. But for most others, the continuous evaluation and frequent rejection make a good time all but impossible, undermine one's self image, and lead to self-protective behavior patterns and mental games that probably carry over into later intimate relationships. [Schwartz, Lever]

If you are a student, whether male or female, according to this 1986 survey of two hundred college students, you strongly prefer to date a mate with low to moderate sexual experience. If your potential date has gone only as far as moderate petting, you probably prefer him or her over someone with either more experience—or still less. Regardless of your own sexual past, you are likely to hope that your marriage partner will be a virgin. What previous experience of your future mate do you dread even more than the loss of his or her virginity? Having been in love with someone else. In fact, even if your future mate has had many partners in sex-just-for-the-sake-of-sex, that is apt to bother you significantly less than knowing she or he has previously been intimately in love. Being your mate's first love, if this survey describes you, is clearly more important to you than being your mate's first sexual partner. [Jacoby, Williams]

If you are a teenage male, your attractiveness as a date increases if you watch horror movies without showing signs of distress.

If you are a teenage female, the more distressed you appear to be, the more attractive the boys will find you—and the more they will enjoy the film. [Zillman]

*You began dating someone three months or less after your
first meeting:*

That person is likely to be just about as attractive as you are. [Fein-
gold]

*You began dating someone eight months or more after your
first meeting:*

That person is likely to be either noticeably less attractive than you
are, or noticeably more. [Feingold]

You have been dating someone for an extended period:

You probably rate the attractiveness of your partner just about the
same as her/his self-rating, and your partner's rating of you will agree
with your self-rating. Researchers call this the "matching" effect.
Also, as the relationship gets older, you probably feel more attractive
than you did when it began.

There is one notable kind of departure from this rule of the
"matching effect." If you are an attractive woman, you are more
likely than a man to make an exception. Some attractive women will
continue to date men who do not match them in attractiveness, and
the relationship seems to be unaffected by the disparity. But attractive men almost never continue long in dating women who are less
attractive than the men regard themselves. [Bailey, Kelly]

If you are a woman and you consider your dating partner a "steady
boyfriend," compared to a woman with no steady boyfriend you are
likely to measure as having higher self-esteem, you are more sure of
marrying, you expect to marry sooner, you evaluate marriage higher,
and you are less willing to remain single.

In contrast, the woman with no steady boyfriend is more likely to
seek intimacy outside of courtship, and to derive her self-esteem
from activities other than personal relationships. [Long]

You are a man or woman whose parents have been divorced:

According to this survey of a large number (365) of college students
whose parents divorced, you are more likely than most others to date

frequently and court actively. That is true even if your parents' divorce was acrimonious, even if your relations with them have since deteriorated, and if your custodial parent has remained single. Your age at the time of their divorce appears to have no bearing on the quantity or quality of your dating activity, nor does it matter whether you are male or female. [Booth, Brinkerhoff, White]

You are a man who dates frequently:

You probably rate your own attractiveness very close to the rating others would give you. If you don't date often, you are likely to rate your own attractiveness *higher* than others are likely to rate you. [Bailey, Kelly]

You are a woman who dates frequently:

You have a set of personality characteristics that are opposite to the personality traits of an infrequent dater—and those traits can be spotted almost immediately by almost anyone.

The researchers identified twelve "over-chosen" (frequently dating) women students and thirteen who were "under-chosen," and all were videotaped interacting with a research confederate. The videotapes were shown to judges, who also were given a list of 555 personality traits and were asked to select those traits that appeared to apply to each woman. They were also to rate how much they liked each woman.

The frequent daters came out significantly more "liked." They also were more likely to be described by traits that indicated sociability, positive emotionality, and extraversion. The infrequent daters were more often assigned traits indicating unhappiness, moodiness, depression, negative emotionality, and introversion. [Hewitt, Goldman]

You are a woman drinking at a bar:

Just as a country-and-western hit song suggested in its title—"Don't the Girls Get Prettier at Closing Time"—it seems you really do. Surveyed at hour-and-a-half intervals during the same evening in a country-and-western bar, male patrons at thirty minutes before closing time rated women as significantly more attractive than they had three hours earlier—presumably, the influence of alcohol, or simply of desperation, on the fantasies of the observer. [Nida, Koon]

. . .

But do you have to "go cowgirl" to get better looking at closing time? These researchers decided to check out the preceding finding in another survey, this time at a student bar near a college. This time, not only men, but women too, rated members of the opposite sex better-looking at closing time than they had earlier in the evening. [Pennebaker, Dyer, Caulkins, Litowitz, Ackerman, Anderson, McGraw]

You are a man drinking at a bar:

If you want to open a conversation with an unaccompanied woman, one of the most effective lines for picking her up is, "I feel a little embarrassed but I'd like to meet you." You might even try the harmless, "What do you think of the band?" At the beach, a strong opener is the innocuous, "The water is beautiful today, isn't it?" At the supermarket, "Can you help me decide here? I'm a terrible shopper."

The worst way to go is either cute or smartypants, like, "Is that really your hair?" Or "I bet I can outdrink you." Or "Your place or mine?" Nor will you get far with "You remind me of a woman I used to date." A freezer at the beach: "Let me see your strap marks." At the supermarket: "Do you really eat that junk?"

The author of this study, a psychologist who specializes in first impressions, asked several hundred students at colleges in California and Massachusetts to suggest all the opening lines that male approachers might use. He listed those on a questionnaire, then asked six hundred students to rank them from "excellent" to "terrible." [Kleinke]

So you think, as you survey the unaccompanied women at the bar, that you're choosing among them before you make your move. Ha!

Monica Moore, a psychologist at the University of Missouri–St. Louis, was intrigued by studies showing that in the courtship of elephant seals, fish, rats, mice, monkeys, gorillas, and birds, the initial moves—and, apparently, the selections—are made by females. Moore wondered if the same finding would hold true for humans. She and her co-workers invested one hundred hours at a singles bar watching two hundred women judged to be eighteen to thirty-five years old, all unaccompanied by men, and each in or near a crowd of at least twenty-five people. They turned on videotapes as they followed the actions of each woman for half an hour. Playing back the tapes, they clocked nonverbal acts such as "a movement of body part(s) or whole body that resulted in male attention . . . within 15 seconds of the behavior." The responses of male attention generally were approaching the woman, talking to her, leaning toward her or moving closer, asking her to dance, or touching her. The actions by the women that apparently invited those responses numbered fifty-two, the researchers discovered. They ranged from a smile to skirt hiking, primping, pouting, and knee touching. The most frequent were the smile, a glance that swept the room, the "solitary dance" (keeping time with the music by a subtle jounce or by finger-tapping), a leaning (toward a man while seated, sometimes leading to a brush of the breast), a fixed gaze of at least three seconds, and a head toss. Moore compared the incidence of these singles-bar gestures against their incidence where one might less expect them—in a university snack bar, the library, and a women's center meeting. Not surprisingly, in those places, the gestures were rare—a total count of nineteen flirtatious acts per hour in the snack bar, ten in the library, and five at the women's center meeting, compared to seventy per hour in the singles bar.

And the big conclusion? "Those women who signaled often," Moore found, "were also those who were most often approached by men." [Moore]

You are a woman who goes to the beach hoping to be picked up:

You're choosing an unproductive place. Women polled on Chicago beaches made an average of thirty-five visits a year and were approached an average of once per visit. They dated just two of thirty-five men they encountered that way, and saw each man just twice. (Incidentally, the number of approaches reported by each woman did *not* correlate significantly with how attractive she was rated.) [Jason, Reichler, Rucker]

You are having a getting-to-know-you conversation with a person of the opposite sex:

If you are a man, you are likely to think of her as seductive and even promiscuous. You are more likely than she to feel sexual attraction and feel eager to date. (In fact, if you observe two strangers, a man and a woman, in conversation, you assume their exchanges have a higher sexual content than does a woman who is observing the same scene. You are likely to perceive more sexuality in everyone's behavior, including your own, than women do.)

If you are a woman, you are more likely than he is to regard the same exchanges as simply friendly. [Abbey]

You are an assertive woman:

You have surely heard—and probably believe—that your trait turns men off.

Does it? Both men and women of college age, who were tested for their own personality types and found to encompass a wide range, *favored* women whom they rated as either "assertive" or "moderately assertive." In fact, women who were rated as not assertive were seen unfavorably. [Pendleton]

You are a man on a first date with a new acquaintance:

You are considerably more likely to be anxious about the date than she is. Your anxiety does not center around sex and intimacy (that comes later) but, more likely, on not knowing what to do or say and having unrealistic expectations of what occurs on dates. (And, by the way, if you are anxious about dating, you're also likely to be anxious in your friendships with other men.) [Arkowitz]

You crave power over other people:

There is a psychological test to measure that, and your high score on it would indicate that you have a stable tendency to seek impact on the lives of others. You might seek that impact in a variety of ways: by a direct action of command or coercion, or less directly, through influence, persuasion, charm, or even by making them obligated by doing them favors. People with what these researchers call "Hope of Power" often become leaders of organizations and institutions, even of small groups; they are drawn to competitive athletics, and to causes in which they might persuade and manipulate others. It has also been found that Hope of Power men tend to seek women partners who are weaker than they are, and who seem to promise to avoid conflict and to follow the stronger male partner. Furthermore, these men high in Hope of Power tend to favor pornographic magazines and to have many sexual partners. They also have a high rate of separation and divorce.

In contrast, women who are high in Hope of Power are far less likely than their male counterparts to be dissatisfied in their relationships, and are less likely to separate or divorce. The authors suggest that "whereas men learn to seek power by means of short-term, serial conquests of women (the Don Juan syndrome), women are more inclined to seek lasting relationships"—taking "possession" of the men as tokens of their own power or prestige. "As a result, women high in power motivation may be relatively unlikely to report difficulties or to want to dissolve an intimate relationship." [Stewart, Rubin]

Among people who might date you, word has gone out that you are religious:

Then you're also presumed to be unusually intelligent, better adjusted, less selfish, more trustworthy, and more attractive as a date or friend—at least if your prospective daters are undergraduate students in East Tennessee, like the subjects of this study. But here's a curious wrinkle in the finding: If you're deemed a religious woman dater and you are also described as hard-to-get, then prospective male daters are likely to prejudge you as "personally maladjusted" and "arrogant." [Bailey, Garrou]

Word has gone out that you are too "available"—too eager to date:

Whether you are a man or woman, you're likely to be considered selfish, untrustworthy, and undesirable. [Bailey, Garrou]

YOU AND YOUR LOVER

"So far as love or affection is concerned," wrote Harry F. Harlow in *American Psychologist* in 1958, "psychologists have failed in their mission. The little we know about love does not transcend simple observation, and the little we write about it has been written better by poets and novelists."

"It is surprising to discover," concurred a Ph.D. candidate in his dissertation written twelve years later in 1970, "that social psychologists have devoted virtually no attention to love." The daring young doctoral candidate, Zick Rubin, decided to look at romantic love as an important and distinct way that human beings think, feel, and behave—distinct, for example, from *liking* someone. But think, feel, and behave *how?* How can romantic love be identified, and how can its intensity be measured? Indeed, young Rubin took on the question that has troubled teenagers as well as older romantics for centuries: *How can I know if I'm really in love?*

Rubin assembled—from literature, from psychologists, from lovers—a large pool of statements that might help describe a person's *liking* a particular other, and another large pool that might describe someone's romantically *loving* another. He then asked two successive panels of student and faculty judges to sort the items into categories of liking and loving. From them he drew up a list of seventy statements and put the list before 198 students. Each student was to indicate which items best described the student's feelings about his or her girlfriend or boyfriend (if there was one), and also which ones described feelings toward a "platonic friend" of the opposite sex. Finally, statistical tabulations of the answers led Rubin to a final thirteen questions in each category.

Clearly, the more delicate and risky of the two categories was the one on love. Rubin tested its validity in a surprising and simple way. He relied on a group of findings that the reader of this book will recall from the first section of Chapter 1, "Your Eyes and What They Express." Couples in love spend more time gazing into one another's eyes than couples who simply like each other or who have just become acquainted. He predicted that a high score on his love scale and a high gazing score would largely match. They did. Since 1970 the Rubin Love Scale has been widely accepted as a tool in research.

Here are a few sample items from the Rubin Liking Scale and the Rubin Love Scale, used by permission of the author. For the blanks in the sentences, substitute the name of the person for whom you want to measure your degree of "liking" or "loving."

LIKING SCALE
1. When I am with _____, we are almost always in the same mood.
2. I think that _____ is unusually well adjusted.
3. I would highly recommend _____ for a responsible job.

The remainder of the thirteen sentences ask you to tell how you feel about the subject's maturity, judgment, tendency to win the favorable reaction of others, similarity in personality and interests to your own, tendency to win respect of others, intelligence, and other aspects of general likeability.

LOVE SCALE

1. If _____ were feeling badly, my first duty would be to cheer him (her) up.
2. I feel that I can confide in _____ about virtually anything.
3. I find it easy to ignore _____'s faults.

The remainder of the thirteen statements ask you to tell whether the subject brings out your generosity, possessiveness, protectiveness, forgiveness, desire to gaze at him or her, desire to be trusted with confidences, and other aspects of your needing to be together.

If the taker of the test scores 9 or more out of the 13 in either group, that score measures a high state of "liking," or being in love, respectively.

To live is like to love—all reason is
against it, and all healthy instinct is for it.

SAMUEL BUTLER (1613–80)

He who cannot love must learn to flatter.

JOHANN WOLFGANG GOETHE (1749–1832)

Men always want to be a woman's first love,
women like to be a man's last romance.

OSCAR WILDE (1854–1900)

Love is merely a madness; and, I tell you,
deserves a dark house and a whip
as madmen do; and the reason why they
are not so punished and cured is that
the lunacy is so ordinary that
the whippers are in love too.

WILLIAM SHAKESPEARE (1564–1616)

LOOK YOURSELF UP

You are a romantic who easily falls into love:

You are probably also highly susceptible to being hypnotized and to having mystical experiences. What you seem to have, according to the researchers, is an "ability to suspend contact with objective reality." [Mathes]

If you are a man, you probably were freer than most people in talking with your mother, father, and your best friends, whether male or female, about intimate matters in your life. If you are a woman, having a romantic attitude toward love is not related to how much you disclose to whom. [Lester, Brazill, Ellis, Guerin]

You are in love with someone:

When you and your lovemate feel equally (and increasingly) involved with each other, your relationship is probably growing. When you feel that one of you is more involved than the other, watch out for deterioration. You can also be quite sure that when one of you moves for a breakup, the other will resist. Almost never do both people want to quit.

If you are the man of a heterosexual couple, you probably "fell" more readily and quickly than she did. Despite popular belief, you are more likely than a woman to rate "the desire to fall in love" as an important reason to enter a relationship. Also, you were probably more committed initially to the relationship than she was.

When things start going badly, you are less likely than the woman to suggest breaking up. If you initiate a breakup, the two of you are more likely to stay friends afterwards than if it was suggested by the woman. If your relationship breaks up, you will feel harder hit than the woman and find it harder to believe that you're no longer loved.

If you are the woman, you probably resisted "falling" or were less aware at first that it was happening than he was. After its initial period, you were probably more committed to the relationship than he was.

You have probably been more sensitive than he to problems in the relationship, and more likely to compare it against other relationships, real or potential.

You are more likely than the man to take the initiative in breaking up the relationship.

To find these answers, five thousand students from four Boston area colleges were invited at random to take part in a two-year longitudinal study of dating couples. More than two hundred dating couples responded. Joined by twenty-nine other couples recruited by an ad at one of the schools, they either answered questionnaires or were interviewed at intervals over the course of the study. Eighteen of the 103 couples whose relationships broke up were intensively interviewed by the researchers. [Hill, Rubin, Peplau]

You and your lover probably laugh at the same humor. Two Connecticut College psychologists asked thirty couples (twenty-six single, four married, mostly college-age) to rate the humor in twenty-five jokes, cartoons, and comic strips. Also, all sixty individuals assessed on a questionnaire their love or liking for their partners, and the singles rated their willingness to marry the other. The study showed that couples who agree on what's funny are more likely to like, love, and want to marry each other than those who didn't laugh at the same things. Moreover, it found that couples with a common sense of humor tended to have been together longer than the others.

A shared sense of what's funny, say the authors, "is indicative of many things: values, interests, preoccupations, intelligence, imagination, and needs." [Murstein, Brust]

If you are a man, you are likely to love your lover more than your mother, your father, your brother or sister closest in age to you, and more than your best male friend. (Of all those, you're apt to like your brother or sister least.)

If you are a woman, you are likely to love your lover and your best female friend about the same, but you *like* your best friend more than you like your lover. The researcher, Robert J. Sternberg at Yale, thinks he knows why that last finding turned up: "Women are better at achieving intimacy and value it more than do men, so if women don't get the intimacy they crave in a relationship with a man, they try to find it with other women. They establish close friendships. They can say things to another woman they can't say to a man."

Sternberg and a graduate student, Susan Grajek, arrived at those findings after recruiting thirty-five men and fifty women between the ages of eighteen and seventy, all of whom had reported at least one love relationship. They arrived at their "loving" and "liking" ratings through the Rubin loving and liking scales and an interpersonal involvement scale developed by psychologist George Levinger. [Sternberg]

The most reliable single predictor that you will have a happy relationship, other studies have led Sternberg to conclude, is not how you feel about your lover but the difference between how you ideally like the other person to feel about you and how you think he or she actually feels about you. "In other words," says Sternberg, "relationships tend to go bad when there is a mismatch between what you want from the other person and what you think you are getting. Were you ever the overinvolved person in a relationship? That can be very dissatisfying. What usually happens is that the more involved person tries to think up schemes to get the other person up to his or her level of involvement. But the other person usually sees what's going on and backs off. That just makes the overinvolved person try harder and the other person backs off more until it tears the relationship apart. The good advice in such a situation is for the overinvolved person to scale down, but that advice is hard to follow." [Sternberg]

Every now and then you need to check "where you stand" with your lover:

You may be in the minority (21 percent) who asks him or her directly, or in the smaller minority (13 percent) who asks the opinion of someone who knows both of you well. But it's far more likely that you use one of a variety of secret "tests" that are supposed not to reveal, of course, that your partner is being tested.

The one you are most likely (35 percent) to use is the "endurance" test: testing your partner's willingness to give up something for the sake of the relationship, like canceling a ski weekend and visiting your parents instead. Endurance testing may take the form of testing how much the other will endure of a behavior that comforts you but bothers her or him. ("How much will he/she put up with? What can I get away with and still keep this person interested?") One third of the endurance testers put stress on their relationships by deliberately making the other jealous.

You may also be in the minority (almost 25 percent) given to arranging absences, even separate vacations, to see how partners react. Another favorite evasive technique you may use is to tell something about yourself in a self-deprecating way to see if your partner steps in to justify you. Or you may make wisecracks or drop cutesy hints that touch on sensitive topics, such as where the relationship is going, to see if your lover cares enough to pick up the hint and talk about it.

More than any other time, you are likely to use tests when the relationship is moving from its platonic stage into heavier romance and commitment.

If you are a woman, you are more likely than your male lover to use an indirect test. That is consistent with other research that indicates women monitor relationships more subtly and indirectly than men do. [Baxter, Wilmot]

You have a stronger need than most people for intimacy:

How would you know that? Dan McAdams, psychologist at Loyola University in Chicago, believes he has a way of finding out.

He simply asks people to write stories about themselves and a set of given characters. From these stories, he derives two scores: one, for "intimacy motivation," based on references to intimacy among the characters; another, for its opposite, in a sense, "power motivation." If your story pictures yourself as a lover, a caregiver, a friend, or a peacemaker, those roles indicate your strong need for intimacy. If you cast yourself as an adventurer, warrior, or traveler, those roles mark you as a power seeker.

How does a high sense of intimacy make a person different?

"For men," says McAdams, "intimacy motivation is related to feeling less strain, stress, and somewhat less anxiety and uncertainty about the future, though it isn't related to life satisfaction and happiness. Some of our research does support that people who score high on intimacy motivation are better off. [High scoring] adult women are somewhat happier with their lives, more satisfied with their roles, than women who are somewhat lower in intimacy motivation."

If you are more interested in power than in intimacy, says McAdams, you are more likely than most to be found in such professions as higher education, journalism, and the executive ranks of corporations.

In everyone's life—and especially between the two lives in every love relationship—there is a constant tension between the need for intimacy and the need for power.

"Some would say it isn't good [to study love and intimacy], because we will demystify it and make it cold and calculated," McAdams mused in an interview with the Gary, Indiana, *Post-Tribune*. "A lot of people believe scientists are going to wreck it—and we might! My own work on love is more in the line of how individuals think of it, instead of how people *do* love." [McAdams]

You and your lover lived together before the two of you were married:

The chances of your marriage ending in divorce are the same as if you hadn't first lived together.

To find that out, two UCLA psychologists followed the marital histories of couples who, in 1972, applied for marriage licenses in Los Angeles County. About half of them had not yet shared a home. One third had been living together for three months or more, and 12 percent had jumped the gun on their license by just a few days. Four years later, the researchers tracked down seventy-seven of the 159 couples they had originally interviewed. In that short time, 31 percent of the couples had been divorced. Of them, half had been cohabitants, half had not.

Of those couples still married, measures of marital satisfaction were equal in both groups. The previous cohabitors reported less daily bickering than the others, but they were more susceptible to problems with alcohol, drugs, and infidelity. The researchers also found that cohabitants tended to be more liberal, had more diverse sexual experience, and rated themselves higher than noncohabitants in competence and self-reliance.

This confirms a previous study of newlyweds done at a Florida university which showed that former cohabitors were no more satisfied with their young marriages (most had been wed less than two years) than other couples. [Newcomb, Bentler; Jacques, Chason]

But if you live in Sweden, according to the very different findings of this American study of 4,996 Swedish women, as a former cohabitor you are almost twice as likely to divorce as someone who did not cohabit before marriage. You also have a lower regard for the institution of marriage than the noncohabitors.

"We are not saying in any way that cohabiting causes higher divorce rates," says Neil Bennett, a Yale sociologist and one of the study's three authors. "What we are saying is that it appears that people who cohabit premaritally are less committed to the institution and are more inclined to divorce than people who don't live together."

Swedes were chosen because they tend to anticipate American social trends by ten to fifteen years, said coauthor David Bloom, a Columbia economist. A higher percentage of Swedes cohabit before marriage, but the practice is still on the rise in America. An estimated two million American couples live together unmarried. That is about 4 percent of all household couples, compared with 12 percent in Sweden. In the United States, cohabiting has about quadrupled in the 1980s. [Bennett, Bloom, Blanc]

You have found out your lover has been unfaithful:

If you feel *highly* threatened by your partner's infidelity, and if you are a woman, the chances are you explain the breach to yourself by assuming your lover is dissatisfied sexually and that he is looking for more sexual variety. If you are a man, you probably assume she is dissatisfied with your degree of commitment to her. [White]

You regard your lover as very good-looking:

Perhaps she/he is. But we almost always rate our partners as better-looking than others do. [Feingold]

You want to do for your lover the most romantic thing you can imagine:

You'd probably say "I love you." [Prentice, Briggs, Bradley]

You want your lover to do for you the most romantic thing you can imagine:

Well, when you put it *that* way—the answer comes out much different. *Hearing* "I love you" ranks only as twelfth most desirable in this survey of students. First choice, by far, is "Lying about in front of a fire." The runners-up: "Walking on the beach," and "Taking a shower together." (For whatever surprise it's worth, the subjects cast practically no votes for enhancing romance by taking drugs together, reading pornography together, or praying together.)

The study subjects were 787 college students who were asked to rate various activities on a scale from "very romantic" to "not romantic at all." [Prentice, Briggs, Bradley]

You are in a homosexual love relationship:

Your life together probably defies a persistent and fallacious myth about homosexual couples: that gay and lesbian partnerships usually imitate heterosexual marriage, one partner playing the "wife," the other the "husband." According to that myth, the butch-femme roleplay gives most of the decision-making to the "husband," the household tasks to the "wife," and views your sexual behavior in husband-wife terms, one being the initiator, the other the consenter; one being the "giver," the other the "receiver"; one being usually "on top." Despite the persistence of this image in the "straight" community, many studies have consistently shown that it's quite unlikely to be descriptive of your life.

A survey of many studies of homosexual life has been made by Letitia Anne Peplau, a UCLA psychologist. At least two of those studies suggest that your gay or lesbian relationship is more likely to resemble a best friendship, with the added glow of romantic attraction. Another study indicates that the main factor in the pattern of who leads in decision-making, particularly in male couples, is likely to be age.

Debunking another myth, a study shows that most homosexuals desire a steady love relationship and, like most straights, would choose that over casual liaisons. The main prize of most homosexual relationships is affection and companionship, the same as that sought by most heterosexuals.

In studies that measure "relationship adjustment," or the related issue of loving or liking your primary partner, you are just as likely to measure in the "well-adjusted" range, and as loving or liking of your partner, as the average heterosexual.

One difference between homosexuals and heterosexuals, each taken as a group (while there may be many individual exceptions), is that, especially among gay men, if one partner urges sexual exclusivity, that demand may inhibit the development of a long-term relationship somewhat more than it may in heterosexual life.

If you are a lesbian, you are more likely to be in a steady relationship and to be living with your love partner than if you are a gay man. You are more likely to be sexually exclusive than if you are a gay man, and you are more likely to place greater importance on emotional intimacy and equality in the relationship than most gay men.

Dr. Peplau points out that existing studies are mostly based on small samples of younger, white, middle-class individuals (a short-coming that applies equally to much of all psychological research), perhaps leaving a great deal yet to be learned. They are further limited by largely relying on questionnaires and interviews which assume accurate responses by the subjects. [Peplau]

If you are male, it's almost certain that you recall first thinking that you might be homosexual when you were about seventeen.

If at the time of this study (1982) you were aged thirty-six to forty, you most probably recalled having your first homosexual love relationship when you were about twenty-seven. If you were twenty-six to thirty-five, you recalled having your first at around twenty-five. If you were twenty to twenty-five, it took place at about twenty.

The survey was conducted among 150 homosexual men living in New York City, a suburban county near New York, and Minneapolis. [Troiden, Goode]

Married couples who love each other tell each other a thousand things without talking.

CHINESE PROVERB

WHAT THEY KNOW ABOUT YOUR MARRIAGE

"What counts in making a happy marriage," George Levinger, a University of Massachusetts psychologist, has said to Daniel Goleman of *The New York Times*, "is not so much how compatible you are, but how you deal with incompatibility."

When marriage and marital happiness first began to occupy the attention of researchers, they tended to concentrate on trying to identify the kinds of people who seemed to fit together best. But the more they tried, the more they found no clear relationship between personality traits and happy marriages. Further confounding them, long-range studies also showed that the happiness of a couple before marriage was no predictor of how long the marriage would last. One of the strongest predictors, they did find, was how well the couple communicated before their wedding day.

As far back as 1938, Lewis Terman, the Stanford authority on intelligence (see "Your IQ, Your Memory, and Your Creativity," in Chapter 3), digressed from his famous long-term study of geniuses, to try to bring order to what he called "the chaos of opinion on the determiners of marital happiness." Contrary to most opinions of the day, Terman found that the frequency of sexual intercourse had little or no relationship to marital satisfaction. That 1938 finding was confirmed by another study—in 1978—of a pool of one hundred couples, all of whom checked out, based on psychological testing, as "happily married." The curve of "frequency" spread widely among these happily-marrieds. Eight percent reported having intercourse less than once a month. Close to 25 percent reported lovemaking two or three times a month. More than half, one to three times a week. At the extremes, two of the hundred reported no intercourse, while one couple performed it daily. One third of the men and two thirds of the women felt they had sexual problems; for the men, most often difficulty in becoming or staying erect, and for women, difficulty in reaching orgasm. Of them, both men and women said they had trouble relaxing and felt a lack of interest in sexual activity, itself leading to troubled feelings.

When the marital road gets bumpy, the typical male reaction is to withdraw and clam up, while women are more likely to become more argumentative and coercive, stepping up the emotional pressure, according to Howard Markman of the University of Denver, author of *Marital Interaction*. The cycle of the wife's pressure and the husband's withdrawal escalates, often destructively. But happily married couples seem better than others at preventing that cycle. "All couples go through ups and downs in marriage," said Dr. Markman in an interview with Dr. Goleman of the *Times*. "But it's a couple that doesn't communicate well whose marriage is more likely to be the victim of such a difficult period."

Attraction to marrying is seen as resulting from each partner sensing in the other the potential fulfillment of some deeply held need. The two most important of these needs are in a perpetual state of conflict with the other: the urge for intimacy versus the drive to preserve one's identity as a separate person, to keep from being swallowed up by the other. Thus, virtually daily, the marriage is a negotiation to try to balance those conflicting needs. "There's an inevitable push-pull in marriage," Michael Kolevzon of Virginia Commonwealth University, said to Goleman. "As a couple's intimacy increases, you often see a corresponding increase in the desire for distance. . . . Anger is one means this balancing act is negotiated in marriage. Sometimes it's a way to ask for distance: I'll get angry with you so I can justify being alone for a while. Or with some people their anger is actually a plea for intimacy. They build up to an angry confrontation so it can resolve into intimacy as an affirmation that their spouse loves them despite their faults."

LOOK YOURSELF UP

You are married and living with your spouse:

You are in the healthiest of states, regardless of whether the marriage is satisfactory or not. Regardless of your present age, your life expectancy is higher than that of someone in any other marital state (not living with your spouse, divorced, widowed, or whatever). In contrast, a divorced person is likely to use more health care services than you, even if you are unhappily married. You are statistically likely to go to a doctor 5.4 times a year, and illness interferes with your normal activities 20.2 days a year. A separated or divorced person can be expected to go to a doctor seven times a year and illness will interfere on 38.8 days. [Holmes]

An accurate measure of your comfort in the marriage is the physical distance you find most comfortable between the two of you when you are conversing. The researchers recruited twenty-four married couples and measured their degree of marital happiness through three standard tests: the Marital Status Inventory (MSI), the Locke-Wallace Marital Adjustment Test (MAT), and the Areas of Change (AOC) test, the latter designed to produce an "amount of conflict" score to distinguish between distressed and nondistressed couples. Then the couples were given two space-measure tests: One was the Couples' Stop-Distance Space Measure, widely used in studying preferred personal space, in which the two members of a couple are placed some distance apart and are asked to approach each other and to stop at "a comfortable conversation distance." The distance between the couples' closest toes was then measured. The other test was the Couples' Chair Placement Space Measure. The subject couple removes two chairs from a stack and places them on the floor to have a conversation. After the couple leaves the room, the distance between their chairs is measured. The researchers found reliably that the larger the space between the spouses, the lower the marital adjustment and the more they were distressed. [Crane, Griffin]

If both you and your spouse were teenagers when you married, you are twice as likely to divorce as couples who marry in their twenties.

If you are a woman and married in your thirties, you are more likely to divorce than a woman who marries in her twenties. [Glick, Norton]

You have been married a long time:

. . . And you sometimes wonder if the romantic feelings are dead and gone.

If you are the husband, the length of time of your marriage appears to have no bearing on how romantic you feel about your wife. The more you describe yourself as "committed" to your marriage, however, the longer your romantic feelings are likely to last.

If you are the wife, the longer you have been married, the less likely you are to feel elated or romantic at thoughts of your husband, and the more likely you are to feel generally anxious—not just about the marriage but about almost everything. [Mathes, Wise]

. . . And you sometimes wonder if the two of you are really growing to look alike.

No kidding, there's a good chance you are. Robert B. Zajonc of the University of Michigan randomly collected photographs of two dozen couples, taken when they were just married. Generally, those photos were about twenty-five years old at the time of the study. The researchers then took or collected relatively fresh photos of the subjects, who were generally fifty to sixty years old. College undergraduates were then asked to pair up the married couples, both then and now. With the younger faces, the students did no better than chance at linking husbands with wives. But they did significantly better with the more recent photos.

How does Zajonc explain the results? Over time, husbands and wives deepen in their habit of mimicking one another, especially in facial expressions. This daily imitation, says Zajonc, "would leave wrinkles around the mouth and eyes, alter the bearing of the head, and the overall expression. Eventually [it] would produce . . . changes that make spouses appear more similar than they originally were.

That's not all Zajonc's results show. He also discovered that the greater their acquired facial resemblance, the happier their marriage. [Zajonc]

. . . And you're proud to say that you believe in monogamy, and have been faithful the whole time.

Congratulations for standing fast for your cultural values, even though you have been defying what appear to be the laws of human nature, and certainly of the world of mammals. According to Duke University anthropologist Patricia Wright, 87 percent of human cultures around the world are *not* monogamous. Only 3 to 4 percent of mammal species stay with a single mate—and in most of those species, cheating is common when the partner is not nearby. Western humans who keep the faith are joined in doing so by coyotes, bats, wolves, beavers, muskrats, and certain varieties of moles. [Wright]

If you are the wife, your authority and influence over your husband has probably increased with the passage of time. If you are the husband, your authority has probably diminished. [Birren]

If you are the husband, your caring for and nurturing of your wife has probably increased over the years and you have become less dominant in the relationship. If you are the wife, you used to be cautious in displaying your aggressive tendencies, but in later years you have become more tolerant of that urge. [Neugarten, Berkowitz, and others]

You are a man highly satisfied with your marriage:

If you score that way on a standard test, you're also likely to score as highly jealous.

For this study, middle-class white men at a health club who had been married (or remarried) for a mean of ten years were asked to rate their marriages and how they would feel if their wives had an affair with another man, a friendship with another man, etc. (No companion study was done of women.) [Hansen]

Both you and your spouse have full-time paying jobs:

Each of you probably works about nine hours a day, including commuting time. Then you are likely to miss being together for another hour and a half because of different work times. For all that, compared to the time that single income couples spend together (3.8 hours), you manage to have almost as much time together: 3.2 hours.

Is your marriage better or worse off under that time squeeze? That depends on how you spend the time. "The more time together in activities such as eating, playing, and conversing, the more satisfying the marriage," say Paul William Kingston and Steven Nock of the University of Virginia, who surveyed 321 couples on time spent together and marital satisfaction. On the other hand, for time spent together on duties, such as child care, housework, community service—and in this category, the authors include watching television—no impact on marital happiness is perceived. [Kingston, Nock]

If you are the woman, you do less housework than a woman who is a full-time homemaker—but not much less. You do about 70 percent of the chores, compared to 83 percent completed by the housewife. Those duties take almost thirty hours a week of your time. Your husband puts in four to six hours, about a 14 percent share. If you are in a high-powered, high-paying career, surely your husband takes over more of the housework. Oh, yeah? Not if he's typical of the 1,565 couples in this study. [Berardo]

If you are the wife, you can scarcely avoid knowing that many people think of you as abandoning your home and children and, shame on you, helping create a new social ethic that has already increased the divorce rate and will increase it further in years to come.

Trouble is, research doesn't verify that portrait of you. True, the divorce rate has soared, but not conspicuously among two-paycheck couples. Nor can divorce be especially linked with educational achievements of either spouse, or with no-fault divorce laws. If a finger is to be shaken at couples whose lifestyles are associated with higher divorce rates, try couples who don't attend church regularly and those with no relatives living nearby. [Johnson, Skinner]

You and your spouse have had your first child:

After the baby's arrival, especially during the first six months, you probably feel a modest decline in the quality of your marriage. You both express less affection, feel less romantic, and spend less time in fun activities. If you are the wife, you probably feel these changes more than your husband does. But on the up side, you both probably feel a heightening of your sense of partnership and mutual caretaking. You are likely to have a rise in marital tension during this period, especially if one of you is troubled by problems at work while the other, probably the wife, finds that she is carrying a greater than usual share of household chores.

"We are finding," says Jay Belsky of Penn State University, director of this $500,000 study, "that having babies doesn't turn good marriages into bad ones or bad marriages into good ones. The best marriages seemed to stay the best after the arrival of the baby, and the worst marriages stayed the worst. Couples seem to be giving up a more romantic intimacy as they gain another source of affection. Something's got to give, as they acquire a new role and the joys and burdens of that role. What gives is the marriage." [Belsky]

If that child (or a later one) is a boy, you are less likely to divorce than you will be if you only have daughters. The researcher, a University of Pennsylvania sociologist, theorizes that the explanation may be that fathers tend to take a greater role in raising sons than daughters, and thus the father develops closer ties to his wife and family. [Morgan]

You are the wife of a doctor:

The chances are quite high (52 percent) that you are disappointed by how your marriage turned out, according to this survey of readers by the magazine *Medical/Mrs.*, to which more than a thousand doctors' wives responded. Almost as many (48 percent) gave affirmative answers to the question, "Do you suffer due to the 'God' status your husband enjoys?"

"Everybody hangs on everything they say," wrote one respondent. "They are so used to telling people what to do and standing around while they do it that they expect the same treatment at home." Others reported feeling too intimidated to discuss homely subjects like squabbles between the children or a jammed washing machine with a man who lives his working days on the edge of life and death.

But there's a rosier side suggested by at least one comment: "Who cares about a successful marriage when you get to drive your Lincoln to the club every day?" [*Medical/Mrs.*]

You are a married woman and a successful scientist:

You probably publish fewer articles reporting your research results than most of your male colleagues do, but you can't easily blame it on having a husband or children. Women scientists who have neither children nor husbands turn out to be no more prolific in their publication than married mothers, according to this study by two Columbia University scholars. The researchers counted the papers published each year by seventy-three women scientists, and asked other scientists to divide them into two categories, "eminent" and "rank-and-file," based on peer opinion, membership in honorary societies, and academic rank. Each group of women was as likely to be married and have children as the other. In fact, in the group of eminent scientists, married women accomplished more than their single peers: an average of at least three published articles per year for married women without children; almost three per year for married women with children, and about two per year for the single women. Among rank-and-file scientists, married women with children publish just as often as married women without children— slightly more than one paper a year. Rank-and-file single women outdid the married, averaging nearly two papers a year. [Cole, Zuckerman]

Your parents are of different racial groups:

If you are a woman, you are more likely to choose a husband from your father's racial group than from your mother's.

If you are a man, you are more likely to choose a wife from your mother's racial group than from your father's.

For this study, the racial choices of 3,814 brides and 3,357 grooms in Hawaii who are of multi-racial descent were examined. To find the subjects, the researcher examined 32,000 marriage licenses issued between 1978 and 80. [Jedlicka]

You are a woman who does not smoke and you are married to a smoker:

Your marriage is a hazard to your health. If your husband is a heavy smoker at home, inhaling his secondhand smoke can double your risk of lung cancer. Even if he smokes just moderately, you run a 23 percent greater chance of lung cancer than women married to non-smoking husbands. This finding came out of an American Cancer Society study of 134 women who had lung cancer, but had never smoked. [American Cancer Society]

Your husband or wife has just died:

The chances that you will die during the next year are ten times as high as someone of your age and sex whose spouse is still alive, according to a British study cited in this research report. [Holmes]

You have been divorced:

In contrast with happily married couples, during your marriage the husband probably showed more dominance than the wife in making financial decisions. You are likely to have spent more than happily married couples on home entertainment items like stereos and color television sets, while the happily marrieds tended to spend more in buying a home, major appliances, and recreational vehicles. The researchers suggest that the happily married couples were putting their money into family commitment, while the soon-to-be divorced were buying items that would probably "be worth as much after marital dissolution and . . . to be consistent with individual leisure enjoyment rather than family commitment."

These conclusions came from a study by two marketing professors of 311 couples for ten years after their marriages, each interviewed at regular intervals. After those ten years, fifty-two couples had divorced and in fifty-two others, both spouses were measured as happily married. From those contrasting 104 couples the conclusions were drawn. [Schaninger, Buss]

If you are a mother of dependent children, and if you are of low income, there's a fair chance (25 percent) that after your divorce you moved in with relatives; if you are of moderate income, a 4 percent chance. But if that's what you did, there's an 86 percent chance that you didn't like the live-in arrangements. [Colletta]

If you resemble the forty-eight divorced mothers and fathers in this study, the two of you readily got into conflict with one another during the two months following your divorce, and the arguments generally ignited over finances and support, child-rearing and visitation rights, and real or suspected intimate relations with others. Over time, conflict decreased, but if you are the wife, your anger and resentment lasted longer than your husband's. There's a fair chance (six out of forty-eight) the two of you had intercourse together in the two months following your divorce. If you are the mother, there's a high likelihood (thirty-four of forty-eight) that during those two months you would have called upon your former spouse before asking anyone else's assistance in case of emergency; if you're the father, the probability is only slightly less, twenty-nine of forty-eight, but far less—eight out of forty-eight—that you helped your ex-wife with home maintenance. After two years, however, your interdependence is apt to have sharply decreased. [Hetherington, Cox, Cox]

If you are a woman, there's an 80 percent chance your contacts with your ex-husband's relatives decreased considerably after your divorce, while he probably dropped contact completely with your relatives. An important reason for your continuing contact is that you probably have the principal custody of your children, and you cooperate in maintaining their relations with his family. If not for that, you would probably drop contact with your former relatives, too. [Anspach; Weiss]

During your separation and divorce period, you are highly likely (84 percent) to have felt supported by your friends, you saw more of them than you did while married, and spending more time with them lessened your stress. If you were in the small minority who fell out of contact with friends, your adjustment to the divorce was much harder. You are almost certain to feel that after a while many of your predivorce relationships became less important and you began seeing less of many of those friends. In fact, you are likely to have discovered that many of your previous friendships depended upon your being a "couple." You probably had a total loss of social contact with those people who had been primarily "his" or "her" friends. And, yes, you also found that you lost (or kept exclusively) some friends who took sides out of loyalty to either your former spouse or to you, meaning the other was rejected. Finally, there's a good chance that you eventually isolated yourself from former friends and family, feeling that you no longer "fit in" with them. You found that many friends now viewed you as a threat to their own marriage, a possible sexual competitor, or a reminder that their marriage too might fail. Thus an important casualty of your divorce was a big chunk of your network of friends, especially married friends. [Saunders, in a survey of research that included studies by Spanier, Castro; Raschke; Weiss; Kohen, Brown, Feldberg; Hetherington, Cox, Cox]

You are much more likely to be engaged in a high status occupation than a low one.

Within that high status group, according to California divorce records for a recent year, the likelihood of your divorce changes among occupations. Of twelve lines of professional work studied, the highest rate of divorce was among authors. They were followed in order by social scientists, architects, college faculty, lawyers and judges, engineers, chemists, editors and reporters, accountants and auditors, dentists, and physicians. But doctors with high rates of patient contact and those who must keep the most irregular hours are more likely to divorce than their medical colleagues. Lowest in the list of those divorcing were natural scientists. [Rosow, Rose]

You have never been married:

You are seven times more likely than a married person to be admitted to a mental hospital, especially if you are a man. Despite that, your population group of never-marrieds makes fewer demands on the health-care system than any other group. (A possible contributing reason may be the unlikelihood of your requiring maternity care.) [Holmes]

People tend to see you as a stereotype of being selfish, irresponsible, impotent, frigid, hedonistic, and immature—separately, or in combination.

In trying to maintain a lifestyle that has no support from the general culture, you often feel shadings of guilt and embarrassment, fear of loneliness, and generalized stress that may be related to you missing regular affection, intimacy, and shared activities. If you are older and single, you often feel dissatisfied with friendships, having expected more from them. You also tend to see your relatives less than married people do, and you are less satisfied with your family life than they are. Despite all that, you are likely to feel that freedom and opportunity for personal development are among the most important assets of your lifestyle.

If you are a woman, compared to single men you are happier, better able to meet life's challenges, and, by middle age, you are more educated, earn more money, and work in a more prestigious job.

If you are a man, sad to say, there is no study known that gives you any advantage in any way over the unmarried woman.

Those conclusions are drawn from a broad review of research on the never-married. The review, covering many studies, contains its own lengthy bibliography for those who wish to investigate in more detail. [Johnston, Eklund]

YOUR CHILDREN AND PARENTS
LOOK YOURSELF UP

You breast-feed your newborn baby:

Your baby is probably healthier physically because you do so, but also more irritable and fussy.

Researchers led by Janet DiPietro, University of Maryland psychologist, studied one hundred full-term newborns, averaging a day-and-a-half old. Of them, sixty-nine were breast-feeding, thirty-nine on a bottle. During the babies' sleep, researchers clocked their heart and breathing patterns. After they awoke, the infants were measured for other signs of general health, as well as for responses to lights and rattles, frequency of crying, reflexes, and overall activity. The tests could not be completed on many of the breast-fed infants, DiPietro reported, because they became irritated quickly and remained upset. Even those completing the tests were relatively distressed. The researchers had a notably easier time with the bottle-fed babies. On the other hand, the two groups of infants were indistinguishable in their muscle responses and general alertness.

What the research fell short of showing was whether the breast-fed babies' differences are temporary or long-lasting. [DiPietro]

You have a prenursery-school child and you sometimes wonder if his or her mind is developing at the right pace:

While a question like that could have been answered only by pure guesswork a short time ago, three pediatricians at the Johns Hopkins University School of Medicine have now come up with a definite yardstick that any parent can easily use.

The most reliable early predictor of a child's mental ability, they have found, is progress in developing linguistic skills—including the making of sounds months before the child says a first real word. Their simple measurement can also help call attention to problems in hearing and learning disorders, as well as possibly tipping off more severe hidden problems like cerebral palsy, mental retardation, and autism, which often are not noticed and treated until the child is much older.

The test, which the researchers have dubbed CLAMS, for Clinical Linguistic and Auditory Milestone Scale, first described in a 1987 issue of *Contemporary Pediatrics*, lists the following markers as indications of normal development:

Age in Months	Milestone
FIRST YEAR	
0.25	Makes some response to sound
1.25	Smiles in response to stimulation
1.6	Coos; makes long vowel sounds
4	Turns toward speaker
	Says "ah-goo"
	Makes razzing sound
5	Turns toward ringing bell
6	Babbles
7	Looks up sideways toward ringing bell
8	Says "dada" and "mama," but not as names
9	Plays gesture games, like peek-a-boo
	Looks directly at ringing bell
	Understands word "no"
11	Uses "dada" and "mama" as names
	Responds to one-step command and gesture indicating activity
	Says first word
12	Says gibberish "sentences" without using real words
	Says second word
SECOND YEAR	
13	Says third word
14	Responds to one-step command without gesture

15	Says four to six words
17	Says gibberish sentence with some real words
	Can point to five body parts
	Says seven to twenty words
19	Forms two-word combinations
21	Forms two-word sentences
24	Uses pronouns *I, me, you* indiscriminately

THIRD YEAR	
30	Uses pronouns *I, me, you* discriminately
36	Uses all pronouns discriminately
	Has 250-word vocabulary
	Uses plurals
	Forms three-word sentences

[Capute, Shapiro, Palmer]

You are a parent and you want to exercise authority over your children, but you don't want to be authoritarian:

A University of California psychologist has studied how children turn out when their parents are *authoritarian* and when they are *authoritative*. The differences are pronounced.

Authoritarian parents, by her definition, are "detached and controlling." Their children often turn out to be discontented, withdrawn, and distrustful. Authoritative parents, on the other hand, are "controlling and demanding, but also very warm, rational, and responsive." Their children tend to turn out the most self-reliant, self-controlled, and explorative, according to Dr. Diana Baumrind's eight-year study with three groups of nursery school children.

Then there's a third major category: parents who are so eager not to be authoritarian that they are *permissive*. They make few demands of their children and rarely try to control them. These parents, according to Dr. Baumrind's studies, produced the least self-reliant, explorative, and self-controlled children.

Successful parents, she says, recognize their own special rights as adults as well as the child's individual interests and special ways. "The mother does not base her decisions on group consensus or on the individual child's desires." During the first six years of a child's life, "exercise of power is a legitimate right of the parents." By early adolescence, however, a child "can see clearly many alternatives to parental directives, and a parent must be able to defend rationally, as she would to an adult, a directive with which the adolescent disagrees." Such rationality is the strongest line of defense, Dr. Baumrind concludes, because permissiveness begets license and psychological damage, while the adolescent "cannot be forced physically to obey over any period of time." [Baumrind]

When your child misbehaves, you believe a well-placed whack doesn't do any harm:

Oh, yes it does, according to this study of sixteen fourteen-month-old babies. Babies who were lightly slapped by their mothers or received more severe physical punishment were found more likely to grasp breakable and forbidden objects and were most likely to defy restraining commands. When given an infant development test seven months later, these physically punished babies, as a group, scored lower than others who received little or no punishment. These differences in scores showed up most markedly in questions related to spatial skills and problem solving, such as fitting puzzle pieces together and fixing pegs in a board.

The differences in development may not be the result of punishment alone. The researchers found that punishing mothers also offered their babies fewer objects to play with that might invite exploration, including toys that were unbreakable and safe. By denying the child interesting playthings, say the researchers, the mother limits the child's opportunities to improve visual/spatial skills and problem-solving ability. [Power, Chapieski]

You have a "latchkey" child—one who returns from school to an empty home, staying alone for an extended period:

A stranger who found that out, in keeping with common assumption, would probably assume you are poor, a single parent, and living in a high-risk inner-city neighborhood. The assumption is misguided. If yours is the more typical latchkey child, you are well-educated, middle- to upper-class, and you live in a suburb or in the country. Leaving your child alone is probably your choice, not a necessity.

You may get dirty looks because of a popular belief that latchkey kids number as many as 15 million, that the number keeps growing, and that they are another evidence of the breakdown of the family. All incorrect. A study based on census data indicates that only 2.1 million children between ages five and thirteen (7 percent of the age group) are left unsupervised. Ninety percent of them are nine or older, and most stay alone for a maximum of two hours a day. Furthermore, most are from two-parent families, and it's not to be assumed that the mother is working. The study found no consistent match between a latchkey child and the mother's employment. [Hofferth, Cain]

If your child is twelve or older, the more hours she or he is unsupervised after school, the more likely the youngster is experimenting with sex—considerably more likely than with alcohol or drugs. Sex experimentation is most likely if you are a single parent. According to this study of four hundred middle-school children between ages twelve and fifteen in the Washington area, 40 percent of single-parent teenagers said that at some time they took part in heavy petting or intercourse at home during the parent's working hours. In homes of two working parents, only 15 percent made the same report.

"Teenagers these days," said Thomas Long, a sociologist at Catholic University, "don't get pregnant in motels and cars at ten at night. Sex happens at home at three in the afternoon"—while parents are at work. Lynette Long of American University, coauthor of the study, added, "The phenomenon of children taking care of themselves is happening in upscale communities, rural areas, suburbs, everywhere." [Long, Long]

You are a mother of a child (or children) whose father is absent because of marital breakup, and you wonder how fatherlessness may affect the child's mental and social development:

You are in the same husbandless boat as mothers of almost 15 percent of children under eighteen living in the United States. Those children are believed to number about ten million. A psychologist of the City University of New York who shares your uneasiness notes that "the social scientist is confronted with a problem of epidemic proportions. . . . To simply describe these children as poor, deprived, or as living on welfare is both facile and erroneous. They come from a wide variety of . . . backgrounds. They have been placed in their peculiar position for a wide variety of reasons: the separation, divorce, or death of their parents; or the increasing desire and ability of a single individual to adopt children; or the increased ability of single women to support those natural children who have been born out of wedlock.

"The magnitude of this situation has not diminished over the years nor is it likely to diminish in the foreseeable future. Recent surveys have pointed out that divorce is becoming more and more of an option for all segments of society. In fact, for the upper–middle class, it is approaching the fadistic proportions and status that psychoanalysis once enjoyed. Single parent adoptions, while still rare, are becoming more readily available and fashionable, which over time should lead to greater numbers of both motherless as well as fatherless homes. For the poor and unskilled, the presence of welfare has typically meant the breaking up of stable heterosexual relationships with its resultant destruction of effective male presence in the home."

Mitchell W. Robin reviewed more than one hundred research studies related to father-absent homes. His focus was the impact on the child's mind, emotions, and social development. Here are some of the findings that Robin unearthed in those studies (all of which are listed in the bibliography of his review):

In a British study of 206 male homosexuals and heterosexuals, K. Freund found it slightly more likely for a homosexual than a heterosexual to have lived prior to the age of two in a father-absent home. The same study also showed that, when growing up with a father present in the home, a homosexual was more likely than a heterosexual to have a strained father-son relationship.

Edward Ziegler, the early-development psychologist of Yale, has cited many studies by Urie Bronfenbrenner of Cornell and others which showed that children from middle-class homes without fathers were more likely than other children to exhibit effeminate behavior and diminished aggressiveness. Another study showed that six- to ten-year-old boys whose fathers were away for military service were less aggressive than father-present boys. An even greater lack of aggressiveness was found in boys from divorced homes when compared against boys whose fathers had died. Girls from father-absent homes were found to date at an earlier age and more frequently than girls with a father at home. Father-absent girls also had sexual experiences earlier, especially if their parents were divorced.

If their fathers had died, adolescent girls were notably inhibited, rigid, avoiding, and restrained when encountering males. That was even more true if the separation from father occurred before the girl's adolescence.

All of those findings were more true for white boys and girls than for blacks.

In a study of thirty white lower-class fifth grade boys whose fathers had been absent during the first two years of the children's lives, they were found to be more distrustful of people around them than comparable boys from homes with fathers present. They also scored lower in measures of industriousness, initiative, and self-management than either father-present boys or those who lost their fathers at a later age.

Boys living with their mothers following loss of the father had a significantly higher-than-average rate of delinquency, while a matched sample of boys living with their fathers after losing their mothers had only the average societal rate. In a huge study of 4,995 boys in Aberdeen, Scotland, all eight to eleven years old, father-absent boys were found more likely to engage in delinquent behavior than father-present boys. A 1976 study suggested that one of the causes of the rises of Nazism in Germany might be attributed to the large number of children raised in father-absent homes as a result of the Germans' crushing defeat in World War I. In Dresden, Germany, of a hundred young jailed alcoholics, two thirds came from broken homes and 60 percent had grown up in father-absent homes. In the United States, a sample of twenty-nine male heroin addicts were all found to come from homes where the father was either absent or emotionally distant. American boys from father-absent homes have been found to have more difficulty making friends than boys from intact homes. The research suggested that these father-absent boys were weaker in their development of masculine skills valued by other boys, thus leading to their rejection by peers.

A classic study that spanned contrasting cultures (by H. A. Barry, M. K. Bacon, and I. L. Child) showed that societies in which infants sleep only with their mothers and have minimal or nonexistent father-child relationships have the highest rates of suicide, assaults, murders, rapes, and sorcery. Those societies also measure unusually high in aggressive masculinity.

The presence and absence of fathers seems to have a discernible impact in school performance of children. In the general population, sample groups of girls quite consistently outperform boys in verbal ability, while boys do better than girls in math ability. Quaintly consistent with that, L. Carlsmith, citing other studies as well as her own research, shows evidence that female mathematicians tend to identify strongly with masculine figures in their lives, while male mathematicians are marked by a "loss of relationship to the mother." Still another quirky evidence of that tendency concerned girls whose fathers were only "absent" because they worked on night shifts. Those girls did even more poorly than most girls in the "masculine" activity of math, especially if the girls were under the age of nine. On the other side of that coin, a study of 307 Harvard freshmen (class of 1964) from intact families showed that, when very young, one third of them had long separations from their fathers during World War II. Those males who had such father separation had significantly higher verbal skills than the others, while those not separated produced a greater group ability in math. That finding seemed to further underline the link between father presence and the development of typically male abilities. The study further found that even boys from father-present homes who did noticeably well on verbal skills were likely to have spent relatively little, or passive, time with their fathers. Dr. Robin's long review of research weightily tends to show that father-absence has perceptible costs, but not disastrous ones, for both boys and girls. He sums up with an old Yiddish proverb: "Lack of a father is not as bad as having a good father is good." [Robin]

You grew up on a farm:

You may be surprised to learn (as these researchers were) that your parents were inclined to get considerably less pleasure out of having children than most nonfarm parents do.

Four Colorado State researchers probed the attitudes of 154 farm parents (63 fathers, 91 mothers). These parents, dependent upon ranching, dairying, and crop raising for their chief income, averaged thirty-eight years of age. Fifty-five percent of them had high school diplomas, 6 percent did not, and 39 percent held college and graduate degrees. Their incomes (in dollar values of 1982, when this study was published) ranged from less than $10,000 to more than $35,000, and their family size, from one to six children. In a twelve-item attitude scale about reasons for having children—covering desires for continuity, tradition, and security; parental satisfactions; "role motivations"; happiness and affection; goals and incentives; and social status—both mothers and fathers, as compared to their non-farm counterparts, showed "generally negative attitudes toward children, an unexpected outcome. Even more surprising is the fact that mothers expressed more overall negative attitudes." [Bigner, Jacobsen, Miller, Turner]

You are a woman, and in your childhood and/or teens your father seduced you into an incestuous relationship:

First of all, recent studies reveal that your experience is far more common than it was once thought to be. While most cases probably remain unreported, confirmed cases of incest are now believed to be the "tip of the iceberg" (see next item). What you endured is regarded as the most traumatic of all sexual abuses of children.

The most outstanding general finding of recent research is that to the innocent onlooker your family gave every appearance of an adjusted, normally functioning group. That is because incest is a game played by the entire family, each member putting up a convincing facade of acting its proper role, and, consciously or unconsciously, carrying off a "conspiracy of silence." That conspiracy is a survival technique, protecting the family against disintegration.

Perhaps your victimization began, as it frequently does in families that harbor incest, at a time of a seriously stressful event: an accident, disease, loss of a job, an economic crisis, a mother's unusual absence from home because she deserted the family, fell into a long illness, or needed to work long hours. This research survey hastens to point out that such crises occur in many families that do not turn to incest, and that there's no known explanation for why certain families fall into the pit of incest.

Your father was probably emotionally immature, seeming to focus excessively on the family. Such fathers "seek to control the lives of all family members by whatever means they think effective—threats, intimidations, psychological or material bribes, or seduction," says this 1983 survey of research on incest by Tamar Cohen, a family therapist of West Hartford, Connecticut, who presented it at the First International Conference on Pediatric Social Work. "Fathers may justify their incestuous behavior as protecting the daughter against outside influence, or as teaching her the facts of life the right way. In many cases, the incestuous father feels that the daughter is his exclusive property and is quite surprised at the concern of outsiders." The typical characteristic of fathers who commit long-term incest is "their inability to meet their needs for closeness, attention, and affection through daily human contact in a nonphysical, nonsexual way."

While there are no known ways of predicting your father's behavior from his family history, there's a more-than-average likelihood that he came from a severely deprived background, and that his own father tended to be absent from the home, thus denying him a normal opportunity to get a sure sense of parental responsibility and restraint. One study has come up with the not-easily-explained finding that the healthier the family background of the offending father, the older his daughter at the time he initiates the incest.

Your mother, who psychologists believe was a kind of "enabler" of the incest, would probably fall under such descriptions as weak and submissive, passive, emotionally distant from the family, generally indifferent and insensitive, and perhaps promiscuous. As an adult woman, she would probably be rated as generally incompetent. Her distance from the family may be a symptom of pervasive depression, which probably started long before your father's incest became overt. Although your mother probably denied knowledge of the incest, recent research raises doubts about her denials. There's a growing observation among researchers that your mother might have felt relief at your taking over the sexual role with your father. Another possibility is that your weak, dependent, and intimidated mother simply was terrified to confront your father because she was afraid he would abandon the family. Those speculative observations about wives of incestuous fathers might help explain why most incest is exposed by daughters and not mothers.

Tamar Cohen emphasizes that wives of incestuous fathers display two specific behavior components that are "important to the understanding of incest: her abdication of her role as a mother and housewife while delegating those responsibilities to her daughter, and her backing out of her sexual role as a wife. These two characteristics appear in nearly all mothers of the classic incestuous families."

The chances are quite high—better than even—that you are the eldest daughter in the family. You generally impressed people as very mature, acting older than your years, assuming much of the household responsibility, and caring for the younger children as well as for your parents before the initial incest experiences. There is no known reason to assume that you were sexually mature or seductive before the incidents. The maturity of your behavior was attributable to the role reversal with your mother rather than to any early sexual development. That switching of roles with her gave you a sense of importance and power, and you were probably soon to find, after the sexual attentions from your father, that you felt power over him too, not only for being the keeper of his secret, but also because the attentions played to your need for physical affection and closeness. Underlying those prizes may have been your subtle enjoyment of revenge against your mother, who psychologically abandoned you.

As the incestuous relationship developed, your tensions and difficulties deepened. Because your deep, secret, and perhaps perfectly normal wish that your father would love you more than he does your mother—a wish you felt was probably wrong—had now come true, you felt not only guilty but *responsible* for the secret, wicked carryings-on with your father. A major part of your raging emotional confusion was resentment toward both of them—your father for trapping and using you, and your mother for not protecting you.

The worst of it, perhaps, was that you could not share the most explosive secret of your life with *anyone*, which built a dense wall around you, alienating you from *everyone*. You couldn't share it with relatives. They *liked* your father. They'd believe him. They'd think you were crazy. You would lose their respect, their affection, and any hope they might protect you. Your story might be an invitation to other relatives to come at you. If you talked to your doctor, your teacher, or the police, your father might go to jail, your parents might divorce, and you would have wrecked your family and your home. Where would you go, where would you live, then? Moreover, you felt ripped in two, craving your independence, on the one hand, and needing the rewards, psychological and sometimes material, that your special position gave you. You felt involved with your family in the most complex and distressing ways, yet for all their show of normality, you felt locked out of the "real" family. *Silence* seemed the only tool that made any sense.

Why did you let it go on? Was it your enjoyment, your feelings of power, or fear, or shame, or guilt, or a certainty that your mother would not believe you, or if she did she would do nothing to put a stop to your anguish—was it one of those, or all of them, that kept your lips tight? Surely the psychological web is too intricate to yield a direct answer. But the telling fact is that rarely does the victim of childhood sexual abuse expose it while it is still occurring. More than half the time the exposure waits until after the daughter has left home. The motive for blowing the whistle, that suggests, is hostility and a desire for revenge against the parents—probably both of them.

You may have experienced even further complexities, although researchers have not collected many case stories that shed much light beyond the father-mother-daughter design of incest. There's one published case of a son witnessing incest between his father and sister—and of the son's subsequent incest with *his* daughter. And one description of "incest envy"—a serious psychological disturbance in the daughter *not* chosen by the father.

And perhaps the most important story is what happens later. "Any serious attempts," writes Tamar Cohen in this remarkably comprehensive and lucidly written review of many studies, "to find the long-range consequences of incest in its broadest sense meet with difficulties, because past victims, who understandably do not wish to be reminded of their past incestuous relationship, are not cooperative. A longitudinal [long-range] study of the victims, especially with regard to sexual functioning, marital relationship, and parenting is yet to be undertaken."

The review contains thirty-two references to case studies and other research from which it is drawn. [Cohen]

While reported occurrences of incest may be only the "tip of the iceberg," scarcely any researcher advances an estimate of how widely the crime occurs. But of every thousand children in America, two or three are known to have been victims of sexual abuse within the family, says Dr. Alexander G. Zaphiris, a lawyer, social worker, and associate dean of the Graduate School of Social Work at the University of Houston. The actual number of abuse victims per thousand could number in the dozens, conceivably in the hundreds.

Dr. Zaphiris says he "has never seen an incest victim who was not conditioned as an infant." The conditioning, which the father may have done unconsciously at first, involves sexually stimulating the child as though this were normal affection. [Zaphiris]

YOUR BROTHERS AND SISTERS

"The toughest job in the family goes, hands down, to the firstborn. If you are a firstborn, you know from firsthand experience what I'm talking about." The person talking is Kevin Leman, a Tucson, Arizona, psychologist, youngest of three and father of four, who wrote a bestseller, *The Birth Order Book*. In an interview with Darrell Sifford of Knight-Ridder Newspapers, he amplified: "You know very well that you have always lived your life in the limelight. You've always been the one who is supposed to set the perfect example for everyone else. You know what it's like to have that burning desire within you, that drive that compels you to conquer the world or die trying. . . .

"The firstborn is the kid who takes out the trash. All of his years at home, until he leaves for college, he'll be taking out the trash. When he comes home from college for Christmas, he's likely to find 300 pounds of trash waiting to be carted off. . . . As a rule [firstborns] have it much tougher than their younger brothers and sisters when it comes to discipline and the behavior that is expected of them."

LOOK YOURSELF UP

You are from a large family:

Whatever surprises lurk in this study, they deserve special attention, because the study is impressively large: an entire year's male births in the Netherlands—400,000 nineteen-year-olds, required to appear for an examination to determine their physical and mental fitness for military induction. (Note: This study is drawn from males *only*.) The findings about family size:

First, the larger your family, the lower the intellectual ability of each of you is likely to be. That is especially true if your father was a manual worker. If he was a nonmanual worker, the tendency is still true, but less so.

Second, the older you are in the birth order of your family, the higher your intellectual ability is likely to be. Reminder: This finding describes a *tendency* and *probability*; it is not a prediction for individuals. But the tendency proceeds almost like a straight line on a graph: A firstborn is probably smarter than the secondborn, who in turn is likely to be smarter than the thirdborn, etc.—except for the lastborn. That tendency holds true regardless of whether your father was a manual or nonmanual worker.

The tendency for your birth order to influence your intelligence is most consistent if you are a firstborn; the tendency is also significant if you are the second, third, or fourth child; if you are the fifth or sixth, the tendency is still there, but less so. Lastborns scarcely follow the "rules" at all. The effects on intelligence of birth order are found consistently across the boundaries of social class. [Belmont, Marolla]

. . .

But how about if you are a woman? Two University of Georgia psychologists wondered about that, and studied the SAT scores and family status of 1,811 college freshmen, 848 of them women and 963 men. Their particular interest was in finding the intellectual impact of having many younger brothers and sisters. For male students, their finding was consistent with the preceding study of Dutch men: The larger the number of younger siblings, the lower their probable SAT scores. But for women students, the result was the opposite: The larger the number of younger siblings, the higher the probable SAT scores. Why? The speculation of the researchers is that older girls in a family are more likely than older boys to take on a caretaking role which often involves serving as a teacher of the younger children. [Paulhus, Shaffer]

But the news, if you are a woman, is not all good. As family size increases, later-borns, boys and girls alike, tend to get increasingly less warm and nurturing treatment by their parents. But if you were a later-born girl—and this applies to girls only—the later you came, the more you were likely to feel increased hostile psychological control by your parents. That is because, speculate the researchers, the culture requires that girls be more closely supervised, and the larger the family the more difficult that supervision becomes. [Nuttall, Nuttall]

The larger your family is and the earlier your position in the birth order, especially if you are the firstborn, the more likely you are as an adult to be a Type A personality, making you more prone to heart attacks. (See Chapter 6, "Your 'Type A' Anxiety.") [Strube, Ota]

If you are the firstborn in a family with eight or more offspring, you have a high advantage over all the others in becoming a creative writer. But if you have only one to six brothers and sisters, being the oldest does not give you any particular advantage. This was determined by a survey of the biographies of 286 prominent creative writers born between 1547 and 1932. [Joubert]

You were the first child born in your family:

You are more likely than your sisters and brothers to lean toward "organizing and controlling" the behavior of others—in other words, acting bossy. [National Institute of Mental Health Science Report]

You tend to have higher self-esteem than most who are later-born, and that is especially so if you are a woman. If you are a woman, your self-esteem is especially bolstered if you felt as a child that your father and other close authority figures thought highly of you. If you are a man, you got that special boost if you felt that close peers—classmates, friends, cousins—held you in high esteem. [Schwab, Lundgren]

You probably got better grades in school than your younger sister or brother, especially if your mother valued high achievement. [Gorman]

You are considerably less likely than one of your younger sisters or brothers to win a popularity contest or election. [Cornoldi, Fattori]

If you also have a sister or brother less than three years younger than yourself, you have probably always shown a greater than usual need for company, sympathy, and help from peers and people of higher status than your own, and you continue to do so in your adult life. This thirst for support from others is even greater the closer in age your sister or brother is to you. [Cornoldi, Fattori]

You've probably heard that you'll be happier married to a later-born than to another firstborn. Many "experts" have long believed so. Now, finally comes the word from a series of studies: The birth order of mates, researchers agree, probably has some mysterious bearing on how marriages work out. But they now know with greater certainty than ever before that they don't know what it is. [Pinsky]

You are a firstborn boy:

If you and your younger brothers were to take a test measuring "social and total adjustment," you would probably score higher than they would. But if you and your younger sisters were to take the same test, their scores might land anywhere. Girls' adjustment appears unrelated to their birth order. [Corsello]

. . .

You tend to be far more interested in job security and benefits than your younger brothers and sisters. [Stenger]

You have probably felt (and openly complained) that your parents came down harder on you than on the secondborn and thirdborn in your family. (But if you are a firstborn girl, you probably did not feel treated differently than the younger children.) [Corsello]

You are likely to have a less favorable attitude than other men toward women as managers in business. [Beutell]

You are a firstborn girl:

If you have a brother less than two years younger than yourself, the chances are better than average that you're trustworthy, loyal, helpful, kind, cheerful, brave, and reverent (no kidding, that's the list reported in the study) and that you're successful in public activities (meetings, parties, etc.). That's the good news. The bad news is that if you also have one or more younger sisters, you're probably inclined to be more quarrelsome, critical, demanding (especially about your rights), jealous, and competitive than they are. [National Institute of Mental Health]

If you are now of college age, you prefer to have significantly fewer children than later-born women do. The apparent reason is that you have a stronger sense of moral responsibility than later-borns do, and you feel that fewer children contribute to the general good. [Joesting, Joesting]

If you are now an adolescent, you are significantly more likely than other teenagers to attempt suicide. This is especially true if you have lost your father. [Cantor]

You were your family's only child:

You are likely to score higher on intelligence tests than do non-onlies from comparable families. You are also likely to have higher academic aspirations, go farther in school, and hold more prestigious jobs. [Falbo]

You know that you have long been assumed to lean toward selfishness, loneliness, and maladjustment. A cluster of recent family studies, however, shows that if you're an "only" you show the same range of happiness, popularity, and physical health as others. [Falbo]

As a child you were considerably more likely than other children to create imaginary playmates. (While boys and girls among "onlies" are equally likely to invent imaginary friends, boys typically create only boy playmates; girls create playmates of both genders—and more of them.) Moreover, if you did create imaginary playmates, you tended to be a leader of others in real play, and more of a "self-starter" than most. [Manosevitz, Prentice, Wilson]

You are much more likely than people who have brothers and sisters to make personal decisions instead of going along with group decisions. Also, you tend to have fewer friends and join fewer clubs than other people, but you don't usually think of yourself as unpopular. [Falbo]

You tend to be more trusting than most other people, which this researcher attributes to your not having brothers and sisters whose interests clashed with yours. In addition, you got your parents' concentrated help and nurturance, which led to your expectation that others would be good to you. [Falbo; Sutton-Smith, Rosenberg]

You are more likely than people with brothers and sisters to have experienced the divorce of your parents or the death of one of them. [U.S. Bureau of Census]

You are a firstborn or an "only":

If you still doubt that that fact influences your personality, you might want to try explaining this: Out of the first twenty-three astronauts who flew on the earliest space missions, twenty-one were either firstborn or "only" children. [National Institutes of Health]

You are likely to have gone further in your education, including college attendance, than most people who are later-born. This is the most consistent finding in all of the birth-order research. [Adams]

You are more likely than later-borns to want to have another person accompany you when you're going to the dentist, the hospital emergency room, or anticipating some other discomfort. This suggests your heightened need for "affiliation" with others. [Schachter]

The way people regard you often governs the way you behave. All right then, here is how people have a tendency to regard you:

A pool of 275 adults—half of them parents of preschool children, the rest childless—were asked to choose adjectives that best described what oldest children, "only" children, and youngest children were like. Oldests were seen as obedient, responsible, outgoing, self-confident, and unspoiled. "Onlies" were described as academically oriented, self-centered, and spoiled. Youngests won marks as likable, sociable, disobedient, and nonacademic. [Baskett]

You were the second child born in your family:

If your mother valued high achievement (thus probably contributing to superior school grades for the firstborn in your family, as described above), the chances are you didn't do as well in school as your older brother or sister. Indeed, the author of this study speculates that your mother may be the cause of your lower grades, a common but not altogether understood reaction of the secondborn to mother's pressure on the firstborn. He determined this in a study of mothers of fifty-six firstborn and forty-eight secondborn unrelated boys in grades five through eight. All were of close to average intelligence from predominantly upper middle-class two- and three-child families. [Gorman]

If you are also a high-achievement woman, you are more likely to have a big sister than a big brother. [Berger]

You are the youngest in your family:

As a child, you were probably selected more frequently by others as a playmate or class seatmate. According to this study of 1,750 children in grades three, four, five, and six, your popularity was followed, in order, by onlies, the second of two children, second of more than two, first-borns, and least of all, others between the oldest and youngest of a family's children. The finding was consistent across all boundaries of age, sex, and racial/ethnic backgrounds (black, Mexican-American, and white). Also, your teacher probably considered you more sociable than others who were earlier-borns. [Miller, Maruyama]

You are a man with one or more sisters:

You attach higher importance to getting a job of high status and responsibility than do men who have only brothers. [Stenger]

You are a man with an older sister, or a woman with an older brother:

You are more likely than others to look and feel self-confident and suave when you first meet a member of the opposite sex. [Ickes, Turner]

You are a twin:

It's perfectly obvious, of course, that you and your twin are similar in many ways, and you assume (as most of the world does) that much of that similarity is because you grew up in the same home, were treated like twins and made to feel like twins. So you constantly reacted like twins.

But don't be so sure, says Thomas J. Bouchard, Jr., director of the University of Minnesota Center for Twin and Adoption Research. Bouchard's center has collected detailed questionnaires and psychological tests of fifty pairs of identical twins who grew up in separate homes, usually not even knowing each other, as well as twenty-five pairs of fraternal twins, and matched them against comparison groups of twins who were reared together. Among those identical twins who knew nothing about each other, Bouchard's research discovered similarities "you would never think of looking at if you were going to study the genetics of behavior." In posture and expressive style alone, he says, "we were amazed at the similarity. It's probably the feature of the study that's grabbed us the most." The identical twins, though uninfluenced by one another, frequently resembled each other strikingly in mannerisms, gestures, habits, speed and rhythms of speech, and even in styles of jokes.

Coincidences that almost anyone would attribute to accident turned up among them too often for reasonable explanation. One pair of brothers who had never previously met finally did so (in England). They were wearing identical shirts, haircuts, beards, and wire-rimmed glasses. Another pair, also meeting for the first time, had in their toilet-articles cases the same brand of cologne and a

Swedish brand of toothpaste. One pair were both volunteer fire-fighters, another were deputy sheriffs; two brothers had almost identical workshops in their distant basements, and two sisters had strikingly similar kitchen layouts. One pair of twins shared a fear of water and had devised to cope with it in the same unusual way: backing into the ocean until they were up to their knees. One twin had been reared by his natural impoverished family; the other by a family in the "good solid upper-middle-class." Both are considered antisocial personalities; both suffer from lack of impulse control, and both have criminal histories. Twin sisters who grew up separately each have a son who won a statewide mathematics contest, one in Wyoming, the other in Texas. A colleague of Bouchard's, Auke Tellegen, devised a personality test to measure similarities and differences in twins reared apart, measuring such tendencies as "social closeness" and "harm avoidance." One such trait, "traditionalism"—conservatism, respect for authority—came out clearly influenced by genes, as were about ten other personality traits. [Bouchard]

YOU AND YOUR PET

Only from pedestrians on the sidewalks of New York do we sometimes hear the protest that America is overrun by dogs. But the numbers are jolting evidence that perhaps we are: At last estimate, in the early 1980s, 40 million dogs were watching for the mail carrier, one for every six human beings, more than half of the households in the English speaking world. Good Lord! Has anyone counted the cats? In fact, yes: 23 million American households own cats.

We know from fossil remains that humans made dogs their companions more than twelve thousand years ago; cats, at least six thousand years ago. Pets have been beloved in the newspapers, movies, and children's stories—but not in science. Researchers have often reported on pet animals as carriers of diseases and hazards to public health. But nobody paid attention to pets as a *measurable* tonic for the human spirit until two English researchers, R. A. Mugford and J. G. M'Comisky, in 1975, distributed caged birds to twelve presumably lonely pensioners, and distributed plants to an equal number. After three months, physical examinations and mood questionnaires revealed that consistently the bird owners showed an improvement in attitudes toward other people and toward their own mental health, while plant owners did not. In another study five years later, patients admitted to a hospital for heart disease were more likely to be alive one year after their discharge if they owned a pet than if they didn't. In fact, ownership of a pet was stronger than any other predictor. The finding held firmly whether the patient was rich or poor, married or single, or with or without access to other friends and social support. And a recent study by the same team (Erika Friedmann and a group that included James J. Lynch, the same psychologist who demonstrated that talking raises blood pressure [see Chapter 1, "What Your Manner of Speech Says"]) showed that children engaged in a mildly stressful task, reading, had a lower blood pressure and heart rate if a friendly dog was in the room than if one was not.

After a study found that impatient patients in the waiting rooms of doctors and dentists relax more in the presence of fish tanks, a company called The Candle Corporation began selling videotapes of fish tanks complete with sound effects. Sales appeal: The tanks never had to be cleaned.

Some people describe their pets as family members. Odd? Neurotic? One researcher, R. L. Wille, found that such "odd-balls" score significantly higher than most in a standard measure called the Purpose in Life Test and the Health Opinion Survey. Wille concluded that pet ownership of a certain intensity of attachment contributed concretely to the health and well being of the pet owner. Actually, fully 99 percent of dog owners in a study of five hundred owners of pets considered the dog to be a family member. In 56 percent of their families, the dog was allowed to sleep on the bed of one of the human members; 64 percent fed the dog tidbits from the table; 86 percent shared their snacks with the dog; and 54 percent celebrated the dog's birthday. (Those findings have been esoterically criticized, however, because the researcher, V. L. Voith, used a "select" population, "all being clients at a major veterinary referral center, and there is no way to know if her respondents belonged to functional or dysfunctional families.") Another study showed that dog ownership is likely to contribute to a strong sense of self, as measured by the Ego Strength Scale of the widely used Minnesota Multiphasic Personality Inventory (MMPI).

LOOK YOURSELF UP

You own a horse, a snake, or a bird:

So you want to know if your choice says something about who you are? It does.

A research team located twenty-five male and twenty-five female owners of those pets and gave them a personality test called the Adjective Check List as well as another questionnaire designed for this study.

If you are a horse owner, whether male or female, you tend to be assertive and introspective, but low in warmth and as a nurturer of others. If you are male and a horse owner, you tend to be aggressive and bossy; if you are female, you are probably easygoing and nonaggressive.

If you own a snake, you are apt to be a breaker of the rules of conventionality, and a seeker of novelty.

If you own a bird, you tend to be socially outgoing and expressive. If you are female, you have something in common with male horse owners: You're bossy. [Kidd, Kelley, Kidd]

CHAPTER
*6*_____

Your Personality Type

*The characteristics of what is male and female
can only be demonstrated in anatomy,
and not in psychology.*

SIGMUND FREUD (1856–1939),
CIVILIZATION AND ITS DISCONTENTS

WHAT IS MASCULINE? WHAT IS FEMININE?

The book *Real Men Don't Eat Quiche* was a big hit, at least in part, because its title touched a nerve. In fact, two nerves. First, the preposterous assertion twitched our funnybones. Second, statements about what real men do, or what real women do, worry us—almost all of us, men and women alike. They pry open those ancient, troubling, slippery questions:

- What is a real man?
- What is a real woman?
- What is masculine? What is feminine?
- And most important: Do I measure up?

Who is the expert anyway who first convinced us to expect that throwing a ball gracefully is a talent that belongs only to men? Who decided that only women have a license to talk from the bottom of the heart, and to weep tears doing it? And who gave whomever it was the right to decide?

All those questions had long hung in the air when Sandra Bem, a Stanford University psychologist, began exploring some striking new questions about "real men" and "real women" and the "desirable" traits for each. But before posing her questions she first had to confirm the presumed answers to old ones: What traits are habitually perceived as "feminine," and what others as "masculine"? And no matter how she or anyone else felt emotionally about male and female stereotypes, she had to cope with the answers factually, impersonally, and fairly.

So first she had to decide: Who decides? Since these were "cultural" decisions, Dr. Bem let *us,* the members of the culture, set the groundwork for her study. She drew up a long, far-ranging list of two hundred adjectives—like *gentle, leaderlike, forceful, sensitive, self-sufficient, expressive*—and she asked representative panels of American women and men to rate, on a seven-point scale, the desirability of each quality for a woman and for a man. Also she asked the panelists to rate each trait for its "social desirability," independently of whether it was thought masculine or feminine. By checking off the long list, the panelist—or, in a polling sense, *we*—named the twenty qualities rated as most "desirable" for each sex. In addition, Dr. Bem wound up with still another twenty terms from the "social desirability" checkmarks, that denoted "good," "bad," or neutral behaviors that didn't differentiate between men and women. These helped determine the level of respect most of us hold for the traits we consider masculine and/or feminine.

For traits perceived as *feminine,* Bem's panels (we) chose items like *warm, understanding, compassionate, gentle, sensitive to feel-*

ings, neat, able to express tenderness, dependent, subjective, interested in art and books.

As masculine traits the panels voted items like aggressive, dominant, assertive, independent, objective, competitive, decisive, adventurous, ambitious, acting as a leader.

Another important outcome of panel choices was that feminity was notably marked by an absence of those traits perceived as masculine; and, conversely, "real men" were relatively free of those traits voted as feminine.

Those starting-point results probably surprised nobody, including Dr. Bem.

Next she developed a scale called the Bem Sex-Role Inventory (BSRI) consisting of three subscales. It asked an individual subject to answer a series of questions about personal preferences and tendencies. Based on the previous survey, the Inventory would score that person for perceived traits of femininity, masculinity, and the "social desirability" of that individual's traits. Dr. Bem administered her newly-devised BSRI to large numbers of subjects.

In beginning to do so, Dr. Bem proposed a hypothesis: True, the stereotypes of "what is feminine" and "what is masculine" may be opposite from one another. But in reality, any particular person rating high in either cluster of traits may also possess traits from the other. For example, society seems to have decided that thinking with precise logic is "masculine"; that revealing emotions is "feminine." Yet a male of perfectly sound manhood who scores high as masculine may wear his heart on his sleeve; a woman may have the fullest dance card at the ball, yet be a math or gene-splicing whiz.

Scores soon confirmed the hypothesis. While femininity and masculinity are usually seen as mutually exclusive opposites, they are actually two independent dimensions. They are not either/or polarities. In fact, significant numbers of people do score high in both dimensions. Moreover, those who come out high in both frequently are measured especially high in emotional well-being and ability to adjust to people and events.

The issue of "Who's In Control Here?," discussed in a later section, turns out to be a major running theme that spreads into this area of life, too. Dr. Bem found that a person who scores high in masculine traits has an increased likelihood of feeling largely in control of the events of her or his life (I-Control-Me), regardless of whether that person is a man or woman. On the other hand, a high score in feminine traits gives no statistical clue as to whether the person feels in control of what happens.

Fortified by those findings, Dr. Bem created a label for people scoring high on both feminine and masculine scales. She calls them psychologically *androgynous*. Her concept of androgyny has since taken deep root in psychological research. The word, however, is often misused or misconstrued to connote homosexual tendencies. Bem's concept seems to puzzle and confuse many people, sometimes even embarrass them. High scores (or low scores) in "masculine" or "feminine" traits of personality have nothing necessarily to do with one's appearance, or sex appeal, or sexual orientation or preference. And to go a step further, to be high in both in no way suggests that a person is "unisexual" or bisexual. Therefore I am substituting for androgyny a more direct term of my own, *high-in-both*, to denote a person who scores high on both masculine and feminine scales.

If scoring high in masculine or feminine personality traits—or both—is not necessarily related to whether you are a man or a woman, which traits are better to have? Feminine or masculine? The best way to an answer is to read the list of traits associated with each label, and ask yourself which ones *you* value most. If you have a strong combination of both—if you're a *high-in-both*—you are considerably more apt to like yourself, as the first research finding listed below shows. And that is clearly one of the direct paths to a happier life.

LOOK YOURSELF UP

You are either a woman or a man and you score high in both masculine and feminine traits:

You are more likely to enjoy a high level of self-esteem and personal adjustment than most other people—whether *they* are men or women, and whether they score high as feminine or high as masculine, or not high as either.

If you rank high in masculine but not in feminine traits, whether you are a man or a woman your strong masculine traits are likely to be accompanied by higher-than-average self-esteem.

If you are a man and you rank high in femininity but not in masculinity, your strong feminine traits do not have any predictable effect on your self-esteem.

How to interpret all that? Apparently most of us—including most women—have been deeply conditioned to value traits thought of as masculine more highly than we value feminine traits—no matter in whom they appear, and including when they appear in ourselves. [Orlofsky, Windle]

If you live in Sweden, your personal traits would be judged masculine or feminine by people around you just about the same as they would in the United States, according to a study designed to verify whether the American-born Bem Scale is valid for Swedish conditions. [Carlsson, Magnusson; Swedish study]

If you are married and both you and your spouse rate high in feminine traits, an Australian study suggests you are likely to have a far happier marriage than if either one of you rates low in feminine traits. The key to long-term marital happiness appears to be the male partner's higher-than-average ability to *nurture*—to respond sensitively and give emotional support. According to the stereotypes, nurturing is listed as a "feminine" characteristic. [Antill; Australian study]

You are a "high-in-both" woman:

While you show a high level of emotional expressiveness (considered a feminine trait), you probably also rank with the highest of female groups—and male groups, for that matter—in assertiveness (considered a masculine trait). [Orlofsky, Windle]

Your mother is more likely than most of her contemporary women to have held a paying job while you were attending grades one to eight. Also both your parents are more likely than most to have emphasized self-reliance and achievement in your upbringing. [De Fronzo, Boudreau]

If the masculine side of your Bem score is high, you are more likely than women with lower scores to favor passage of the Equal Rights Amendment. Also you are more likely than others to take action toward passing ERA. [Gibb, Lambirth]

You are a "high-in-both" man:

You are only moderately assertive compared to men who rack up especially high masculinity scores. Among men, however, you probably rank very high as emotionally expressive. [Orlofsky, Windle]

You are more likely than most men to have grown up emotionally close to your mother (although that does not mean that you might not also have identified closely with your father).

Also, you are considerably more likely than a masculine-only man to favor assistance for the aged, expansion of opportunities for the poor, more help from rich nations to poor nations, and increased liberalism in economics and politics. [De Fronzo, Boudreau]

If the masculine side of your Bem score is high, you are more likely than lower-scoring men to oppose passage of the Equal Rights Amendment. Also you are more likely to take action against ERA. [Gibb, Lambirth]

FEMININITY AND FEMINISM

Before leaving this subject, there's one additional question that may have hooked your curiosity—and that research has tried to answer.

How well did the age-old conceptions of masculine and feminine traits withstand the rise of the women's movement that started in the mid-1960s and threw traditional sex roles into a state of flux?

A group of New England researchers, led by Paul S. Rosenkrantz of the College of the Holy Cross and Inge and Donald Broverman of Worcester State Hospital, suspected, not surprisingly, that the shift in attitudes might affect responses to earlier sex-role scales. So they devised a "modern" questionnaire to try to detect and measure revised views of what was "feminine" and "masculine." They surveyed almost a thousand subjects, culled the results of many other studies, and in 1972 published the following broad conclusions. (If you find these results disagreeable, as many do, please remember they are presented here neither to please nor upset, but to report on what one group of researchers, presumably sympathetic to the women's revolution, found in one study.)

• A "strong consensus" (the researchers' words) about masculine and feminine characteristics clearly persisted through that historic period. The mass perceptions held firm despite the sex, age, religion, marital status, or educational level of those surveyed.

• Masculine characteristics were more often rated "socially desirable" than feminine characteristics, regardless of whether men or women did the rating. The desirable traits ascribed to men appeared to cluster in what might be generalized as qualities of *competence* (the tendencies toward being independent, objective, active, competitive, logical, skilled in business, worldly, adventurous, able to make decisions easily, self-confident, ambitious, acting as a leader). The stereotypical woman's traits considered desirable clustered as general qualities of *warmth* and *expressiveness* (gentle, sensitive to the feelings of others, tactful, religious, neat, quiet, interested in art and literature, able to express tender feelings, dependent, subjective, passive, noncompetitive, nonlogical).

• The idealized man is marked by an *absence* of the admired feminine traits, and the idealized woman is marked by an *absence* of the admired masculine traits.

• While most respondents agreed on the traditional images of proper femininity and masculinity, *few rated themselves as measuring up*. Most women and men rated themselves as significantly less feminine or masculine than their stereotypical perceptions. [Broverman, Vogel, Broverman, Clarkson, Rosenkrantz]

THE EXTROVERT AND THE INTROVERT IN YOU

Most people have heard the terms *extrovert* and *introvert*, and know at least in broad terms what they mean. These two personality types are somewhat opposite in their way of meeting life, therefore in their very experience of it. Some psychologists heretofore have thought of the line between extroverts and introverts as the Great Divide between the styles of human personality. By definition, an extrovert is likely to be sociable, needs people to talk to, craves excitement, and acts impulsively. An introvert maintains a reserve and distance from others, doesn't like high stimulation or surprises, and stays "properly serious" about everyday life.

Studies by Hans J. Eysenck of London University, father of the widely accepted scale that distinguishes introverts from extroverts, show that extroverts, notably more than introverts, are lured by rewards and prizes, and are tempted to go for them even when it's risky to do so. They tend to minimize the threatened price of losing. The extrovert feels a relatively high degree of *power to control results of what they undertake*, thus making potential rewards more likely. In contrast, introverts are more interested in avoiding risks and punishment than in winning rewards. They tend to *feel relatively powerless to control outcomes*.

LOOK YOURSELF UP

You are an extrovert:

Your capacity as an extrovert for tolerating, even enjoying, stimulation and excitement may be genetically programmed in your brain, specifically in a part called the reticular activating system. You are lifted to high levels of excitement by the same conditions of stimulation that may only mildly stimulate an introvert.

You are probably less disturbed than an introvert at encountering disagreements with others. In evaluating other people, you recall more positive information than introverts do, thus you rate them higher. You enjoy competition, whether in games or real-life situations, more than introverts do. In social situations, you are far less inclined than the introvert to instantly recall previous social terrors that you have experienced. So, as a plunger toward reward, you take social gambles with relative confidence.

The introvert, in contrast, habitually shrinks back in the face of social risk. [Graziano, Feldesman, Rahe, in a review of research]

You are less likely than an introvert to be religious. [Francis, Pearson, Carter, Kay; British study]

You are more likely than an introvert to support capital punishment, especially if you're a man. This study buttresses findings by others that as an extrovert you're likely to lean toward tough-mindedness. [McKelvie, Daoussis; Canadian study]

Although it may appear to contradict the last two findings, you are more likely than an introvert to be a social and political radical. This tendency is probably related to your higher willingness to take risks. [Furnham]

. . .

If you are young and male as well as an extrovert, you are unusually prone to automobile accidents. The researchers attribute their finding to the extrovert's generally reduced vigilance and caution. [Smith, Kirkham; Australian study]

Suppose you are taking a psychological test (namely, the Eysenck Personality Inventory) and you are asked, "Do you mind filling in this questionnaire?" As an extrovert you are considerably more likely than an introvert to answer "No." Those who answer "yes" are not only more probable introverts, but are likely to score higher than most on the same test in the section that measures tendency toward neuroticism and psychoticism. [Rim; Israeli study]

You are more likely than an introvert to participate as a subject in a psychology experiment. [Zuckerman]

YOUR "TYPE A" ANXIETY

The clearest way to type what is called "Type A" is to tell how its discoverers discovered it.

In the late 1950s in California, a medical secretary informed her employers, Drs. Meyer Friedman and Ray Rosenman, both cardiologists, that they needed new waiting-room chairs. The old ones were worn down and, oddly, only on their front edges.

The doctors knew, as cardiologists do, that many heart patients in a sense are misnamed, because they are noticeably *im*patient. They tend to arrive on the minute for their appointments, then can scarcely wait to get out, always having some urgent thing to do next. In the examining room, they fidget and twitch, nod nervously while listening to the doctor (or *not* listening, the doctor often feels), interrupting explanations, and completing the doctors' sentences for them. The waiting-room furniture was tell-taling an apt diagnostic truth about many cardiac patients: They *live on the edge of their chairs*—literally.

Drs. Friedman and Rosenman began calling this behavioral syndrome "the hurry sickness." Later, they renamed it the "Type A behavior pattern." It contained attitude combinations of "ambitiousness, aggressiveness, competitiveness, and impatience," and observable behaviors that included "muscle tenseness, alertness, rapid and emphatic speech," and an accelerated living pace; also, often, the emotions of irritation, hostility, and anger. According to a list of typical behaviors compiled by Jane E. Brody, the health writer, a Type A:

- Often tries to do two things at once.
- Walks fast, eats fast, leaves the table right after eating.
- Has trouble just sitting and doing nothing.
- Blinks or moves eyes rapidly and/or sucks air while speaking.
- Often jiggles a knee or taps fingers.
- Interrupts the speech of others habitually.
- Talks with hands or pounds fist for emphasis.
- Sighs deeply, especially when talking about a frustrating topic.
- Often bumps into or trips over objects while moving rapidly.
- Gets irritated when kept waiting for any reason.
- Is suspicious of other people's motives.
- Plays to win, even in games with children.
- Shows signs of rage when describing past events that caused anger.
- Has periodic bulging of eyes, showing white above and below pupils.

(Type B people—all those substantially free of the dominant symptoms of being Type A—are "more relaxed, easygoing, readily satisfied," not likely driven by "any habitual need for achievement and acquisition.")

After the Friedman-Rosenman typing of Type A, a parade of studies elaborated a connection between Type A behavior and coronary heart disease. Long-term studies of large samples of subjects showed that:

- A Type A man or woman is more than twice as likely as a Type B to die prematurely from heart disease;
- An extreme Type A is more likely than a mild Type A to have heart disease;
- A Type A who survives a first heart attack is more likely to have a second one than a Type B who has had a first heart attack; and
- A Type A's heart attack is likely to be more severe than a Type B's.

LOOK YOURSELF UP

You are a Type A:

Around the clock, you probably invest more of your energy, attention, and thinking in your job, or in other work activities, than the average Type B does. [Chesney, Rosenman]

You probably work more hours per week and travel more days per year than the average Type B. [Howard, Cunningham]

If you are discussing a controversial subject (such as "Should merit pay be installed for teachers?" or "Should abortion be made illegal?"), far more frequently than most people you state phrases or sentences that defend, support, or advance your own belief or position ("pro-self"). Also, you more frequently state phrases or sentences that directly contradict, dismiss, or otherwise belittle your adversary's belief-defending argument ("anti-other"). This finding, say the researchers, supports previous studies suggesting that Type A people lean markedly toward competitiveness, hostility, dominance, and control of others. [Yarnold, Mueser, Grimm]

Your Type A tendency to hostility may pull you toward physical aggression. In this experiment, subjects who were pronounced Type A's and Type B's, all of whom were undergraduate males, donned instruments that measured pulse rates and blood pressure. Then the researcher had confederates make critical comments or accusations that gratuitously angered half of the subjects, until those subjects recorded measurable levels of anger. Next, all the subjects were instructed in administering a test to other research confederates who had been falsely introduced to them as subjects. They were instructed in how to bestow rewards (points toward cash) or punishments (negative points toward a painful screech in their headphones) as responses for correct and incorrect answers. Of those subjects who had not been insulted and angered consistently, Type A's gave more punishment points than Type B's gave. Of those who had been angered, both Type A and Type B subjects inflicted the same degrees of punishment. [Holmes, Will]

You are reluctant to give up control, even when doing so may demonstrably help your cause. ("Control" in this sense means dominance over another person or a task.)

In this experiment, Type A and Type B undergraduate males were randomly assigned to partnership teams in playing a blinking-lights reaction-time game. Each partner was periodically "informed" of how well he was doing compared with the other partner (the reports had no relationship to the truth). Those who had been identified as Type A's (by a separate test, its results unknown to the experimenters) resisted relinquishing their turn or giving up control to a "superior" partner, even though doing so would probably have helped win the game and a valuable prize. [Strube, Werner]

If you and a Type B both are scheduled for an appointment at the same time in the same place, you are likely to show up first. [Gastorf]

You are a Type A woman:

You probably have a better and more demanding job than a Type B woman. If you are married, you probably feel less healthy than a Type B woman. [Kelly, Houston]

If you are engaged in a college courtship, and if the relationship is fairly new, there's merely a 45 percent chance you'll still be dating him six months after it began. But if you're Type B, you feel more committed to the relationship and there's an 83 percent chance. "It may be," says psychologist Michael J. Strube of Washington University, who studied thirty-one college couples, "that female Type A behavior is particularly threatening early in the relationship because it violates the traditional expectations that serve to guide partners who don't know each other well. As couples proceed in the relationship they have to find effective ways to deal with conflict." [Arffa, Strube]

Not Type "A", But Type "I"?—Or Type "Me"?

An important vein of research suggests that maybe the cardiac-killer is not Type A at all, but something hiding within it, smaller and finer.

In 1974, a team at the University of Wisconsin was doing a study of anger and physiological reactions. Using as subjects fifty-nine students divided between Type A and Type B, they stumbled on something unexpected. In their structured interview, when a student frequently said "I," "me," "my," or "mine," his or her blood pressure shot up. The experimenters then discovered that Type A's used those words of self-reference twice as often as non-A's. More striking still, Type A's referred to themselves even more often than usual when they were stimulated to anger—and their blood pressure soared to levels of hypertension. This was not true of Type B subjects.

Pursuing this evidence, the University of Wisconsin team interviewed 150 men who had checked into a hospital for an angiogram to diagnose blocked arteries (a common companion of prolonged high blood pressure). Sure enough, those who said "I" and "me" and other self-references more often than usual had more extensively blocked arteries than those who didn't.

A Yale psychologist, Lynda Powell, while still a graduate student at Stanford, soon refined the Wisconsin discovery. Looking to find which of forty-nine conditions—physical as well as psychological—might foreshadow a second heart attack in men, she found that the strongest predictor was a high rating of observed emotional intensity in responding to her structured interview questions. The second strongest was hidden in the way men answered the question, "About what do you feel insecure?" The more often the men used the words "I" and "me," in answering, the more likely these men were to have a second heart attack. A combination of the two elements was a still better predictor than either one alone. [Fischman]

(Important additional information on intense talkers and heart disease may be found in "What Your Manner of Speech Says," in Chapter 1.)

CAN TYPE A'S BE CURED—OR AT LEAST HELPED?

A three-year study of eight hundred men who had suffered heart attacks has shown that psychological counseling to reduce the evidences of Type A behavior can cut in half the chances of a second attack.

Of that sizeable group studied, some were given only standard therapeutic advice about diet and exercise. Of those, 19 percent had a recurrent attack in the three-year study period. Of those who also were given psychological counseling, only 9 percent had a second attack. The counseling resulted in a far greater protective effect than that achieved by a national cholesterol-lowering study as well as in *any other* coronary intervention project up to the time of this study, which was completed in 1984.

The finding is all the more remarkable because it was directed by Dr. Meyer Friedman, the original "typer" of Type A—who is not a psychiatrist, but a cardiologist, and thus might be expected by training to lean toward medicinal or surgical solutions for heart problems.

Some of the new habits coaxed upon Type A's to replace their old behaviors were:

- Smile at people in the street.
- Take fifteen minutes alone and do nothing but listen to music.
- Show interest in your children's schoolwork—not their grades.
- Admit to being wrong—even if you're not.
- Listen to someone talk without letting your mind skip to something else, and don't say anything until they're done.
- Let someone's minor error slip by without harping on it.
- Play a game and plan to lose.
- Laugh at yourself.
- Avoid other angry Type A's.
- Remind yourself daily that life by its nature is unfinished.

[Brody]

WHO'S IN CONTROL HERE?

Like almost everyone else, psychologists sometimes claim that the world divides basically into two types of people. When psychologists make the claim, however, they usually have a test to prove it. We have just seen in the preceding sections of this chapter how they divide us into either feminine or masculine personalities—and can test which each of us is. They divide us into extroverts and introverts—and can test us. Into either optimists or pessimists—and can label us with a test. Into Type A hot reactors or cooler heads—and, yes, they have a test. Their tests are valuable, not only to them, but to us. Each typing they invent can help us make better sense of strange behaviors we see in members of our families, in relatives and friends, in co-workers and bosses—and perchance in ourselves.

There is one little-known two-typing that I suggest may be of greatly underestimated importance in understanding our personalities. In the preface to this book I said it might be "the biggest little-known idea in all of psychology."

In the mid-1960s a University of Connecticut psychologist, Julian B. Rotter, observed that people use two different styles of sentences for describing important events in their lives. The two modes of description separate two essential personality types. The people who use the contrasting kinds of sentences live in contrasting worlds because they actually *experience* the events of their lives in opposite ways.

One group describes an important event—say, an auto accident, a broken relationship, winning an athletic event, a school exam, a personal bankruptcy for unpaid credit cards—as something that happened *to* them, caused by other people or outside forces.

The other group describes personal events in "I did" terms, suggesting that the happening was under their own control, wholly or in part. We know little or nothing of what caused either group to get that way, but each of these ways of thinking—of *experiencing*—leads to remarkably different life consequences. Before looking at those different consequences, we need to look at how we have been hampered by language.

Rotter assigned a label to each style. The first group of people, he said, has an *external locus of control*, because they imagine that control of their lives is located mainly with some force outside themselves. The second group is said to have an *internal locus of control*; they are mostly "in charge" of their lives most of the time.

Other scholars have been drawn to similar ideas, have tilted them in different ways to give off different reflections, and they have given them different brand names: *personal efficacy, hardy personality, explanatory style, learned optimism, learned helplessness*, and more. Those names are unfortunate. While they have a ring of importance and elevation that impresses scientific peers, their meanings don't easily click into place in the brain. Being nondescriptive abstractions, they hide from us, the studied, what scholars are learning about our personalities. But perhaps worse than that, those vague, imprecise, ambiguous labels may keep the scholars themselves somewhat in the dark about the full implications of the work of the others. The language of those high-flown labels obfuscates and conceals more successfully than it communicates.

So I'm going to take a liberty and assign a single and simpler pair of names to the personality types—not only Rotter's labels for them, but those of the others who have done significant work exploring roughly the same concepts. Those "external locus of control" and "internal locus of control" personalities shall hereinafter be known as *"They*-Control-Me's" and *"I*-Control-Me's."

How do you tell an I-Control-Me from a They-Control-Me? One way is simply to listen to them talk, particularly to the phrases and sentence structure with which they explain the *causes* of events in their lives. People who consistently ascribe responsibility for happenings to *them* or *they*, or to "luck," or to the "system," or who portray themselves with suspicious frequency as *victims of what others do to them* are all hinting clearly that they feel as if their lives are driven primarily by outside "forces."

Rotter devised a more precise way to separate I-Control-Me's from They-Control-Me's. He has people tally answers on a simple psychological test called the Rotter Internal-External Scale. The Rotter Scale presents a long list of belief statements and asks subjects to mark that they "agree" or "disagree" with each. The belief statements go like these:

> Who gets to be the boss often depends on who was lucky enough to be in the right place first.
> I have often found that what is going to happen will happen.
> Sometimes I can't understand how teachers arrive at the grades they give.
> In the long run people get the respect they deserve in this world.
> This world is run by the few people in power, and there is not much the little guy can do about it.

A consistent pattern of answers in the Rotter Scale tends to nail a subject into one of the two polar types. By 1974, however, another psychologist, Barry E. Collins of UCLA, saw deeper possibilities in the test. He concluded that by grouping Rotter's questions into *subtypes* and tallying subtype answers, the same test could be used to separate and explain us more finely. They-Control-Me's may be broadly similar in their feelings of relative powerlessness, but they seem to get there for different reasons. Collins discovered that They-Control-Me's tend to explain their feelings through one of four separate underlying beliefs:

(1) The world is difficult, or
(2) The world is unjust, or
(3) The world is governed by luck, or
(4) The world is politically unresponsive.

Persons who explain the world so differently experience it differently.

Research evidence is mounting that the way a person experiences control has important consequences for physical as well as mental health, and much more. In fact, health can be affected by how much a person *feels* that she or he has a real say over what happens in his or her life, whether the degree of control is real or merely felt. The findings go still further: Broad traits of personality can go hand-in-hand with a person's *desire* for control.

Regarding the last of those, Dr. Jerry Burger, a psychologist at the University of Santa Clara, has developed a questionnaire-test to measure the intensity of a person's *desire* to feel control. He has found that those who score high in *desire* for control also tend to:

• Be high achievers in school,
• Hold opinions more rigidly than others,
• Engage in sex more frequently and report a wider variety of sexual experiences,
• Be more likely to use contraceptives, and choose "more reliable methods, such as pills and diaphragms (while low scorers in desire for control) more often rely on ineffective methods, like withdrawal, douching, guessing whether it's a safe time of month, or nothing at all," and have a higher tendency to fall into depression, especially when they feel that control of events in their lives has slipped away.

While Burger was measuring desire for control, Judith Rodin, a psychologist at Yale, was experimenting to find the effects of *actual* control on elderly residents of a convalescent home, both men and women. For eighteen months these residents were given increased control of simple daily activities normally denied them: choices of their food, hours for permitting their room telephones to ring, and arrangement of room furniture. The residents who were permitted increased control measured in standard psychological tests as happier and more alert than residents in the same home who were not given the same choices. Moreover, those given the increased control had a *50 percent lower mortality rate* over the eighteen-month period of the experiment.

Aged people, of course, are generally more susceptible than others to disease, but Dr. Rodin found evidence (detailed below) that stress resulting from absence of control had effects on the immune system of elderly people. That evidence dovetails with earlier findings that the immune system functioned less well in laboratory rats that suffered from lack of control over the severity or duration of electric shocks. (When a comparable group of rats, given the same total amount of shock, were permitted to learn how to stop the jolts, there was no adverse effect on their immune system.)

The They-Control-Me personality, having surrendered to the *felt* power of external forces, therefore *feels* as helpless as the convalescent-home resident. A person who feels stressed or depressed because of a controlling boss or spouse or parent may respond to the world exactly as the person who only *imagines* that "They" are in control. Thus, a real lack of control and an imagined lack of control may have the same consequences.

Another set of connections between They-Control-Me and I-Control-Me personalities, on the one hand, and physical illness and immunity, on the other, has been established by a University of Chicago graduate student who wrote an unusually bold dissertation. Suzanne C. Ouellette Kobasa, puzzled by ambiguous findings that some people get sick under stress while others seem to stay healthy and even thrive on it, set out to discover whether those who stay healthy have a *definable personality structure* that is different from those who get sick.

For seven years she studied middle-aged managers, both male and female, at the Illinois Bell Telephone Company. She devised questionnaires that helped her map personalities and attitudes, and kept careful track of her subjects' physical health. Sure enough, Kobasa found a clear connection between certain clusters of personality characteristics and the incidence of illnesses. To check it out further, she conducted parallel studies with groups of bus drivers, printers, and lawyers—and the correlation held consistently.

Here is what she found: Whether or not the managers got sick under emotional pressure had no predictable connection to health habits like exercise or diet, nor to family histories of illness. The only predictor she found was a cluster of attitudes, to which Kobasa gave the name *hardiness*. "Hardy" personalities showed high levels of what Kobasa and her thesis supervisor, Salvatore R. Maddi, have come to call "the three C's": Control, Commitment, and positive response to Challenge.

"Hardy persons," wrote Kobasa in the *Journal of Personality and Social Psychology*, "are considered to possess three general characteristics: (a) the *belief that they can control or influence the events of their experience* [italics mine], (b) an ability to feel deeply involved in or committed to the activities of their lives, and (c) the anticipation of change as an exciting challenge to further development."

"For all these reasons," says Kobasa, who soon went on to teach at the City University of New York, the person "is not just a victim of a threatening change but an active determinant of the consequences it brings about."

Clearly, our newly labeled I-Control-Me personality remarkably resembles Kobasa's "hardy" personality. With either label we may be talking about a person on an inside track to superior health and longevity.

Still another prominent psychologist, Martin E. P. Seligman of the University of Pennsylvania, after more than twenty years of exploring a similar research region, has produced yet a different set of labels—and strikingly similar conclusions. Seligman says almost identically what Rotter proposed: The way people *explain* events in their lives—especially bad events, he emphasizes—may be more important than the events themselves. For distinguishing one personality type from another, Seligman introduces the term *explanatory style*.

Sometimes a bad event is clearly outside the victim's control and easily explained: "That truck driver was drunk, crossed into my side of the road, and smashed into my car." But in other instances, reality may be *ambiguous*: "My boss fired me because business was off and he had to cut expenses." Or, based on the same facts the person might say more passively, "He fired me because he didn't like my work, and used expense cutting as an excuse." Or, possibly, another person might conclude from the same circumstances, "He didn't like *me*, and I was doomed in that job no matter what."

The heart of Seligman's personality theory is that when reality is ambiguous, each person has a *characteristic* style of explaining it. Seligman, too, has developed a test—his aimed at measuring explanatory style. He calls it the Attributional Style Questionnaire (ASQ). It describes a series of hypothetical events, some good, some bad.

Subjects taking the test are asked to imagine themselves in each of these situations. Then they are asked to rate, on a scale of 1 to 7, each of a series of statements that explain the probable cause of each event.

Seligman, too, correlated the personality style with measurable mental health. In his first round of trying out the ASQ, Seligman administered it to 143 college students, and then asked them to fill out a short version of the Beck Depression Inventory, a standard test to identify symptoms of clinical depression. Sure enough, students who scored high as They-Control-Me's *also consistently scored as more depressed*.

To make sure the correlation held true for people other than college students, Seligman and his research team gave the same pair of tests to women on welfare, inmates of a maximum security prison, grade school children who gave appearances of depression, college students who did poorly on midterms, and patients hospitalized for depression. Since the first trial run, the pair of tests has been given to almost fifteen thousand subjects, with overwhelming confirmation that an explanatory style of pessimism is a marker of depression.

In contrast, answers akin to an I-Control-Me explanatory style were more accurate than the Scholastic Aptitude Test (SAT) and other conventional methods in helping identify University of Pennsylvania students who got high grades, as well as in spotting insurance salespeople who sell more insurance than average and keep their jobs for a year or more.

Far more significant, perhaps, is that Seligman's "explanatory style," like Rotter's "locus of control" and Kobasa and Maddi's "hardy personality," appears to play a role in a person's physical health, resistance to infectious disease, and length of life. Seligman and a University of Pennsylvania associate, Leslie Kamen, working with Judith Rodin of Yale, produced a link between explanatory style and susceptibility to illness, including cancer. They took blood samples from a group of elderly people, whom they also interviewed about life changes, stresses, and health. The interviews were evaluated for explanatory style. Those measuring as They-Control-Me's also showed a larger percentage of suppressor cells that are believed to inhibit the body's ability to fight the growth of tumors.

Later, Christopher Peterson of the University of Michigan tested 172 students for explanatory style and questioned them at two points in time—one month later and one year later—about how many days they had lost to illness and how many times they had visited a doctor.

He found a "strong correlation" between They-Control-Me explanatory styles and frequency of illnesses.

One month later? One year? How about, say, half a lifetime—or more? To look into that, Seligman formed a partnership with George Valliant, a Dartmouth Medical School psychiatrist who had been tracking the long-term health histories of the Harvard graduating classes of 1939 through 1944, starting with questionnaires he sent them in 1946 asking about their experiences in World War II. Seligman contacted the same group in 1980 for responding to his ASQ. The "preliminary" results, Seligman reports, confirm that explanatory style continues as a reliable predictor of physical health over a twenty- to thirty-five-year period.

"Reliable"? How reliable? As Seligman recently assessed it for an editor of *Psychology Today*, "If a crane falls on you, it doesn't matter what you think. If the magnitude of your cancer is overwhelming, your psychological outlook counts for zero. On the other hand, if your cancer is marginal or if an illness is just beginning, your psychological state may be critical."

Can explanatory style be changed? "If you learned it," asserts Seligman, "you can unlearn it." (See the next chapter, "Can We Change Our Personalities?")

Salvatore Maddi, Kobasa's former advisor at the University of Chicago, not only believes people can learn to develop a "hardy" personality, he now teaches how to do it. The teaching of it works and the results stick, he claims. At Illinois Bell headquarters in Chicago, Maddi has given a fifteen-week course to small groups of men and women in management, one hour at a time. His course encouraged trainees to take charge of events in their lives, become conscious of their success in doing so, and extend their "I-Control-Me" experiences outside of class. Before the course he gave the trainees a new test he devised with Kobasa. When retested at the end, the trainees showed more than a doubling in job satisfaction. Scores for their levels of anxiety, depression, and obsessiveness dropped markedly, and so did some physical symptoms commonly associated with stress, such as headaches and insomnia. Blood pressures dropped as well, from an average of 130/82 to 120/77. A control group of managers who did not take the course showed none of those changes.

When Illinois Bell managers were tested two and six months after Maddi's course, they still scored high on the hardiness scale, even improving slightly. Maddi predicts that the techniques of learned hardiness will become second nature to people who use them regularly.

Participants who resisted the instruction, of course, as well as those of poor attendance, showed little or no improvement in hardiness scores.

Still others besides Rotter, Collins, Burger, Rodin, Kobasa, Maddi, and Seligman have come along with slightly modified concepts and still other brand names, such as *high personal efficacy* for what closely resembles an internal locus of control (and *low personal efficacy* for an external locus). When the political scientists learned of that appealing concept, they further modified the labels. A person who feels she or he can exert influence in a group or community has *political efficacy*. (Those who don't, don't.)

The explanatory styles of I-Control-Me and They-Control-Me, under still other names, have been continual themes of the "human potential movement" that emanated from Northern California starting in the mid-sixties: the Esalen Institute, "self-actualization" seminars, transactional analysis, gestalt therapy, est, the Forum, Insight Transformational Seminars, and still others. Their curricula speak of "taking responsibility" for what happens in your life, a phrase sometimes sadly misconstrued as meaning to take *blame* for what happens. Werner Erhard, creator of est and the Forum, preaches that a person has a choice of being *at cause* (I-Control-Me) or being *at effect* (the victim, the done-to, They-Control-Me). It's an incendiary subject that, for some people, touches their most precious defenses—especially when they hear the suggestion that being an I-Control-Me or a They-Control-Me is largely a matter of *choice*.

But the research evidence mounts that this matter of control— that whether *I* Control Me or *They* Control Me—*is* open to choice, that the techniques of that choice can be taught or self-learned, and that the choice may approach the importance of life and death.

LOOK YOURSELF UP

You generally feel your life is controlled and buffeted about by outside forces and unpredictable events (translation: You are a They-Control-Me type):

As a They-Control-Me, you are apt to fear death (both your own and of people close to you) more than those who feel they control their own lives.

If you also feel that life is governed mostly by luck, you are likely to be fearful of the death of others, but not especially your own.

This series of conclusions was drawn by matching scores on a Rotter Internal-External scale with those on a fear-of-death scale, both tests given to two hundred subjects in four occupation groups: fifty business students, fifty-one college faculty members, forty-three firefighters and fifty-six police officers. (The firefighters showed far stronger fears of their own death than any of the other occupation groups.) [Hunt, Lester, Ashton]

If you visit a game room or amusement arcade, as a They-Control-Me you are slightly more likely than an I-Control-Me to choose a game governed by chance rather than by skill. (If you're a woman, you're even more likely than a man to choose a chance game.) [Zenker, Wolfgang]

You are a man and you have had your first heart attack:

If you are an I-Control-Me type who believes that the attack was caused by a combination of circumstances, some controllable by you and some not (like "pressure at work" or letting yourself get angered too easily) you are more likely to return to work and to other activities than a They-Control-Me man who attributes the attack to "fate" or "bad luck." I-Control-Me men tend to change attitudes and activities they think caused the heart attack. They-Control-Me men are more likely to trust their recovery to fate or luck.

That was the conclusion of an Israeli psychologist, Dan Bar-On of Ben Gurion University, who interviewed eighty-nine first-time heart attack patients and their physicians. [Bar-On; Israeli study]

You were an adult during the late sixties:

If you are an American woman, you may have participated in a great "cultural shift" regarding your feelings of control, and not in the direction you might think. Having gone through the women's revolution of the sixties, women in the mid-seventies, measured as a group, shifted significantly toward the They-Control-Me (or powerlessness) end of the scale. Previously women's scores, as a group, were distributed about the same as those of men.

The researchers discovered this shift by locating and examining almost two decades of scores of a large-scale long-term continuing survey of fourteen thousand men and women, from younger (as young as fourteen) to older (up to age fifty-nine), which contained the Rotter Internal-External Scale (first published in 1966). Each subject had been requestioned three times over a seven- to eight-year period. In the late 1960s and the early 1970s, all groups, men and women, old and young, produced similar Rotter scores. In 1973, the scores of women, older and young alike, diverged notably from those of men—towards They-Control.

The shift was generated, speculate the researchers, by a consequence of the women's movement: the mass entry of women into the world of work-for-pay. Women thus acquired, they suggest, a heightened awareness of the "perceived disparities in wages and advancement possibilities between men and women . . . coupled with perceived limited individual ability to effect change," leading "many women to feel less in control of their lives during the 1970s. White women changed more rapidly than black women did, perhaps reflecting new awareness of obstacles among women who previously had not felt part of a group that faced discrimination in American society. Because men as a group presumably did not experience new awareness of barriers to personal achievement during this period, on the average they did not change much in locus of control orientation." [Doherty, Baldwin]

You became a mother before the age of nineteen:

You probably feel less effective at controlling your life (you're more likely to be a They-Control-Me) than a woman whose first child was born later. [McLaughlin, Micklin]

You have had an abortion:

Despite widespread belief, the chances are very slim—only 15 percent—that you suffered significant physical or emotional distress as a result. In fact, the major feeling was "relief," reports Brenda Major, a psychologist at the State University of New York at Buffalo, who interviewed six hundred women before and immediately after they underwent abortions. Most of the women were in their early twenties and from a wide range of social and economic backgrounds. Follow-up interviews with 179 of the women showed that three weeks after the abortion, the emotional state of the participant tended to be still better.

Now here's the I-Control-Me and They-Control-Me part: Of those 15 percent who did report moderate to severe depression, most blamed some fixed (stable) trait in their character as the reason they felt "down." That fixed-trait person is the kind most likely to say, "I can't do anything about it because that's the way I am." Thus, that person is saying, "It's outside of my control." [Major]

On a scale that measures optimism versus pessimism, you score high as an optimist or positive thinker:

If you're a college student, you report fewer end-of-semester symptoms of stress—like muscle tightness, fatigue, dizzy spells, and coughs—than pessimistic students do.

If you've recovered from coronary bypass surgery, you showed fewer signs of complication on the operating table and recovered at a "significantly faster rate" than pessimists.

If you're an alcoholic in a ninety-day "after-care" program, you're more likely to complete the program and stay sober than pessimists.

If you have been involved (say, through an immediate-family relationship) in caring for a stroke victim, regardless of how the patient progressed, *you* came out less depressed and healthier after a year of such personal service than pessimists with similar responsibilities did.

"People's optimistic or pessimistic orientations," says Charles Carver, a University of Miami psychologist and codeveloper of a scale for pessimism versus optimism, "are not just faces we display to the world. They have lots of implications for what people do, how they feel, and potentially they may have important health implications as well."

"If I were lost at sea in a lifeboat," adds his codeveloper, Michael Scheier, a psychologist at Carnegie-Mellon University, "I'd much rather be stuck with an optimist than a pessimist, because as a more likely believer in a payoff, he'd probably row longer." [Carver, Scheier, Steck]

You are a generally dependent kind of person:

When you run into serious problems, you're more apt (as a They-Control-Me) than an independent person to consider seeing a psychiatrist. [Darden]

You are a generally independent kind of person:

When you run into serious problems, you're more apt (as an I-Control-Me) than a dependent person to want to see a lawyer. [Darden]

You like salt on your food:

If you test on the Rotter scale as an I-Control-Me person, you're likely to salt your food before you taste it.

If you're a They-Control-Me type, you're likely to taste your food first, then sprinkle salt on it. [McGee, Snyder]

CHAPTER
7 _____

Can We Change
Our Personalities?

*The Master said, It is only the wisest
and the very stupidest who cannot change.*

CONFUCIUS (551–479 B.C.)

The studies in these pages, more than five hundred, are distilled
from almost half a million that have occupied scholars over the past
two decades and more.

What have they learned about us that can help us live better?

Or does that question ask too much of research? Should helping
us live better be the goal of social science? And even if research came
up with better rules for better living, are we humans capable of
changing our personalities?

Since Freud, a vast industry of psychoanalysis, psychiatry, psychotherapy, and social work has constructed itself on the turf of the improvability of human personality. Yet a deep contradictory tradition runs through psychology stating that, in the main, we are stuck with being who we are.

"In most of us, by the age of 30 the character has set like plaster, and will never soften again," wrote William James, the nineteenth-century psychology pioneer. That judgment remained widely held for much of the twentieth century and it remains defensible.

A few years ago an adherent of that tradition, Jack Block, a psychologist of the University of California at Berkeley, found records of several hundred people in Berkeley and nearby Oakland who had been tracked since they were junior high school students in the 1930s. When those subjects reached their late teens, the Berkeley Institute of Human Development interviewed and tested them again, and again in their mid-thirties, and still again in their mid-forties. Such long-term follow-ups of the same people are extremely rare.

The general finding of this large-scale California study: Subjects showed a remarkable record of stability. Those whose early lives, for whatever reasons, led them to dig self-defeating holes for themselves as adolescents were still undoing themselves in the same ways as adults; optimistic teenagers grew into optimistic middle-agers; youngsters with wide swings of mood developed into mood swingers in midlife.

Even more convincing, some feel, is the work of Paul T. Costa, Jr., and Robert R. McCrae, both psychologists at the National Institute on Aging in Baltimore. They learned of the existence of two large-scale, long-term studies, one by the Veterans Administration in Boston, another by the Baltimore Longitudinal Study of Aging. Those agencies had followed subjects beyond middle age into late adulthood, interviewing them repeatedly over six-, ten-, and twelve-year intervals—and the subjects held to their basic characteristics with extremely high consistency. "The assertive 19-year-old," concluded Costa, "is the assertive 40-year-old is the assertive 80-year-old." The report covering his and McCrae's findings is titled to parody a Paul Simon song: "Still Stable After All These Years."

Those conclusions have done little to dissuade the believers in human perfectability. After all, goes their argument, people died of recurring plagues for hundreds of years. Was that a reason to believe people would always die of plagues? Was medical research pointless and hopeless?

Independent of the Freudian movement, the 1970s opened what psychologist-writer Zick Rubin has called "an aquarian explosion of behavior modification from TA to TM, from AA to Zen. . . . At bottom, it seems, the debate is not so much methodological as ideological. . . . The potential for growth [is] the hallmark of humanity. . . . People are trying, perhaps for the first time in history, to change *themselves*."

"When you focus on stability," adds Orville G. Brim, Jr., a sociologist who heads the Foundation for Child Development, "you're looking at . . . the people who have gotten stuck. You want to look at how a person grows and changes, not at how a person stays the same."

People may not have always known how to grow and change, but their desire to do so seems inherent. In showing the manuscript of this book to friends—including psychology professionals—I have noticed consistently that they soon drop their critical detachment and begin going through these studies with a remarkable degree of subjectivity, of self-involvement. They are *looking themselves up*. They seem to be asking, "Am *I* like that?" Then: "Is that the way I *want* to be?"

Again, take the example of this book's opening study about the "game of 'chicken' played with the eyes." In my experience of showing the manuscript, people have read studies like that with surprise. Women seem to say, with a faint trace of anger, "I'm not going to let them do that to me." Perhaps that is the simple beginning of self-change.

If that first example sheds light on a revealing specific behavior, the closing discussion—of I-Control-Me's and They-Control-Me's—pierces to the roots of personality structure. To change that structure is to change the way a person lives. And the research shows that They-Control-Me's can *learn to become* I-Control-Me's.

The psychologists whose studies appear here have not decided—as a group, as a professional discipline, as an industry—whether the purpose of their research is to "improve" our behavior or simply to advance better "understanding" of it. Every now and then in the professional journals some brave scholar protests that research is not purposeful enough, indeed not even *serious* enough. One learned rebel complained recently (in a journal) that the chief criterion for getting a study published is that it be amusing, even frivolous, as long as it's *clever*—and that a "serious" study has a harder time making the grade.

Is that charge valid? Who can say? But to avoid intellectual rioting among themselves, the high priests of human behavior research have fastidiously avoided defining the goals of their research. So each of *us* has to decide for ourselves what all *their* marvelous discoveries mean.

What do *we* want to do with the immense pile of bits and pieces of knowledge, fascinating but largely unsorted, that *they* have gathered about *us*?

We can, if we choose, try to use the jigsaw pieces to design some personal self-change, some self-improvement. True enough, *most* people may live lives that are "set like plaster." But who doesn't know *someone* who at some critical point took a hard look at his or her life, decided there was a better one to live, then wrestled herself or himself into a substantially new shape? If everyone knows *someone* who has succeeded in doing that, perhaps everyone can learn to. As Kenneth Boulding, the economist-philosopher, once declared (thus hatching Boulding's Law): "Anything that exists is possible."

But there's another possible value to playing with this picture puzzle of a million fragments: not as a guidebook to changing ourselves into what we *ought* to be, but as a reality check on who we *are*. Perhaps the best use of these 33,000 studies a year is to clarify what we may *expect*, without too many surprises, of the behavior of our relatives and co-workers and friends and neighbors—and, consequently, how we may accommodate ourselves more successfully to the real world of real people.

Whether our goal is to understand ourselves and others or the more ambitious one of remolding ourselves, either aim must begin with accurate observation. The studies in this book, drawn from what is only the first century in the life of a young science, are the beginnings of accurate observation.

These studies and their possible uses go far beyond anything I had in mind when I accidentally stumbled over those first studies about mothers and fear of death; when I found myself wondering how many more glimpses into the mystery of the human soul other research scholars had turned up. This project started many years ago with no intention of producing "self-help" or advice, and it ends with no such intention. Its mission was then, as it is now, to entertain, to enliven the mind, to stimulate and feed curiosity about ourselves—and perhaps to make us a mite gladder that we are human.

THE STUDIES AND
WHERE TO FIND THEM

CHAPTER 1: YOUR OUTER SELF AND WHAT IT SAYS ABOUT YOU

Academy of Management Journal, v25, no3, reported in "Beauties, Beasts, and Job Markets," *Psychology Today*, April 1983.

Adams, G. R., "Social Psychology of Beauty: Effects of Age, Height and Weight on Self Reported Personality Traits and Social Behavior," *Journal of Social Psychology*, 1980, v112, no2, p287–94.

Allon, Natalie, "Latent Social Services in Group Dieting," *Social Problems*, 1975, v23, no1, p59–69.

Apple, W., L. A. Streeter, and R. B. Krauss, "Effects of Pitch and Speech Rate on Personal Attributions," *Journal of Personality and Social Psychology*, 1979, v37, p715–27.

Argyle, Michael, and Janet Dean, Oxford University, "Eye-Contact, Distance and Affiliation," *Sociometry*, 1965, v28, p289–304.

Argyle, Michael, and R. Ingham, "Gaze, Mutual Gaze and Proximity," *Semiotics* 6, 1972, p32–49.

Argyle, Michael, L. Lefebvre, and Mark Cook, "The Meaning of Five Patterns in Gaze," *European Journal of Social Psychology*, 1974, v4, p125–36.

Bakan, Paul, "The Eyes Have It," *Psychology Today*, 1971, v4, p64–67,96.

Baron, Robert A., National Science Foundation and Purdue University, "Olfaction and Human Social Behavior: Effects of a Pleasant Scent on Attraction and Social Perception," *Personality and Social Psychology Bulletin*, December 1981, v7, no4, p611–16.

Bar-Tal, Daniel, Tel-Aviv University, and Leonard Saxe, Boston University, "Perceptions of Similarly and Dissimilarly Attractive Couples and Individuals," *Journal of Personality and Social Psychology*, 1976, v33, no6, p772–81.

Beaman, Arthur L., University of Montana, and Bonnel Klentz, University of West Florida, "The Supposed Physical Attractiveness Bias Against Supporters of the Women's Movement: A Meta-Analysis," *Personality and Social Psychology Bulletin*, December 1983, v9, no4, p544–50.

Berkowitz, Leonard, and Ann Frodi, University of Wisconsin, Madison, "Reactions to a Child's Mistakes as Affected by Her/His Looks and Speech," *Social Psychology Quarterly*, 1979, v42, no4, p420–25.

Berry, Diane S., and Leslie Zebrowitz McArthur, Brandeis University, "Some Components and Consequences of a Babyface," *Journal of Personality and Social Psychology*, 1985, v48, no2, p312–23.

Berscheid, Ellen, University of Minnesota, Elaine Walster, University of Wisconsin, and R. Campbell, "Grow Old Along with Me," mimeographed, 1972. Cited in Berscheid and Walster, 1974.

Berscheid, Ellen, University of Minnesota, and Elaine Walster, University of Wisconsin, "Physical Attractiveness," in *Advances in Experimental Social Psychology*, L. Berkowitz (ed.), v7, New York: Academic Press, 1974, p157–215.

Bonuso, Carl, in *Phi Delta Kappan*, v64, no5, as reported in "The Image of a Leader," *Psychology Today*, September 1983.

Boyanowsky, Ehor O., and Curt T. Griffiths, Simon Fraser University, "Weapons and Eye Contact as Instigators or Inhibitors of Aggressive Arousal in Police-Citizen Interaction," *Journal of Applied Social Psychology*, 1982, v12, no4, p398.

Brant, Sandra J., Cleveland State University, "Name Recall as a Function of Introduction Time," *Psychological Reports*, 1982, v50, p377–78.

Breytspraak, L. M., J. McGee, J. C. Conger, J. L. Whatley, J. T. Moore, "Sensitizing Medical Students to Impression Formation Processes in the Patient Interview," *Journal of Medical Education*, 1977, v52, p47–54.

Bruch, Hilde, *The Importance of Overweight*, New York: W. W. Norton and Co., 1957.

Burns, Jo Ann, and B. L. Kintz, Western Washington State College, "Eye Contact While Lying During an Interview," *Bulletin of the Psychonomic Society*, 1976, v7, no1, p87.

Buss, David, Harvard University, "Human Mate Selection," *The American Scientist*, 1985, v73, no1, p47–51.

Busse, T. V., and J. Helfrich, "Changes in First Name Popularity Across Grades," *Journal of Social Psychology*, 1975, v89, p281–83.

Busse, T. V., and Louisa Seraydarian, Temple University, "Frequency and Desirability of First Names," *Journal of Social Psychology*, 1978, v104, p143–44.

Busse, T. V., and Louisa Seraydarian, "First Names and Popularity in Grade School Children," *Psychology in the Schools*, 1979, v16, no1, p149–53.

Byrne, Donn, C. R. Ervin, and J. Lamberth, "Continuity Between the Experimental Study of Attraction and Real-Life Computer Dating," *Journal of Personality and Social Psychology*, 1970, v16, p157–65.

Cash, Thomas F., Old Dominion University, Norfolk, Va., as reported in "On Corporate Ladder, Beauty Can Hurt," Georgia Dullea, *The New York Times*, June 3, 1985.

Cash, Thomas F., and J. Kehr, "Influence of Nonprofessional Counselors' Physical Attractiveness and Sex on Perceptions of Counselor Behavior," *Journal of Counseling Psychology*, 1978, v25, p336–42.

Cash, Thomas F., J. Kehr, J. Polyson, and V. Freeman, "Role of Physical Attractiveness in Peer Attribution of Psychological Disturbance," *Journal of Consulting and Clinical Psychology*, 1977, v45, p987–93.

Chen, E., and S. Cobb, "Family Structure in Relation to Health and Disease: A Review of the Literature," *Journal of Chronic Disease*, 1960, v12, p544–67.

Chetwynd, S. J., R. A. Stewart, and G. E. Powell, "Social Attitudes toward the Obese Physique," in A. Howard (ed.), *Recent Advances in Obesity Research*, Westport, Conn.: Technomic, 1975, p223–26.

Clifford, M. M., and Elaine Walster, "The Effects of Physical Attractiveness on Teacher Expectation," *Sociology of Education*, 1973, v46, p248–58.

Cochran, C. D., and Sally Urbanczyk, Stetson University, "The Effect of Availability of Vertical Space on Personal Space," *The Journal of Psychology*, 1982, v111, p137.

Connolly, Patrick, Ph.D. thesis, University of Iowa, reported in *Behavior Today*, November 5, 1973, p2.

Cook, Mark, "Gaze and Mutual Gaze in Social Encounters," *American Scientist*, May–June 1977, v65, p328–33.

Cook, Mark, and J. M. C. Smith, "The Role of Gaze in Impression Formation," *British Journal of Social and Clinical Psychology*, 1975, v14, p19–25.

Craddock, D., "Psychological and Personality Factors Associated with Successful Weight Reduction: A 10-Year Follow-Up of 134 Personal Cases," in A. Howard (ed.), *Recent Advances in Obesity Research*, Westport, Conn.: Technomic, 1975, p220–23.

Cunningham, Michael, University of Louisville, "Measuring the Physical in Physical Attractiveness: Quasi-Experiments on the Sociobiology of Female Facial Beauty," *Journal of Personality and Social Psychology*, May 1986, v50, no5, p925–35.

Darwin, Charles, *The Expression of Emotion in Man and Animals*, London: Murray, 1872.

Davis, Leslie L., and Sharron J. Lennon, Utah State University, "Social Stigma of Pregnancy: Further Evidence," in *Psychological Reports*, 1983, v53, p997–98.

Deaux, K., and E. Farris, "Attributing Causes for One's Own Performance: The Effects of Sex, Norms, and Outcomes," unpublished paper, Purdue University, cited in Kahn, McGaughey.

Dermer, Marshall, and Darrel L. Thiel, University of Wisconsin, "When Beauty May Fail," *Journal of Personality and Social Psychology*, 1975, v31, no6, p1168–76.

Dion, Karen K., University of Minnesota, "Physical Attractiveness and Evaluations of Children's Transgressions," *Journal of Personality and Social Psychology*, 1972, v24, p207–13.

Dion, Karen K., and Ellen Berscheid, University of Minnesota, and Elaine Walster, University of Wisconsin, "What Is Beautiful Is Good," *Journal of Personality and Social Psychology*, 1972, v24, p285–90.

Douven, E., and J. Adelson, *The Adolescent Experience*, New York: Wiley, 1966.

Driskell, James E., Jr., U.S. Navy Human Factors Laboratory, "Beauty as Status," *American Journal of Sociology*, v89, no1, p141–65.

Durham, Thomas W., and William Grossnickle, East Carolina University, "Attitudes Toward Masturbation," in *Psychological Reports*, 1982, v51, p932.

Ekman, P., and W. V. Friesen, *Unmasking the Face*, Englewood Cliffs, N.J.: Prentice-Hall, 1975.

Ekman, P., and H. Oster, "Facial Expressions of Emotion," in M. R. Rosenzweig and L. W. Porter (eds.), *Annual Review of Psychology*, 1979, v30.

Elder, G. H., Jr. "Appearance and Education in Marriage Mobility," *American Sociological Review*, 1969, v34, p519–33.

Ellsworth, Phoebe C., J. Merrill Carlsmith, and Alexander Henson, Stanford University, "The Stare as a Stimulus to Flight in Human Subjects," *Journal of Personality and Social Psychology*, 1972, v21, no3, p302–11.

Ellyson, Steve L., Linfield University; John F. Dovidio, Colgate University; and

Randi L. Corson, Beaver College; in "Visual Behavior Differences in Females as a Function of Self-Perceived Expertise," in *Journal of Nonverbal Behavior*, 1980, v5, no3, p164.

Exline, Ralph V., J. Thibaut, C. B. Hickey, and P. Gumpert, "Visual Interaction in Relation to Machiavellianism and an Unethical Act," *Studies on Machiavellianism*, R. Christie and F. L. Geis (eds.), Academic Press, 1970.

Exline, Ralph V., and L. C. Winters, "Affective Relations and Mutual Glances in Dyads," in *Affect, Cognition and Personality*, S. S. Tomkins and C. Izard (eds.), New York: Springer Publishing Co., 1965.

Exline, Ralph V., and others (several studies), as cited by Frances J. Anderson and Frank N. Willis, University of Missouri, Kansas City, in "Glancing at Others in Preschool Children in Relation to Dominance," *The Psychological Record*, 1976, v26, p467.

Fallon, April, and Paul Rozin, University of Pennsylvania, *Journal of Abnormal Psychology*, 1984, reported in "Dislike of Own Body Found Common Among Women," *The New York Times*, March 19, 1984.

Feingold, Alan, City University of New York, "Do Tall Men Have Prettier Girl Friends?" *Psychological Reports*, 1982, v50, p810.

Feldman, Saul, Case Western Reserve, at American Sociological Association convention, reported in "The Non-Tall Caught Up Short," *Behavior Today*, September 6, 1971.

Fellman, Bruce, "Talk: The Not-So-Silent Killer," *Science 85*, December 1985, p70–71.

Fisher, J. D., M. Rytting, and R. Heslin, "Hands Touching Hands: Affective and Evaluative Effects of an Interpersonal Touch," *Sociometry*, 1976, v39, p416–21.

Fisher, Jeffrey David, and Donn Byrne, Purdue University, "Too Close for Comfort: Sex Differences in Response to Invasions of Personal Space," *Journal of Personality and Social Psychology*, 1975, v32, no1, p15.

Ford, C. S., and F. A. Beach, *Patterns of Sexual Behavior*, New York: Harper & Row, 1951, p86.

Forden, Carie, State University of New York, Stony Brook, "The Influence of Sex-Role Expectations on the Perception of Touch," *Sex Roles*, 1981, v7, no9, p889.

Frieze, Irene, and Josephine Olson, University of Pittsburgh Graduate School of Business, as reported by the Associated Press and published in the *Centre Daily Times* (State College, Pa.), February 25, 1987.

Frommer, Myrna, "Names," *Etc*, 1982, v39, no2, p106–8.

Fugita, Stephen S., Thomas A. Agle, Isadore Newman, and Nancy Walfish, University of Akron, "Attractiveness, Self-Concept, and a Methodological Note on Gaze Behavior," *Personality and Social Psychology Bulletin*, 1977, v3, p240.

Gallucci, Nicholas T., McNeese State University, "Effects of Men's Physical Attractiveness on Interpersonal Attraction," *Psychological Reports*, 1984, v55, p935–38.

Garn, S. M., S. M. Bailey, and I.T.T. Higgins, "Effects of Socioeconomic Status, Family Line and Living Together on Fatness and Obesity," in R. M. Laur and R. B. Shekelle (eds.), *Childhood Prevention of Atherosclerosis and Hypertension*, New York: Raven Press, 1980, p187–204.

Garn, S. M., and D. C. Clark, "Trends in Fatness and the Origins of Obesity," *Pediatrics*, 1976, v57, p443.

Garn, S. M., P. E. Cole, and S. M. Bailey, "Living Together as a Factor in Family Line Resemblances, *Human Biology*, 1979, v51, p565–87.

Garwood, S. Gary, Lewis Cox, Valerie Kaplan, Neal Wasserman, and Jefferson L. Sulzer, Tulane University, "Beauty Is Only Name Deep: The Effect of First-Name on Ratings of Physical Attraction," *Journal of Applied Social Psychology*, 1980, v10, no5, p431–35.

Garwood, S. Gary, Susan Baer, Douglas Levine, Sudie Carroll, and Ed O'Neal, Tulane University, "Sex-Role Expectations of Socially Desirable First Names," *Sex Roles*, 1981, v7, no3, p257–62.

Geiselman, R. Edward, Nancy Haight, and Lori Kimata, University of California, Los Angeles, *Journal of Experimental Social Psychology*, v.20, no5, reported in "Beauty by Association," *Psychology Today*, August 1985, p66.

Genthner, R., and J. Moughan, "Introverts' and Extroverts' Responses to Nonverbal Attending Behavior," *Journal of Counseling Psychology*, 1977, v24, p144–46.

Gibbins, Keith, and Jeffrey R. Coney, Murdoch University, "Meaning of Physical Dimensions of Women's Clothes," *Perceptual and Motor Skills*, 1981, v53, p720–22.

Giles, Howard, and Kathryn Farrar, University of Bristol, "Some Behavioural Consequences of Speech and Dress Styles," *British Journal of Social and Clinical Psychology*, 1979, v18, p209.

Gitter, A. George, Jack Lomranz, and Leonard Saxe, Boston University and Tel-Aviv University, "Factors Affecting Perceived Attractiveness of Male Physiques by American and Israeli Students," *The Journal of Social Psychology*, 1982, v118, p167–75.

Goffman, Erving, *Interaction Ritual*, Garden City, N. Y.: Anchor Books, 1967.

Goldberg, Philip A., and Marc Gottesdiener, Connecticut College, and Paul Abramson, University of Connecticut, "Another Put-Down of Women? Perceived Attractiveness as a Function of Support for the Feminist Movement," *Journal of Personality and Social Psychology*, 1975, v32, no1, p113.

Goldstein, Melvin A., M. Catherine Kilroy, and David Van de Voort, "Gaze as a Function of Conversation and Degree of Love," *Journal of Psychology*, 1976, v92, p227–34.

Gordon, David Paul, University of California, Berkeley, "Hospital Slang for Patients: Crocks, Gomers, Corks, and Others," *Language in Society*, 1983, v12, no2, p173–85.

Gross, A. E., and C. Crofton, "What Is Beautiful Is Good," *Sociometry*, 1977, v40, p85–90.

Haase, R. F., and D. T. Tepper, "Nonverbal Components of Empathic Communication," *Journal of Counseling Psychology*, 1972, v19, p417–24.

Haber, Gilda Moss, University of the District of Columbia, "Spatial Relations between Dominants and Marginals," *Social Psychology Quarterly*, 1982, v45, no4, p219–28.

Hai, Dorothy M., St. Bonaventure University School of Business, "Sex and the Single Armrest: Use of Personal Space During Air Travel," *Psychological Reports*, 1982, v51, p743–49.

Hansell, Stephen, Johns Hopkins University; Jack Sparacino and Don Ronchi, Ohio State University, "Plain Girls' High Blood Pressure," *Psychology Today*, October 1981.

Hayduk, Leslie A., University of Western Ontario, and Steven Mainprize, University of British Columbia, "Personal Space of the Blind," *Social Psychology Quarterly*, 1980, v43, no2, p216–23.

Heilman, Madeline, and Melanie Stopeck, New York University, "Attractiveness and Corporate Success: Different Causal Attributes for Males and Females," *Journal of Applied Psychology*, May 1985, v70, no2, p379–88.

Henley, Nancy M., "Status and Sex: Some Touching Observations," *Bulletin of the Psychonomic Society*, 1973, v2, p91–93.

Henley, Nancy M., *Body Politics: Power, Sex, and Nonverbal Communication*, Englewood Cliffs, N.J.: Prentice-Hall, 1977.

Hewitt, Jay, University of Missouri, Kansas City, "Liking for Touchers as a Function of Type of Touch," *Psychological Reports*, 1982, v50, p917–18.

Hocking, John E., University of Georgia; Barbara Walker, Florida State University; and Edward Fink, Michigan State University, "Physical Attractiveness and Judgments of Morality Following an 'Immoral' Act," in *Psychological Reports*, 1982, v51, p111.

Hoover, Michele Lanza, Pittsburgh, Pa., "The Self-Image of Overweight Adolescent Females," *Maternal-Child Nursing Journal*, 1984, v13, no2, p125–37.

Hughey, Aaron Wilson, Western Kentucky University, "Effects of Living Accommodations of High Proximity on the Self-Perceptions of College Students Residing in University Housing Facilities," *Psychological Reports*, 1983, v53, p1013–14.

Jones, Warren H., Robert O. Hansson, and Anita L. Phillips, University of Tulsa, "Physical Attractiveness and Judgments of Psychopathology," *Journal of Social Psychology*, 1978, v105, p79–84.

Jourard, S. M., "An Exploratory Study of Body Accessibility," *British Journal of Social and Clinical Psychology*, 1966, v5, p221.

Kahn, Arnold, and Timothy A. McGaughey, "Distance and Liking: When Moving Close Produces Increased Liking," *Sociometry*, 1977, v40, no2, p138–44.

Kallen, David J., and Andrea Doughty, Michigan State University, "The Relationship of Weight, the Self Perception of Weight and Self Esteem with Courtship Behavior," *Obesity and the Family*, 1984, p93–114.

Kassarjian, Harold H., University of California, Los Angeles, "Voting Intentions and Political Perception," *Journal of Psychology*, 1963, v56, p85–88.

Keating, Caroline F., Allan Mazur, and Marshall H. Segall, Syracuse University, "Facial Gestures Which Influence the Perception of Status," *Sociometry*, 1977, v40, no4, p374–78.

Kemper, Susan, University of Kansas, "When to Speak Like a Lady," in *Sex Roles*, 1984, v10, no5/6, p435–43.

Kendon, A., "Movement Coordination in Social Interaction," *Acta Psychologica*, 1970, v32, p100–25.

Kirkpatrick, C., and J. Cotton, "Physical Attractiveness, Age, and Marital Adjustment," *American Sociological Review*, 1951, v16, p81–86.

Kleinke, Chris, Wheaton College, "Effects of Dress on Compliance to Requests in a Field Setting," *Journal of Social Psychology*, 1977, v101, p223.

Kleinke, Chris L., "Interaction Between Gaze and Legitimacy of Request on Compliance in a Field Setting," *Journal of Nonverbal Behavior*, Fall 1980, v5, no1, p3–11.

Kleinke, Chris L., Wellesley College, and Richard A. Staneski, Chaffey College,

"First Impressions of Female Bust Size," in *Journal of Social Psychology*, 1980, v110, p123.

Kness, Darlene, and Barbara Densmore, Pennsylvania State University, "Dress and Social-Political Beliefs of Young Male Students," in *Adolescence*, Fall 1976, v11, no43, p431.

Krebs, D., and A. A. Adinolfi, "Physical Attractiveness, Social Relations, and Personality Style," *Journal of Personality and Social Psychology*, 1975, v31, p245–53.

Kroch, Anthony S., "Toward a Theory of Social Dialect Variation," *Language in Society*, April 1978, v7, no1, p17–36.

Kunzendorf, Robert G., and Joseph Denney, "Definitions of Personal Space— Smokers versus Nonsmokers," in *Psychological Reports*, 1982, v50, p818.

Labov, W., *Sociolinguistic Patterns*, Philadelphia: University of Pennsylvania Press, 1972.

Labov, W., "Language Change as a Form of Communication," in M. Silverstein (ed.), *Human Communication: Theoretical Explorations*. Hillsdale, N.J.: Lawrence Erlbaum Associates, 1974.

La France, Marianne, "Nonverbal Synchrony and Rapport: Analysis by the Cross-lag Panel Technique," *Social Psychology Quarterly*, 1979, v42, p66–70.

La France, Marianne, and M. Broadbent, "Group Rapport: Posture Sharing as a Nonverbal Indicator," *Group and Organization Studies*, 1976, v1, p328–33.

La France, Marianne, and Clara Mayo, Boston University, "Racial Differences in Gaze Behavior During Conversations: Two Systematic Observational Studies," *Journal of Personality and Social Psychology*, 1976, v33, no5, p547–52.

Lamb, Theodore, Wittenberg University, "Nonverbal and Paraverbal Control in Dyads and Triads: Sex or Power Differences?" in *Social Psychology Quarterly*, 1981, v44, no1, p49.

Langlois, Judith H., University of Texas, *Developmental Psychology*, May 1987, v23, p363–69.

Lawson, E.D., "Men's First Names, Nicknames, and Short Names: A Semantic Differential Analysis," *Names*, 1973, v21, p22–27.

Lee, Alan B., and Morton Goldman, University of Missouri, Kansas City, "Effect of Staring on Normal and Overweight Students," in *Journal of Social Psychology*, 1979, v108, p165.

Lindman, Ralf, Abo Academy, Finland, "Alcohol and Eye Contact," in *Scandinavian Journal of Psychology*, 1980, v21, p201.

Lipson, Adam, State University of New York, Albany; David Przybyla, Colgate University; and Donn Byrne, State University of New York, Albany, "Physical Attractiveness, Self-Awareness and Mirror-Gazing Behavior," *Bulletin of the Psychonomic Society*, 1983, v21, p115.

Lockard, Joan S., Renate I. McVittie, and Lisa M. Isaac, University of Washington, "Functional Significance of the Affiliative Smile," *Bulletin of the Psychonomic Society*, 1977, v9, no5, p367.

Lucker, Gerald, University of Texas at Austin, Ph.D. thesis, "Physical Attractiveness, Individual Differences and Personality Stereotyping," *Dissertation Abstracts*, 1976.

MacLachlan, J., "What People Really Think of Fast Talkers," *Psychology Today*, 1979, v13, no6, p113-14, 116–17.

Maier, Richard A., Loyola University of Chicago, and Paul J. Lavrakas, Northwestern University, "Attitudes Toward Women, Personality Rigidity, and Idealized Physique Preferences in Males," *Sex Roles*, 1984, v11, no5/6, p425–33.

Marcus, Mary G., "The Power of a Name," *Psychology Today*, October 1976, p75–76, p108.

Marshall, J. R., and J. Neill, "The Removal of a Psychosomatic Symptom: Effects on the Marriage," *Family Process*, 1977, v16, no3, p273–80.

Mashman, Robert C., Counseling and Psychological Services, University of California, "The Effect of Physical Attractiveness on the Perception of Attitude Similarity," *Journal of Social Psychology*, 1978, v106, p103–10.

McGinley, H., R. LeFevre, and P. McGinley, "The Influence of a Communicator's Body Position on Opinion Change in Others," *Journal of Personality and Social Psychology*, 1975, v31, p686–90.

McMillan, Julie R., A. Kay Clifton, Diane McGrath, and Wanda S. Gale, Illinois State University, Norman, "Women's Language: Uncertainty or Interpersonal Sensitivity and Emotionality?" *Sex Roles*, 1977, v3, no6, p545–59.

Mehrabian, A., "Inference of Attitudes from the Posture, Orientation, and Distance of a Communicator," *Journal of Consulting and Clinical Psychology*, 1968, v32, p296–308.

Mehrabian, A., "Relationship of Attitude to Seated Posture, Orientation, and Distance," *Journal of Personality and Social Psychology*, 1968, v10, p26–30.

Mehrabian, A., "Significance of Posture and Position in the Communication of Attitudes and Status Relationships," *Psychological Bulletin*, 1969, v71, p359–72.

Mehrabian, Albert, and Shirley G. Diamond, University of California, Los Angeles, "Effects of Furniture Arrangement, Props, and Personality on Social Interaction," *Journal of Personality and Social Psychology*, 1971, v20, no1, p18–30.

Mehrabian, A., and S. R. Ferris, "Inference of Attitudes from Nonverbal Communication in Two Channels," *Journal of Consulting Psychology*, 1967, v31, p248–52.

Middlemist, R. Dennis, Oklahoma State University; Eric S. Knowles, Ohio State University; and Charles F. Matter, University of Wisconsin, Green Bay, "Personal Space Invasions in the Lavatory: Suggestive Evidence for Arousal," *Journal of Personality and Social Psychology*, 1976, v33, no5, p541–46.

Milgram, S., *Obedience to Authority*, New York: Harper & Row, 1974.

Miller, Arthur G., Miami University, "Role of Physical Attractiveness in Impression Formation," *Psychonomic Science*, 1970, v19, no4, p241–44.

Miller, A. R., and R. A. Stewart, "Perception of Female Physiques," *Perceptual and Motor Skills*, 1968, v27, p721–22.

Miller, G., R. Beaber, and K. Valone, "Speed of Speech and Persuasion," *Journal of Personality and Social Psychology*, 1976, v34, 615–24.

Millman, M., *Such a Pretty Face: Being Fat in America*, New York: W. W. Norton, 1980.

Mueser, Kim T., Barry W. Grau, Steve Sussman, and Alexander J. Rosen, University of Illinois, "You're Only as Pretty as You Feel: Facial Expression as a Determinant of Physical Attractiveness," *Journal of Personality and Social Psychology*, 1984, v46, no2, p469–78.

Murrell, Mary E., Trenton State College, and David Lester, Richard Stockton State College, "The Personalities of Short People," *Psychological Reports*, 1982, v50, p1034.

Natale, M., "Convergence of Mean Vocal Intensity in Dyadic Communication as a Function of Social Desirability," *Journal of Personality and Social Psychology*, 1975, v32, p790–804.

Neill, J. R., J. R. Marshall, and C. E. Yale, "Marital Changes after Bypass Surgery," *Journal of the American Medical Association*, 1978, v240, p447–50.

Newman, Parley W., and Darwin F. Gale, Brigham Young University, as reported in *Psychology Today*, September 1961, p.84.

Nguyen, Tuan D., Richard Heslin, and Michele L. Nguyen, "The Meaning of Touch: Sex Differences," *Journal of Communication*, 1975, v25, p92–103.

Noller, Patricia, University of Queensland, Australia, "Gaze in Married Couples," in *Journal of Nonverbal Behavior*, 1980, v5, no2, p115.

Noppa, H., and C. Bengtsson, "Obesity in Relation to Socioeconomic Status," *Journal of Epidemiology and Community Health*, 1980, v34, p139–42.

Noppa, H., and T. Hallstrom, "Weight Gain in Adulthood in Relation to Socioeconomic Factors, Mental Illness and Personality Traits: A Prospective Study of Middle-Aged Women," *Journal of Psychosomatic Research*, 1981, v25, no2, p83–89.

Nylander, I., "The Feeling of Being Fat and Dieting in a School Population," *Acta Sociologica Medica Scandonacia*, 1971, v1, p17–26.

O'Neal, Edgar C., Mark A. Brunault, Michael S. Carifio, Robert Troutwine, and Jaine Epstein, Tulane University, in "Effect of Insult Upon Personal Space Preferences," *Journal of Nonverbal Behavior*, 1980, v5, no1, p56.

Owens, G., and J. G. Ford, "Further Consideration of the 'What Is Good Is Beautiful' Finding," *Social Psychology*, 1978, v41, p73–75.

Page, Richard A., and Joseph L. Balloun, "The Effect of Voice Volume on the Perception of Personality," *The Journal of Social Psychology*, 1978, v105, p65–72.

Paulsess, Shari, and Morton Goldman, University of Missouri, Kansas City, "The Effect of Touching Different Body Areas on Prosocial Behavior," *Journal of Social Psychology*, 1984, v122, p269–73.

Petty, Richard E., University of Missouri, Columbia; Gary L. Wells, University of Alberta; Martin Heesacker, Southern Illinois University, Carbondale; Timothy C. Brock, Ohio State University; and John T. Cacioppo, University of Iowa, "The Effects of Recipient Posture on Persuasion," *Personality and Social Psychology Bulletin*, June 1983, v9, no2, p209–22.

Reece, M., and N. Whitman, "Warmth and Expressive Movements," *Psychological Reports*, 1961, v8, p76.

Reece, M., and N. Whitman, "Expressive Movements, Warmth, and Verbal Reinforcement," *Journal of Abnormal and Social Psychology*, 1962, v64, p234–36.

Reingen, P. H., J. B. Kernan, L. Gresham, C. Narashmhan, I. Ronkainen, "Cognitive and Behavioral Consequences of the Physical Attractiveness Stereotype in Personal Selling," unpublished paper, School of Business, University of South Carolina, 1978.

Reis, Harry T., University of Rochester; John Nezlek, College of William and Mary; and Ladd Wheeler, University of Rochester, "Physical Attractiveness in Social Interaction," *Journal of Personality and Social Psychology*, 1980, v38, no4, p604.

Rimm, I. J., and A. A. Rimm, "Association between Socioeconomic Status and Obesity in 59,556 Women," *Preventive Medicine*, 1974, v3, p543–52.

Robinson, Janet, and Leslie Zebrowitz McArthur, Brandeis University, "Impact of Salient Vocal Qualities on Causal Attribution for a Speaker's Behavior," *Journal of Personality and Social Psychology*, 1982, v43, no2, p236–47.

Rokeach, Milton, *The Open and Closed Mind*, New York: Basic Books, 1960.

———, *Beliefs, Attitudes, and Values*, San Francisco: Jossey-Bass, 1968.

———, *The Nature of Human Values*, New York: Free Press, 1973.

———, P. W. Smith, and R. I. Evans, "Two Kinds of Prejudice or One?" in Rokeach, *The Open and Closed Mind*, New York: Basic Books, 1960.

Rosenfeld, H. M., and M. Hancks, "The Nonverbal Context of Verbal Listener Responses," in M. R. Key (ed.), *The Relationship of Verbal and Nonverbal Communication*, The Hague: Mouton, 1980.

Royce, W. Stephen, University of Portland (Oregon), "Behavioral Referents for Molar Ratings of Heterosocial Skill," *Psychological Reports*, 1982, v50, p139–46.

Rutter, D. R., and G. M. Stephenson, University of Kent, "The Functions of Looking: Effects of Friendship on Gaze," in *British Journal of Social and Clinical Psychology*, 1979, v18, p203.

Sanders, J. S., and W. L. Robinson, "Talking and Not Talking about Sex: Male and Female Vocabularies," *Journal of Communication*, 1976, v29, p22–30.

Scheflen, A. E., *How Behavior Means*, Garden City, N.Y.: Anchor Press–Doubleday, 1974.

Schwartz, R. A., D. B. Hershenson, and W. G. Shipman, "The Sexual Behavior of Obese Married Women," *Proceedings of the Annual Convention of the American Psychological Association*, 1971, v6, p445–46.

Severy, Lawrence, University of Florida, Donelson R. Forsyth, Virginia Commonwealth University, and Peggy Jo Wagner, Pennsylvania Hospital, "A Multimethod Assessment of Personal Space Development in Female and Male, Black and White Children," *Journal of Nonverbal Behavior*, 1979, v4, no2, p68.

Sewell, Edward H., Jr., Virginia Polytechnic Institute, "Appreciation of Cartoons with Profanity in Captions," *Psychological Reports*, 1984, v54, p583–87.

Sherman, Mark, and Adelaide Haas, State University of New York at New Paltz, "Man to Man, Woman to Woman," *Psychology Today*, June 1984, p72.

Sigall, Harold, and Nancy Ostrove, University of Maryland, "Beautiful but Dangerous: Effects of Offender Attractiveness and Nature of Crime on Juridic Judgment," *Journal of Personality and Social Psychology*, 1975, v31, no3, p410.

Skotko, Vincent P., University of Cincinnati, "Conversational Intimacy and Interpersonal Attraction as a Function of the Manipulation of Interaction Distance," *Dissertation Abstracts*, 1975, order 75-3368.

Smith, David E., Frank N. Willis, and Joseph A. Gier, "Success and Interpersonal Touch in a Competitive Setting," *Journal of Nonverbal Behavior*, 1980, v5, no1, p26.

Solomon, Michael R., and John Schopler, University of North Carolina, *Personality and Social Psychology Bulletin*, v8, no3, as reported in *Psychology Today*, April 1983, p27.

Sommer, R., *Personal Space: The Behavioral Basis of Design*, Englewood Cliffs, N.J.: Prentice-Hall, 1969.

Sroufe, Ralph, Alan Chaikin, Rita Cook, and Valerie Freeman, Old Dominion University, "The Effects of Physical Attractiveness on Honesty: A Socially Desirable Response," *Personality and Social Psychology Bulletin*, 1977, v3, p59.

Stewart, Mark A., University of Notre Dame; Ellen Bouchard Ryan, McMaster University; and Howard Giles, University of Bristol, "Accent and Social Class Effects on Status and Solidarity Evaluations," *Personality and Social Psychology Bulletin*, March 1985, v11, no1, p98–105.

Stier, Deborah S., and Judith A. Hall, Harvard University, "Gender Differences in Touch: An Empirical and Theoretical Review," *Journal of Personality and Social Psychology*, 1984, v47, p440–59.

Stone, Gerald L., and Cathy J. Morden, University of Western Ontario, "Effects of Distance on Verbal Productivity," in *Journal of Counseling Psychology*, 1976, v23, p486.

Stuart, Richard B., and Barbara Davis, *Slim Chance in a Fat World: Behavioral Control of Obesity*, Champaign, Ill.: Research Press, 1972.

Stunkard, Albert J., University of Pennsylvania, as reported in "Fat or Fit? Study May Confirm Suspicions It Is in the Genes," Jane E. Brody, *The New York Times*, January 23, 1986, pA-24.

Sussman, M. B., "Psycho-social Correlates of Obesity: Failure of Calorie Collectors," *Journal of the American Dietetic Association*, 1956, v32, p423–28.

Tepper, D. S., "The Communication of Counselor Empathy, Respect, and Genuineness through Verbal and Nonverbal Channels," doctoral dissertation, University of Massachusetts, 1972, in *Dissertation Abstracts International*, 1973, v33, 4858A. (University Microfilms No. 73–6710.)

Terry, Roger L., and Judy S. Davis, Hanover College, "Components of Facial Attractiveness," *Perceptual and Motor Skills*, 1976, v42, p918.

Trout, Deborah L., and Howard M. Rosenfeld, "The Effect of Postural Lean and Body Congruence on the Judgment of Psychotherapeutic Rapport," *Journal of Nonverbal Behavior*, 1980, v4, no3, p176–90.

Tucker, Larry A., New Mexico State University, "Cigarette Smoking Intentions and Obesity Among High School Males," *Psychological Reports*, April 1983, v52, no2, p530, reported in *Developmental Psychology*, v71, p1123–31.

U.S. Food and Drug Administration, *A Nationwide Study of Food Shoppers' Knowledge, Beliefs, Attitudes and Reported Behavior Regarding Food and Nutrition*, DHEW Publication No. (FDA) 76-2058, 1976.

Udry, J. Richard, and Bruce K. Eckland, University of North Carolina, Chapel Hill, "Benefits of Being Attractive: Differential Payoffs for Men and Women," *Psychological Reports*, 1984, v54, p47–56.

Udry, J. Richard, and Bruce K. Eckland, University of North Carolina, Chapel Hill, reported in *Psychology Today*, April 1983.

Valentine, Mary E., and Howard Ehrlichman, City University of New York, "Interpersonal Gaze and Helping Behavior," in *Journal of Social Psychology*, 1979, v107, p193.

Vander Zanden, J. W., *Sociology*, New York: John Wiley and Sons, 1979.

Waldron, J., "Judgment of Like-Dislike from Facial Expression and Body Posture," *Perceptual and Motor Skills*, 1975, v41, p799–804.

The Wall Street Journal, as reported in "The Non-Tall Caught Up Short," *Behavior Today*, September 6, 1971. Source of the survey unspecified.

Walster, Elaine, University of Wisconsin, "Did You Ever See a Beautiful Conservative?" unpublished paper, 1971, cited in Berscheid and Walster, 1974.

Webster, Murray, Jr., University of South Carolina, and James E. Driskell, Jr.,

U.S. Navy Human Factors Laboratory, "Beauty as Status," *American Journal of Sociology*, v89, no1, p140–65.

West, K. M., "Culture, History and Adiposity, or Should Santa Clause Reduce?" *Obesity and Bariatric Medicine*, 1974, v3, no2, p48–52.

Willis, Frank N., University of Missouri, Kansas City; Lois A. Willis, Ozanam Home for Boys; Joseph A. Gier, also U.M.–K.C.; "Given Names, Social Class, and Professional Achievement," *Psychological Reports*, 1982, v51, p543–49.

Wilson, Darrell, M.D., Stanford University, *Pediatrics*, 1987, v78, p646–50.

Worringham, Charles J., and David M. Messick, University of California, Santa Barbara, "Social Facilitation of Running: An Unobtrusive Study," *Journal of Social Psychology*, 1983, v121, p23–29.

Wurtman, Judith, Massachusetts Institute of Technology, *International Journal of Eating Disorders*, March 1985, reported in "A Candy Bar a Day Keeps Fat Away," *Centre Daily Times* (State College, Pa.), March 4, 1984.

Yates, James S., and Robert S. Miller, "Effects of Seating Orientation on Appreciation of Humor," *Psychological Reports*, 1982, v51, p567.

Zweigenhaft, Richard L., Guilford College, "The Other Side of Unusual First Names, *Journal of Social Psychology*, 1977, v103, p291–302.

CHAPTER 2: YOUR MOODS AND MENTAL STATES

Albin, Rochelle Semmel, McLean Hospital, Harvard Medical School, "The Holiday Blues—A Christmas Fable?" *Psychology Today*, December 1981, p10–12.

Aneshensel, Carol, University of California School of Public Health, as reported in *Litchfield County Times*, March 22, 1985.

Arizona State University, researchers unspecified, in a paper delivered at American Psychological Association convention, as reported in "Pinups and Letdowns," *Psychology Today*, September 1983.

Beck, Aaron, University of Pennsylvania School of Medicine, article in *American Journal of Psychiatry*, 1985, as reported in "Test Is Called Successful in Predicting Suicide," *The New York Times*, February 10, 1985.

Beck, Alan, ecologist, and Aaron Katcher, psychiatrist, University of Pennsylvania Center for the Interaction of Animals and Society, School of Veterinary Medicine, as reported in *Psychology Today*, May 1981.

Behavior Today, June 19, 1972, researchers not identified.

Benham, Lee, and Alexandra Benham, quoted in "Handsome Is as Handsome Doesn't," in *Psychology Today*, April 1983.

Blazer, Dan, psychiatrist, Duke University Medical Center, reported in "Depression Is Twice as Frequent in Cities as in Rural Areas, Study Says," *The New York Times*, August 6, 1985.

Blotnick, Srully, *Ambitious Men: Their Drives, Dreams and Delusions*, 1987; and from an interview with the Associated Press.

Boor, Myron, Brown University, *American Sociological Review*, v46, no5.

Borys, Shelley, University of Waterloo, and Daniel Perlman, University of British Columbia, "Gender Differences in Loneliness," *Personality and Social Psychology Bulletin*, 1985, v11, no1, p63.

Boyanowsky, Ehor, and Curt Griffiths, Simon Fraser University, "Weapons and Eye Contact as Instigators or Inhibitors of Aggressive Arousal in Police-Citizen Interaction," *Journal of Applied Social Psychology*, 1982, v12, no4, p398.

Braff, David L., and June Sprock, University of California, San Diego, Medical Center, and Dennis Saccuzzo, San Diego State University, in a paper presented to the 1981 meeting of the American Psychological Association, as reported in *University of California Clipsheet*, June 2, 1981.

Center for Disease Control, as reported in "Increase in Young Men's Suicides Arouses Concern of Health Aides," *The New York Times*, June 24, 1985.

Christie, Daniel, Ohio State University, and Carl Glickman, University of Georgia, reported in *Psychology in the Schools*, v17, no3.

Cohen, Sheldon, "Sound Effects on Behavior," *Psychology Today*, October 1981, p38, 41–44, 48.

Cory, Christopher T., "Newsline," *Psychology Today*, November 1981, p22; researchers were not specified.

Coyne, James, University of California, Berkeley, and Stephen Strack, University of Miami, as reported in "Shunning the Depressed," *Psychology Today*, March 1982.

Cumming, David C., Faculty of Medicine, University of Iberta, as reported in "Runner's Love Slump," *Self*, February 1985.

Cutler, Winnifred B., and George Preti, Monell Chemical Senses Center, Philadelphia, *Hormones and Behavior*, 1987, v20, p463–82.

Darnton, Nina, "Women and Stress on Job and at Home," *The New York Times*, August 7, 1985.

DeLongis, Anita, and others, Stress and Coping Project, University of California, Berkeley, "Relationship of Daily Hassles, Uplifts, and Major Life Events to Health Status," *Health Psychology*, 1982, v1, no2, p119–36.

DeMartino, M. F., *Sex and the Intelligent Woman*, New York: Springer, 1974.

Dittrich, Gerhard, Urban Planning Institute, Nuremberg, Germany, a 250-page report published by West German Ministry of Housing and Urban Development, as reported in *The New York Times*, May 9, 1971.

Donnerstein, Edward, and Gary Barrett, Iowa State University, "Effects of Erotic Stimuli on Male Aggression Toward Females," *Journal of Personality and Social Psychology*, 1978, v36, no2, p180.

Dutton, Donald G., and Arthur P. Aron, University of British Columbia, "Some Evidence for Heightened Sexual Attraction under Conditions of High Anxiety," *Journal of Personality and Social Psychology*, 1974, v30, no4, p510–17.

Earls, Felton, professor of child psychiatry, Washington University School of Medicine, and director, Martha's Vineyard Child Health Survey, as reported in *The New York Times*, October 3, 1983.

Eron, Leonard, and Rowell Huesmann, University of Illinois, reported in " 'Class Bully' More Likely to Break Laws as an Adult," *Centre Daily Times* (State College, Pa.), August 17, 1985.

Fichten, Catherine S., and Betty Sunerton, Dawson College, "Popular Horoscopes and the 'Barnum Effect,' " *Journal of Psychology*, 1983, v114, p123–34.

Fischer, C. S., and Phillips, S. L., "Who Is Alone? Characteristics of People with Small Networks," in *Loneliness: A Sourcebook of Current Theory, Research and Therapy* (L. A. Peplau and D. Perlman, eds.), New York: Wiley, p21–39.

Fischman, Joshua, "Getting Touch," *Psychology Today*, December 1987, p26–28.

Fisher, William A., and Donn Byrne, Purdue University, "Sex Differences in

Response to Erotica? Love versus Lust," in *Journal of Personality and Social Psychology*, 1978, v36, no2, p117.

Gove, Walter R., and Michael R. Geerken, Vanderbilt University, "The Effect of Children and Employment on the Mental Health of Married Men and Women," in *Social Forces*, 1977, v56, no1, p66.

Harris Poll, "The Nuprin Pain Report," as reported in *Centre Daily Times*, (State College, Pa.), July 30, 1987.

Hatfield, Elaine, Sue Sprecher, and Jane Traupmann, University of Wisconsin, "Men's and Women's Reactions to Sexually Explicit Films: A Serendipitous Finding," *Archives of Sexual Behavior*, 1978, v7, no6, p583–92.

Hicks, Robert, San Jose State University, *Perceptual and Motor Skills*, 1983, v56, no1.

Hollender, Marc H., Vanderbilt University, at Mid-South Medical Association meeting in Memphis Tenn., as reported in the *Pittsburgh Post-Gazette*, March 1, 1971.

Holmes, T. H., and R. H. Rahe, University of Washington, "Social Readjustment Scale," *Journal of Psychosomatic Research*, v2, 1967, p213–18.

Hoon, Peter W., University of Tennessee, and Emily Franck Hoon, University of Florida, "Effects of Experience in Cohabitation on Erotic Arousability," *Psychological Reports*, 1982, v50, p255–58.

Inman, Marjorie, Purdue University, as reported in *Self*, February 1985, p40.

Ivancevich, John M., and Michael T. Matteson, "Occupational Stress, Satisfaction, Physical Well-Being, and Coping: A Study of Homemakers," *Psychological Reports*, June 1982, v50, no3, p995–1005.

Iwata, Osamu, "The Relationship of Noise Sensitivity to Health and Personality," *Japanese Psychological Research*, 1984, v26, no2, p75–81.

Jenks, Richard J., Indiana University Southeast, *Journal of Sex Research*, 1986, v21, no2.

Jones, Warren H., J. E. Freemon, and R. A. Goswick, "The Persistence of Loneliness: Self and Other Determinants," *Journal of Personality Assessment*, 1983.

Jones, Warren H., Steven A. Hobbs, and Don Hockenbury, University of Tulsa, "Loneliness and Social Skill Deficits," *Journal of Personality and Social Psychology*, 1982, v42, no4, p682.

Kleinke, Chris L., Edith Nourse Rogers Memorial Veterans Hospital, Bedford, Mass.; Richard A. Staneski, Old Dominion University; and Jeanne K. Mason, Caffey College, "Sex Differences in Coping with Depression," *Sex Roles*, 1982, v8, no8, p877.

Lazarus, Richard S., University of California, Berkeley, "Little Hassles Can Be Hazardous to Your Health," *Psychology Today*, July 1981, p58–62.

Lewy, Alfred J., psychiatrist, Oregon Health Sciences University, *Science*, 1987, v235, p352–53.

McCormack, S. H., and A. Kahn, "Behavioral Characteristics of Lonely and Non-Lonely College Students," paper presented at Midwestern Psychological Association, St. Louis, May 1980.

Miller, Gus H., director, Studies on Smoking, Inc., Edinboro, Pa., as reported by the Associated Press and appearing in *Centre Daily Times* (State College, Pa.), February 23, 1986.

Monk, Timothy H., University of Sussex, Brighton, England, and Lynne C.

Aplin, King's College, University of London, London, England, "Spring and Autumn Daylight Saving Time Changes: Studies of Adjustment in Sleep Timings, Mood, and Efficiency," *Ergonomics*, 1980, v23, no2, p167–78.

Morokoff, Patricia J., Uniformed Services University of the Health Sciences (Department of Defense), "Effects of Sex Guilt, Repression, Sexual 'Arousability,' and Sexual Experience on Female Sexual Arousal During Erotica and Fantasy," *Journal of Personality and Social Psychology*, 1985, v49, no1, p177-87. (Some additional findings and interview quotations are from Daniel Goleman, "New Studies Examine Sexual Guilt," *The New York Times*, August 20, 1985.)

New York Hospital–Cornell Medical Center, White Plains, N.Y., a study reported in *American Journal of Orthopsychiatry*, 1984, v54, no3.

Newsweek (cover story), "Depression," May 4, 1987, p48–54, 57.

Nolen-Hoeksema, Susan, Stanford University, as reported in *Centre Daily Times* (State College, Pa.), January 29, 1987.

Paoli, a study in a Paoli, Pa., hospital, as reported (without identifying the researcher) in the *Centre Daily Times* (State College, Pa.), October 7, 1984.

Peplau, Letitia Ann, University of California, and Daniel Perlman, University of British Columbia, "Perspectives on Loneliness," in *Loneliness: A Sourcebook of Current Theory, Research and Therapy*, New York: Wiley, 1982, p1–20.

Persinger, Michael A., *The Weather Matrix and Human Behavior*, New York: Praeger Publishers, 1980.

Phillips, David P., and John S. Wills, University of California, San Diego, *Suicide and Life-Threatening Behavior*, 1987, v17, p1–12.

Range, Lillian M., Howard N. Anderson, and Andrea L. Wesley, University of Southern Mississippi, "Personality Correlates of Multiple Choice Answer-Changing Patterns," *Psychological Reports*, 1982, v51, p523–27.

Rassidakis, N. C., as reported in *Behavior Today*, October 2, 1972.

Repetti, Rena, University of Southern California, paper delivered at 1985 annual meeting, American Psychological Association, as reported in *Litchfield County Times*, December 27, 1985.

Rooney, John J., La Salle College, reported in *Psychology Today*, November 1981.

Rosenthal, Norman E., and Thomas A Wehr, as presented to the 1985 annual meetings of the American Psychiatric Association and the Association of Biological Psychiatry.

Russell, D. W., Letitia Ann Peplau, and Carolyn E. Cutrona, "The Revised UCLA Loneliness Scale: Concurrent and Discriminant Validity Evidence," *Journal of Personality and Social Psychology*, 1980, v39, p472–80.

Saft, Marcia, "When Depression Calls at Christmas," *The New York Times*, December 8, 1985.

Salk, Lee, Cornell University Medical College, article in *Lancet*, reported in "Teen-Age Suicide," *The New York Times*, April 30, 1985.

Sanders, Jeffrey L., and Mary S. Brizzolara, Towson State University, "Relationships Between Weather and Mood," *Journal of General Psychology*, July 1982, v107, no1, p155–56.

Seiden, Richard H., University of California (Berkeley) School of Public Health, an article in *International Journal of Aging and Human Development*, 1982, reported in *University of California Clip Sheet*.

Seiden, Richard H., and Mary Spence, University of California, Berkeley, "A

Tale of Two Bridges: Comparative Suicide Incidence on the Golden Gate and San Francisco–Oakland Bay Bridges," *Crisis—International Journal of Suicide and Crisis Studies*, v3, no1, p32–40.

Sex Over Forty (a newsletter published in Chapel Hill, N.C.), Paul A. Fleming, M.D., ed., "How Women Feel About Sex: What Surveys Show," February 1988, v6, no9.

Shaver, Philip, and Jonathan Freedman, "Your Pursuit of Happiness," *Psychology Today*, August 1976, p26–32, 75.

Shneidman, Edwin S., UCLA School of Medicine, as indirectly and directly quoted from his book, *Definition of Suicide*, in an article, "Clues to Suicide: A Brain Chemical Is Implicated," Daniel Goleman, *The New York Times*, October 8, 1985, pC-1, C-8.

Simpson and Schill (1977), cited in Harold Holzman, Rutgers University, and Sharon Pines, Montgomery County Health Department, "Buying Sex: The Phenomenology of Being a John," *Deviant Behavior: An Interdisciplinary Journal*, 1982, v4, p89.

Solano, Cecilia H., Phillip G. Batten, and Elizabeth A. Parrish, Wake Forest University, "Loneliness and Patterns of Self-Disclosure," *Journal of Personality and Social Psychology*, 1982, v43, no3, p524.

Stack, Steven, Pennsylvania State University, paper presented at 1984 annual meeting, American Sociological Association.

Stokes, Joseph P., University of Illinois at Chicago, "The Relation of Social Network and Individual Difference Variables to Loneliness," *Journal of Personality and Social Psychology*, 1985, v48, no4, p981.

Strack, Stephen, Paul H. Blaney, and Ronald J. Ganellen, University of Miami; and James C. Coyne, Mental Research Institute, Palo Alto, California, "Pessimistic Self-Preoccupation, Performance Deficits, and Depression," *Journal of Personality and Social Psychology*, 1985, v49, no4, p1076–85.

Stramler, Carlla, James Kleiss, and William Howell, reported in *Journal of Applied Psychology*, v68, no1.

Wasserman, Ira, Eastern Michigan University, *American Sociological Review*, 1985, v49, no3.

Weinberg, Martin S., Rochelle Ganz Swensson, and Sue Kiefer Hammersmith, Indiana University, "Sexual Autonomy and the Status of Women: Models of Female Sexuality in U.S. Sex Manuals from 1950 to 1980," *Social Problems*, February 1983, v30, no3, p312–24.

Wheeler, Ladd, and Harry Reis, University of Rochester, and John Nezlek, College of William and Mary, "Loneliness, Social Interaction and Sex Roles," *Journal of Personality and Social Psychology*, 1983, v45, no4, p943.

White, Gregory, University of Maryland; Sanford Fishbein, Notre Dame University; and Jeffrey Rutstein, Rutgers University, "Heartbeat and Your Perceptions of the Opposite Sex," *Journal of Personality and Social Psychology*, 1981, v41, no1.

Williams, Janice G., and Cecilia H. Solano, Wake Forest University, "The Social Reality of Feeling Lonely: Friendship and Reciprocation," *Personality and Social Psychology Bulletin*, 1983, v9, no2, p237.

Wilson, Wayne, and Valette Liedtke, Stephen F. Austin State University, "Movie-Inspired Sexual Practices," in *Psychological Reports*, 1984, v54, p328.

CHAPTER 3: THE SECRET LIFE OF YOUR MIND

Altman, Irwin, "Reciprocity of Interpersonal Exchange," *Journal of Theory of Social Behaviour*, 1973, v3, no2, p249.

Amabile, Teresa M., Brandeis University, "Brilliant but Cruel: Perceptions of Negative Evaluators," *Journal of Experimental Social Psychology*, 1983, v19, p146–56.

Amerikaner, Martin, University of Houston, "Self-Disclosure: A Study of Verbal and Coverbal Intimacy," in *Journal of Psychology*, 1980, v104, p221.

Andreasen, Nancy C., University of Iowa College of Medicine; Kay Jamison, University of California at Los Angeles; and Kareen and Hagop Akiskal, in separate studies reported in *Science News*, October 24, 1987, v132, p262; also reported by wire service news items, November 1984 and March 1987.

Asbell, Bernard, "Is Your Child Brighter Than Teachers Think?" *Redbook*, March 1973, p92–93, 153–56.

Barefoot, John C., Lloyd H. Strickland, Paul Guild, and Allen Turnbull, Carleton University, Ottawa, Canada, "The Effect of Severity of Exertion on Liking for a Cause," *Journal of Social Psychology*, June 1976, v99, no1, p51–56.

Beale, Claudette J., and David Baskin, Bronx-Lebanon Hospital Center, Crotona Park Community Mental Health Center, N.Y., "What Do Our Teenagers Fear?" *Child Psychiatry Quarterly*, 1983, v16, no1, p1–8.

Cadwell Davis Partners (advertising agency) survey on attitudes toward aging, commissioned after the marketing failure of a "senior citizen" food line and shampoo for "over-forty hair." Reported in "Most Feel Their Age Is Unreal," *The New York Times*, November 10, 1982.

Cameron, Paul, University of Louisville, reported in *Behavior Today*, December 17, 1970.

Chaikin, Alan L., Valerian J. Derlega, Benjamin Bayma and Jacqueline Shaw, Old Dominion University, "Neuroticism and Disclosure Reciprocity," *Journal of Consulting and Clinical Psychology*, 1975, v43, no1, p13.

Cozby, Paul C., University of Minnesota, "Self-Disclosure: A Literature Review," *Psychological Bulletin*, February 1973, v79, no2., p73.

Darley, John, and C. Daniel Batson, Princeton University, *Journal of Personality and Social Psychology*, v27, no1.

Davidson, William, University of South Carolina, Aiken; and Patrick Cotter, University of Alabama; "Adjustment to Aging and Relationships with Offspring," *Psychological Reports*, 1982, v50, p731. (Survey involved "structured" interviews with eighty-three elderly people, mostly white, female, and living with a spouse, who participate in a senior citizens discount program in Aiken, S.C.)

Davis, John D., University of Sheffield, England, "Self-Disclosure in an Acquaintance Exercise: Responsibility for Level of Intimacy," *Journal of Personality and Social Psychology*, 1976, v33, no6, p787.

Davis, Kingsley, and Pietronella van den Oever, University of Southern California, in *Population and Development Review*, v7, no1, as reported in *Psychology Today*, December 1981.

Derlega, Valerian J., Midge Wilson, and Alan L. Chaikin, Old Dominion University, "Friendship and Disclosure Reciprocity," *Journal of Personality and Social Psychology*, 1976, v34, no4, p587.

Feldman, David, Tufts University, as reported in "Does 180 Mean Supergenius?" *Psychology Today*, May 1983, p18.

Fell, Larry; Mark Dahlstrom, D. Campbell Winter, Kenosha (Wisconsin) Unified School District No. 1, "Personality Traits of Parents of Gifted Children," *Psychological Reports*, 1984, v54, p383–87.

Flynn, James R., University of Otago, New Zealand, *Psychological Bulletin*, v101, p171–91.

George, Pamela, Department of Special Education, North Carolina Central University, and James Gallagher, Frank Porter Graham Child Development Center, University of North Carolina, *Journal for the Education of the Gifted*, v2, no1.

Gold, Norman, and Julie Shaw, Malvern Clinic, Malvern, Victoria, Australia, *Medical Journal of Australia*, v1, no13.

Goldenson, Robert M., *The Encyclopedia of Human Behavior*, Garden City, N.Y.: Doubleday, 1970.

Goleman, Daniel, "Forgetfulness Is Seen Causing More Worry Than It Should," *The New York Times*, July 1, 1986, pC-1.

Goleman, Daniel, "In Memory, People Re-Create Their Lives to Suit Their Images of the Present," *The New York Times*, June 23, 1987, pC-1.

Goleman, Daniel, " 'Social Chameleon' May Pay Emotional Price," *The New York Times*, March 12, 1985.

Gondola, Joan, Baruch College of the City University of New York, and Bruce Tuckman, Florida State University, *Journal of Social Behavior and Personality*, v1, no1.

Grigsby, James P., and Donald Weatherley, University of Colorado, "Gender and Sex-Role Differences in Intimacy of Self-Disclosure," *Psychological Reports*, 1983, v53, p891.

Gruber, Howard, Director, Institute for Cognitive Studies, Rutgers University, interviewed by Howard Gardner, Boston University School of Medicine, "Breakaway Minds," *Psychology Today*, July 1981, p64–73.

Harvey, Joan, University of Pennsylvania Medical School, a paper presented before the annual meeting of the American Psychological Association, Toronto, 1984, as reported in *The New York Times*, September 11, 1984.

Hoelter, Jon W., University of Cincinnati, "Relative Effects of Significant Others on Self-Evaluation," *Social Psychology Quarterly*, 1984, v47, no3, p255–62.

Hoffman, Martin L., University of Michigan, "Altruistic Behavior and the Parent-Child Relationship," *Journal of Personality and Social Psychology*, 1975, v31, p937–43.

Hogan, H. Wayne, Tennessee Technological University, "I.Q. Self-Estimates of Males and Females," *Journal of Social Psychology*, 1978, v106, p137–38.

Hosch, Harmon M., and Stephanie J. Platz, "Self-Monitoring and Eyewitness Accuracy," *Personality and Social Psychology Bulletin*, June 1984, v10, no2, p289–92.

Ickes, William, and Richard D. Barnes, University of Wisconsin, "The Role of Sex and Self-Monitoring in Unstructured Dyadic Interactions," *Journal of Personality and Social Psychology*, 1977, v35, no5, p315.

Jackson, Jeffrey M., and Bibb Latane, Ohio State University, *Personality and Social Psychology Bulletin*, v7, no3.

Johnson, David L., Baylor University, "College Students' Scores on Torrance's Tests of Creative Thinking," *Psychological Reports*, 1974, v35, p65–66.

Jourard, Sidney M., and Lasakow, P., "A Research Approach to Self-Disclosure," *Journal of Abnormal Psychology*, 1958, p56.

Kaltsounis, Bill, Middle Tennessee State University, "Race, Socioeconomic Status and Creativity," *Psychological Reports*, August 1974, v35, no1, p164–66.

Kaufmann, Walter, *Beyond Guilt and Justice*, as reported in *Behavior Today*, February 7, 1972.

Loewenstine, Harold V., George D. Ponticos, and Michele A. Paludi, University of Cincinnati and Kent State University, "Sex Differences in Graffiti as a Communicative Style," *Journal of Social Psychology*, 1982, v117, p307–8.

Lynn, Richard, "The Social Ecology of Intelligence in the British Isles," *British Journal of Social and Clinical Psychology*, 1979, v18, p1–11.

Maas, Henry, and Joseph Kuypers, *From Thirty to Seventy*, published 1975 by Jossey-Bass, Inc., San Francisco, as reported in the *University of California Clip Sheet*, June 24, 1975.

Mewaldt, Steven, Marshall University, paper delivered before the 1987 annual meeting of the American Psychological Association, as reported in "Tranquil Daze," *Psychology Today*, January 1988, p12.

Pedersen, Dahrl, Brigham Young University, *Perceptual and Motor Skills*, v62, no1.

Perkins, David N., codirector, Project Zero, Harvard University, as reported in "The Spark: Personal Testimonies of Creativity," *Science News*, November 7, 1987, p297–99.

Piechowski, Michael M., Northwestern University; Linda K. Silverman and R. Frank Falk of the University of Denver, "Comparison of Intellectually and Artistically Gifted on Five Dimensions of Mental Functioning," *Perceptual and Motor Skills*, 1985, v60, p539–49.

Psychology Today, "Wellness Is All, a Report on *Psychology Today*'s Survey of Beliefs about Health," by Carin Rubenstein, October 1982, p28–37.

Rafferty, Carole, "Study of Gifted from Childhood to Old Age," *The New York Times*, April 23, 1984.

Rosner, Mordecai, and Michael Belkin, *Archives of Opthalmology*, 1987, as reported by the Associated Press, November 1987, and T. W. Teasdale, Copenhagen University and Danish Institute of Myopia Research, "Study Links Intelligence and Myopia," by Cory Dean, *The New York Times*, December 20, 1988.

Rossi, Alice, University of Massachusetts, Amherst, in *Signs*, v6, no1, as reported in "Women's 40-Year Itch to Be 34," *Psychology Today*, February 1982, p82.

Rotter, Julian B., University of Connecticut, "Interpersonal Trust, Trustworthiness, and Gullibility," *American Psychologist*, January 1980, v35, no1, p1–7.

Rubin, Zick, Harvard University, "Disclosing Oneself to a Stranger: Reciprocity and Its Limits," *Journal of Experimental Social Psychology*, 1975, v11, p233.

Schaie, K. Warner, and Sherry L. Willis, Pennsylvania State University, a study supported by the National Center of Aging, as reported in "Resharpening Mental Skills," *The New York Times*, February 26, 1986, pC-3.

Shaffer, David R., University of Georgia; Jonathan E. Smith, Akron University; and Michele Tomarelli, University of Georgia, "Self-Monitoring as a Determinant of Self-Disclosure Reciprocity During the Acquaintance Process," *Journal of Personality and Social Psychology*, 1982, v43, no1, p163.

Shaw, Jeffrey S., Frances Francois, Hadassa Filler, and Vincenza Sciarillo, City

University of New York, "The Thoughts of Persons in an Urban Environment," in *Journal of Social Psychology*, 1981, v115, p293.

Snyder, Mark, University of Minnesota, "Self-Monitoring of Expressive Behavior," in *Journal of Personality and Social Psychology*, 1974, v30, no4, p526. (The Snyder test for self-monitoring is included in this article.)

Snyder, Mark, Ellen Berscheid, and Peter Glick, University of Minnesota, "Focusing on the Exterior and Interior: Two Investigations of the Initiation of Personal Relationships," *Journal of Personality and Social Psychology*, 1985, v48, no6, p1427–39.

Snyder, Mark, Steve Gangestad, and Jeffrey A. Simpson, University of Minnesota, "Choosing Friends as Activity Partners: The Role of Self-Monitoring," *Journal of Personality and Social Psychology*, 1983, v45, no5, p1061–72.

Snyder, Mark, and Thomas C. Monson, University of Minnesota, "Persons, Situations and the Control of Social Behavior," *Journal of Personality and Social Psychology*, 1975, v32, no4, p637.

Snyder, Mark, and William B. Swann, Jr., University of Minnesota, "When Actions Reflect Attitudes: The Politics of Impression Management," *Journal of Personality and Social Psychology*, 1976, v34, no5, p1034.

Sobol, Dava, "For Some People, Studies Find, 'One True Self' Isn't Enough," *The New York Times*, November 24, 1981, pC-1.

Solano, Cecelia H., Phillip G. Batten, and Elizabeth A. Parrish, Wake Forest University, "Loneliness and Patterns of Self-Disclosure," *Journal of Personality and Social Psychology*, 1982, v43, no3, p524.

Streufert, Siegfried, Pennsylvania State University College of Medicine, as reported by Daniel Goleman, "Successful Executives Rely on Own Kind of Intelligence," *The New York Times*, July 31, 1984, pC-1.

"The Tampax Report," compiled for Tampax Inc. by Research and Forecast, the research arm of Ruder and Finn, a public relations firm, as reported in *The New York Times*, June 22, 1981.

Wales, Elizabeth, and Barbara Brewer, University of Cincinnati, "Graffiti in the 1970's," *Journal of Social Psychology*, 1976, v99, p115–23.

Weinrich, James D., Harvard University, "Nonreproduction, Homosexuality, Transsexualism, and Intelligence: A Systematic Literature Search," *Journal of Homosexuality*, Spring 1978, v3, no3, p275–89.

Winstead, Barbara A., and Valerian J. Derlega, Old Dominion University, and Paul T. P. Wong, Trent University, "Effects of Sex-Role Orientation on Behavioral Self-Disclosure," *Journal of Research in Personality*, 1984, v18, p541.

Won-Doornink, Myong Jun, Washington State University, "On Getting to Know You: The Association Between the Stage of a Relationship and Reciprocity of Self-Disclosure," *Journal of Experimental Social Psychology*, 1979, v15, p229.

Wortman, Camille B., Peter Adesman, Elliot Herman, and Richard Greenberg, Northwestern University, "Self-Disclosure: An Attributional Perspective," *Journal of Personality and Social Psychology*, 1976, v33, no2, p184.

CHAPTER 4: CRIME, VIOLENCE, AND AGGRESSION

Allen, Vernon L., and David B. Greenberger, University of Wisconsin, "Enjoyment of Destruction: The Role of Uncertainty," *Journal of Nonverbal Behavior*, 1979, v4, no2, p87.

Anderson, Craig A., Rice University, and Dona C. Anderson, Houston Veterans Administration Medical Center, "Ambient Temperature and Violent Crime: Tests of the Linear and Curvilinear Hypotheses," *Journal of Personality and Social Psychology*, 1984, v46, no1, p91–97.

Bart, Pauline, and Patricia H. O'Brien, University of Illinois at Chicago, as reported by Valerie J. Phillips, Chicago Tribune Syndicate, *Centre Daily Times*, (State College, Pa.) March 31, 1986.

Behavior Today, April 26, 1971, p2.

Block, Richard, Loyola University, and Wesley Skogan, Northwestern University, as reported in "Best Tactics for Talking to Assailants," *The New York Times*, August 16, 1983.

Brutz, Judith L., Iowa State University, and Bron B. Ingoldsby, Ricks College, Rexburg, Id., "Conflict Resolution in Quaker Families," *Journal of Marriage and the Family*, February 1984, p21–26.

Calhoun, Lawrence G., Arnie Cann, James W. Selby, and David L. Magee, University of North Carolina at Charlotte, "Victim Emotional Response: Effects on Social Reaction to Victims of Rape," *British Journal of Social Psychology*, 1981, v20, p17–21.

Cann, Arnie, Lawrence G. Calhoun, and James W. Selby, University of North Carolina at Charlotte, "Attributing Responsibility to the Victim of Rape: Influence of Information Regarding Past Sexual Experience," *Human Relations*, 1979, v32, no1, p57–67.

Clifford, Brian R., and Clive R. Hollin, North East London Polytechnic, "Effects of the Type of Incident and the Number of Perpetrators on Eyewitness Memory," *Journal of Applied Psychology*, 1981, v66, no3, p364.

Cook, Philip, Duke University, as reported in "Best Tactics for Talking to Assailants," *The New York Times*, August 16, 1983.

Curtis, Gary, Greater Washington D.C. Board of Trade, reported in "When You Least Expect It . . . ," *Chain Store Age Executive*, February 1985, p18.

DePaulo, Bella, University of Virginia, and Roger Pfeifer, Federal Law Enforcement Training Center, Glynco, Ga., *Journal of Applied Social Psychology*, v16, no3.

Dodge, Kenneth, Vanderbilt University, *Child Development*, 1987.

Eron, Leonard, and Rowell Huesmann, University of Illinois, reported in " 'Class Bully' More Likely to Break Laws as an Adult," *Centre Daily Times* (State College, Pa.), August 17, 1985.

Feldman-Summers, Shirley, and Karen Lindner, University of Washington, "Perceptions of Victims and Defendants in Criminal Assault Cases," *Criminal Justice and Behavior*, June 1976, v3, no2, p135–50.

Grayson, Betty, Hofstra University, *Journal of Communication*, Winter 1981, as reported in "Do Body Actions Invite Assault?" by Jane E. Brody, *The New York Times*, February 3, 1981.

Hassett, James, Boston University, "But That Would Be Wrong," *Psychology Today*, November 1981, p34–48.

Heath, Linda, Loyola University, "Impact of Newspaper Crime Reports on Fear of Crime: Multimethodological Investigation," *Journal of Personality and Social Psychology*, 1984, v47, no.2, p263.

Jacobson, Marsha, University of Dayton, "Effects of Victim's and Defendant's

Physical Attractiveness on Subjects' Judgments in a Rape Case," in *Sex Roles*, 1981, v7, no3, p247.

Jarmon, Robert, College of Medicine and Dentistry of New Jersey, reported in "Crime and Pollution," *Behavior Today*, May 21, 1973.

Johnson, Eric, Carnegie-Mellon University, and Amos Tversky, Stanford University, "Affect, Generalization, and the Perception of Risk," *Journal of Personality and Social Psychology*, 1983, v.45, no.1, p20.

Johnston, Roy, and Burdette Lundy, Veterans Administration Medical Center, *Hospital & Community Psychiatry*, v33, no12.

Kellermann, Arthur, M.D., University of Tennessee, and Donald Reay, M.D., King County Medical Examiner's Office, Seattle, Wash., *The New England Journal of Medicine*, 1986, v314, no24.

Knauft, Bruce M., Emory University, *Current Anthropology*, August–October 1987, as reported in "Murder in Good Company," by Bruce Bower, *Science News*, February 6, 1988, v133, p90–91.

Lewis, Dorothy Otnow, M.D., New York University School of Medicine, *American Journal of Psychiatry*, v143, p838–45.

Lichtenstein, Sarah; Paul Slovic, Baruch Fischhoff, Mark Layman, and Barbara Combs, Decision Research, Eugene, Ore., "Judged Frequency of Lethal Events," *Journal of Experimental Psychology: Human Learning and Memory*, 1978, v4, no6, p551.

Lipton, David, John F. Kennedy Medical Center, Edison, N.J., *Journal of Consulting and Clinical Psychology*, as reported in "Rapists' Blind Spot," *Psychology Today*, October 1986, p14.

Lunde, Donald T., professor of psychiatry and law, Stanford University, as reported by United Press International in *New Haven Journal-Courier*, May 31, 1976.

Lyon, Alec, psychiatrist, Purdysburn Hospital, Belfast, Ireland, reported in "Riot On," *Behavior Today*, February 21, 1972.

Maital, Shlomo, chairman, Economics Department, Technion-Israel Institute of Technology, Haifa, Israel, "The Tax-Evasion Virus," *Psychology Today*, March 1982, p74–78.

Peters, Joseph, University of Pennsylvania, at the American Assocation for the Advancement of Science, reported in *Behavior Today*, January 10, 1972.

Petersilia, Joan, RAND Corporation, reported in "Most Felons Put on Probation Still a Threat, Research Finds," *The New York Times*, February 3, 1985.

Petrovich, Michael, and Donald I. Templer, California School of Professional Psychology, Fresno, "Heterosexual Molestation of Children Who Later Became Rapists," *Psychological Reports*, 1984, v54, p810.

Ray, Joseph B., Gary S. Solomon, Maria G. Doncaster, and Richard Mellina, Lubbock Regional Mental Health Center, Texas, "First Offender Adult Shoplifters: A Preliminary Profile," *Journal of Clinical Psychology*, September 1983, v39, no5, p769–70.

Rizzo, Nicholas D., Lowell District Court Clinic, Mass., "Murder in Boston: Killers and Their Victims," *International Journal of Offender Therapy and Comparative Criminology*, 1982, v26, p36–42.

Russell, Gordon W., University of Lethbridge, "Crowd Size and Density in Relation to Athletic Aggression and Performance," *Social Behavior and Personality*, reported in *Experimental Social Psychology*, v71, no6712, p710.

Shannon, Lyle W., University of Iowa, *Science News*, reported in "Crimefighting That Doesn't Pay," *Psychology Today*, February 1983, p62.

Sigelman, Carol K., Carol J. Berry, and Katharine A. Wiles, Eastern Kentucky University, "Violence in College Students' Dating Relationships," *Journal of Applied Social Psychology*, 1984, v5, no6, p530–48.

Slovic, Paul, Baruch Fischoff, Sarah Lichtenstein, "Facts versus Fears: Understanding Perceived Risk," *Judgment Under Uncertainty: Heuristics and Biases*, New York: Cambridge University Press, 1982.

Steffensmeier, Darrell J., Pennsylvania State University, "Trends in Female Crime: It's Still a Man's World," *The Criminal Justice System and Women*, Barbara Price and Natalie Sokoloff (eds.), New York: Clark Boardman, 1982.

Thornton, B., "Effect of Rape Victim's Attractiveness in a Jury Simulation," cited in Jacobson, above.

Wells, Gary L., University of Alberta; Tamara Ferguson, Catholic University of Nijmegen, The Netherlands; R. C. L. Lindsay, University of Manitoba, "The Tractability of Eyewitness Confidence and Its Implications for Triers of Fact," *Journal of Applied Psychology*, 1981, v66, no6, p688.

Wells, Gary L., University of Alberta, and Michael R. Leippe, St. Norbert College, "How Do Triers of Fact Infer the Accuracy of Eyewitness Identifications? Using Memory for Peripheral Detail Can Be Misleading," *Journal of Applied Psychology*, 1981, v66, no6, p682.

West, Stephen G., Steven P. Gunn, and Paul Chernicky, Florida State University, "Ubiquitous Watergate: An Attributional Analysis," *Journal of Personality and Social Psychology*, 1975, v32, no1, p55–65.

Wyer, Robert S.; Galen V. Bodenhausen, and Theresa F. Gorman, University of Illinois, "Cognitive Mediators of Reaction to Rape," *Journal of Personality and Social Psychology*, 1985, v48, no2, p324–38.

CHAPTER 5: YOUR RELATIONSHIPS

Abbey, Antonia, Northwestern University, "Sex Differences in Attributions for Friendly Behavior: Do Males Misperceive Females' Friendliness?" *Journal of Personality and Social Psychology*, 1982, v42, no5, p830.

Adams, Bert N., University of Wisconsin, Madison, "Birth Order: A Critical Review," *Sociometry*, 1972, v35, no3, p411–39.

American Cancer Society, *The Journal of the National Cancer Institute*, September 1985, as reported in *The New York Times*, September 14, 1985.

Anspach, D. F., "Kinship and Divorce," *Journal of Marriage and the Family*, 1976, v38, p323–30.

Arkowitz, Hal, University of Arizona, *Behavior Therapy* (no date cited), and James Curran, Brown University, as reported in "In Dating, Men Remain the More Troubled Sex," *The New York Times*, April 28, 1981.

Bailey, Roger C., and Donna G. Garrou, East Tennessee State University, "Dating Availability and Religious Involvement as Influences on Interpersonal Attraction," *Journal of Psychology*, 1983, v113, no1, p95.

Bailey, Roger C., and Michael Kelly, East Tennessee State University, "Perceived Physical Attractiveness in Early, Steady, and Engaged Daters," *Journal of Psychology*, 1984, v116, no1, p39.

Baskett, Linda Musun, University of Arkansas, Little Rock, "Sibling Status

Effects: Adult Expectations," *Developmental Psychology*, 1985, v21, no3, p441–45.

Baumrind, Diana, University of California, Berkeley, as reported in *University of California Clip Sheet*, May 20, 1969, v44, no45.

Baxter, Leslie, Lewis and Clark College, and William Wilmot, University of Montana, *Human Communication Research*, v11, no2.

Belmont, Lillian, and Frances A. Marolla, "Birth Order, Family Size, and Intelligence," *Science*, December 14, 1973, p1096–1101.

Belsky, Jay, Pennsylvania State University, as reported in "Changes in a Marriage When a Baby Is Born," Glenn Collins, *The New York Times*, January 6, 1985.

Bennett, Jay, Yale University; David Bloom, Columbia University; and Ann Klimas Blanc, Westinghouse Institute Resource Development, Columbia, Maryland, *American Sociological Review*, February 1988.

Berardo, Donna Hodgkins, University of Florida, *Journal of Marriage and the Family*, v49, p381–90.

Berger, Kathleen Stassen, Bronx Community College of the City University of New York, reported in "The Outlook for Feminism Debated by Vassar Panels," *The New York Times* coverage of the Fifth Berkshire Conference on the History of Women, June 19, 1981.

Beutell, Nicholas J., W. Paul Stillman School of Business, Seton Hall University, "Correlates of Attitudes Toward American Women as Managers," *Journal of Social Psychology*, October 1984, v124, 1st half, p57–63.

Bigner, Jerry J., R. Brooke Jacobsen, Judith A. Miller, and Joseph G. Turner, Colorado State University, "The Value of Children for Farm Families," *Psychological Reports*, 1982, v50, p793–94.

Birren, J., *The Psychology of Aging*, New York: Prentice-Hall, 1964.

Booth, Alan, David B. Brinkerhoff, Lynn K. White, University of Nebraska, Lincoln, "The Impact of Parental Divorce on Courtship," *Journal of Marriage and the Family*, February 1984, p85–94.

Bouchard, Thomas J., Jr., University of Minnesota Center for Twin and Adoption Research, as described in "Genes and Behavior: A Twin Legacy," by Constance Holden, *Psychology Today*, September 1987, p18–19.

Cantor, Pamela, Boston University, "The Adolescent Attempter: Sex, Sibling Position, and Family Constellation," *Life-Threatening Behavior*, Winter 1972, v2, no4, p252–61.

Capute, Arnold J., Bruce K. Shapiro, and Frederick B. Palmer, Kennedy Institute for Handicapped Children, Johns Hopkins University School of Medicine, as reported in "Child Development: Language Takes On New Significance," Jane E. Brody, *The New York Times*, May 5, 1987, pC-1.

Cohen, Tamar, private practitioner in marriage and family therapy, West Hartford, Connecticut, "The Incestuous Family Revisited," *Social Casework: The Journal of Contemporary Social Work* (Family Service Association of America), March 1983, p154–161.

Cole, Jonathan R., and Harriet Zuckerman, Columbia University, *Scientific American*, v256, no2.

Colletta, N. D., "Support Systems after Divorce: Incidence and Impact," *Journal of Marriage and the Family*, 1979, v41, p837–46.

Cornoldi, Cesare, and Lucia Cornoldi Fattori, "Age Spacing in Firstborns and

Symbiotic Dependence," in *Journal of Personality and Social Psychology*, 1976, v33, no4, p431.

Corsello, Philip, St. John's University, Ph.D. thesis, "Birth Order and Children's Perceptions of Love, Authority and Personality Adjustment," in *Dissertation Abstracts*, 1973, Order 73-29, 944.

Crane, D. Russell, Texas Tech University, and William Griffin, Auburn University, "Personal Space: An Objective Measure of Marital Quality," *Journal of Marital and Family Therapy*, 1983, v9, no3, p325–27.

DiPietro, Janet, and others, University of Maryland, *Developmental Psychology*, v23, p467–74.

Falbo, Toni, University of Texas, Austin, "Folklore and the Only Child: A Reassessment," paper presented at 84th Annual Convention, American Psychological Association, Washington, D.C., 1976; also quoted in "Dispelling Myths About the Only Child," *The New York Times*, August 13, 1984.

Feingold, Alan, City University of New York, "Physical Attractiveness and Romantic Evolvement," *Psychological Reports*, 1982, v50, p802.

Folkes, Valerie S., University of California, Los Angeles, "Forming Relationships and the Matching Hypothesis," *Personality and Social Psychology Bulletin*, 1982, v8, no4, p631.

Friedmann, Erika, and Aaron H. Katcher, University of Pennsylvania School of Veterinary Medicine; Sue A. Thomas and James J. Lynch, University of Maryland School of Medicine; and Peter R. Messent, Animal Studies Center, Waltham-on-the-Wolds, Leicestershire, England, "Social Interaction and Blood Pressure," *The Journal of Nervous and Mental Disease*, 1983, v171, no8, p461–65; also "Animal Companions and One-Year Survival of Patients After Discharge from a Coronary Care Unit," *Public Health Report*, 1980, v95, p307–12.

Glick, P. C., and A. J. Norton, "Marrying, Divorcing, and Living Together in the United States Today," *Population Bulletin*, 1979, v32.

Goleman, Daniel, "Marriage: Research Reveals Ingredients of Happiness," *The New York Times*, April 16, 1985.

Gorman, Ira, California School of Professional Psychology, "The Relationship of Mothers' Achievement Orientation to the Academic Achievement of Her First and Second Born Sons," in *Dissertation Abstracts*, 1974, Order 74-7929.

Hansen, Gary L., University of Southern Mississippi, "Marital Satisfaction and Jealousy Among Men," in *Psychological Reports*, 1983, v52, p363.

Harris, J., "Dogs Contribute to Ego Strength," *The Latham Letter*, 1981, v3, p13–15.

Hetherington, E. M., M. Cox, and R. Cox, "Divorced Fathers," *The Family Coordinator*, 1976, v25, p417–28.

Hewitt, Jay, and Morton Goldman, University of Missouri, Kansas City, "Traits Attributed to Over- and Under-Chosen Women," *Psychological Reports*, 1982, v51, p431–39.

Hill, Charles T., University of Washington; Zick Rubin, Harvard University; and Letitia Anne Peplau, University of California, Los Angeles, "Breakup Before Marriage: The End of 103 Affairs," *Journal of Social Issues*, 1976, v32, no1, p147.

Hofferth, Sandra, and Virginia Cain, National Institute of Child Health and Development, a paper presented before the Population Association of America, as reported in *Psychology Today*, December 1987, p12.

Holmes, Thomas, and colleagues, University of Washington, Seattle, as reported in "Marriage Is Good for Health and Longevity, Studies Say," *The New York Times*, May 8, 1979.

Ickes, William, University of Texas, Arlington, and Marilyn Turner, University of Missouri, St. Louis, "On the Social Advantages of Having an Older, Opposite-Sex Sibling: Birth Order Influences in Mixed-Sex Dyad," *Journal of Personality and Social Psychology*, 1983, v45, no1, p210.

Jacoby, Arthur P., sociologist, and John D. Williams, statistician, University of North Dakota, *Journal of Marriage and the Family*, 1986, v47, no4.

Jacques, Jeffrey, and Karen Chason, Florida A&M University, *Family Coordinator*, v28, no1.

Jason, Leonard A., Arnold Reichler, and Walter Rucker, De Paul University, "Territorial Behavior on Beaches," *Journal of Social Psychology*, 1981, v114, no1, p43.

Jedlicka, Davor, University of Texas, "Indirect Parental Influence on Mate Choice: A Test of the Psychoanalytic Theory," in *Journal of Marriage and the Family*, February 1984, p65.

Joesting, Joan, Salisbury State College, and Robert Joesting, Challenge Foundation, "Birth Order and Desired Family Size," *Journal of Individual Psychology*, 1973, v29, p34.

Johnson, William R., and Jonathan Skinner, University of Virginia, *American Economic Review*, 1986, v76, no3.

Johnston, Michael W., and Susan J. Eklund, Indiana University, "Life-Adjustment of the Never-Married: A Review with Implications for Counseling," *Journal of Counseling and Development*, December 1984, v63, p230–36.

Joubert, Charles E., University of North Alabama, "Birth Order and Creative Writing," *Psychological Reports*, April 1983, v52, no2, p617–18.

Kidd, Aline H., Mills College; Helen T. Kelley, St. Mary's College; Robert M. Kidd, V. A. Medical Center, Martinez, California, "Personality Characteristics of Horse, Turtle, Snake, and Bird Owners," *Psychological Reports*, 1983, v52, p719–29.

Kingston, Paul William, and Steven Nock, University of Virginia, *American Sociological Review*, v52, p391–400.

Kitson, Gay C., School of Medicine, Case Western Reserve University, and Helen J. Raschke, Austin College, "Divorce Research: What We Know; What We Need to Know," *Journal of Divorce*, Spring 1981, v4, no3, p1–37.

Kleinke, Chris, Rogers Memorial Veterans Hospital, Bedford, Mass., in *Psychology Today*, August 1981.

Kohen, J. A., C. A. Brown, and R. Feldberg, "Divorced Mothers: The Costs and Benefits of Female Family Control," in *Divorce and Separation*, George Levinger and O. C. Moles, eds., New York: Basic Books, 1979.

Lester, David, Nancy Brazill, Constance Ellis, and Thomas Guerin, Stockton State College, Pomona, N.J., "Correlates of Romantic Attitudes Toward Love: Androgyny and Self-Disclosure," *Psychological Reports*, 1984, v54, p554.

Long, Barbara H., Goucher College, "A Steady Boy Friend: A Step Toward Resolution of the Intimacy Crisis for American College Women," *The Journal of Psychology*, 1983, v115, p275–80.

Long, Thomas, Catholic University, and Lynette Long, American University, as reported in *Washington Post Health*, November 27, 1985, p9.

Manosevitz, Martin, Norman Prentice, and Frances Wilson, University of Texas, "Imaginary Companions," in *Behavior Today*, March 5, 1973.

Mathes, Eugene W., Western Illinois University, "Mystical Experiences, Romantic Love, and Hypnotic Susceptibility," in *Psychological Reports*, 1982, v50, p701.

Mathes, Eugene W., and Paula S. Wise, Western Illinois University, "Romantic Love and the Ravages of Time," in *Psychological Reports*, 1983, v53, p839.

McAdams, Dan, Loyola University in Chicago, as reported by Valli Herman, Gary *Post-Tribune*, appearing in "Intimate Measures," *Centre Daily Times* (State College, Pa.), April 20, 1987.

Medical/Mrs., "A Doctor's Wife: The Myth vs. the Reality," as reported in *Newsweek*, June 11, 1979, p99–99C.

Miller, Norman, and Geoffrey Maruyama, University of Southern California, "Ordinal Position and Peer Popularity," *Journal of Personality and Social Psychology*, 1976, v33, no2, p123–31.

Moore, Monica, University of Missouri, St. Louis, *Ethology and Sociobiology*, 1986, v6, no4.

Morgan, S. Philip, University of Pennsylvania, *American Journal of Sociology*, July 1987.

Murstein, Bernard, Connecticut College, and Robert Brust, *Journal of Personality Assessment*, 1986, v49, no6.

National Institute of Mental Health Science Report, "What Research Shows about Birth Order, Personality, and IQ," 1978, DHEW Publication No. (ADM) 78–638.

National Institutes of Health, study quoted in "Study Finds First-Born Have Higher I.Q.'s," *The New York Times*, February 6, 1979.

Neugarten, B., H. Berkowitz, et al, *Personality in Middle and Late Life*, New York: Atherton, 1964.

Newcomb, Michael, and Peter Bentler, University of California, Los Angeles, *Journal of Personality Assessment*, 1981, v44, no1. Also see Jacques, Chason.

Nida, Steve, Franklin University, and Jack Koon, Georgia College, "They Get Better Looking at Closing Time Around Here, Too," *Psychological Reports*, 1983, v52, p657.

Nuttall, Ronald, and Ena Nuttall, Institute of Human Sciences, Boston College, as reported in *Behavior Today*, September 27, 1971, p3.

Paulhus, Delroy, and David R. Shaffer, University of Georgia, "Sex Differences in the Impact of Number of Older and Number of Younger Siblings on Scholastic Aptitude," *Social Psychology Quarterly*, 1981, v44, no4, p363–68.

Pendleton, Linda, Colorado State University, "Attraction Responses to Female Assertiveness in Heterosexual Social Interactions," *The Journal of Psychology*, 1982, v111, p57.

Pennebaker, J. W., M. A. Dyer, R. S. Caulkins, D. L. Litowitz, P. L. Ackerman, D. B. Anderson, and K. M. McGraw, "Don't the Girls Get Prettier at Closing Time: A Country and Western Application to Psychology," *Personality and Social Psychology Bulletin*, 1979, v5, p122.

Peplau, Letitia Anne, University of California, Los Angeles, "Research on Homosexual Couples: An Overview," *Journal of Homosexuality*, Winter 1982, v8, no2, p3–8.

Pinsky, Harvey, "The Effect of Sibling Constellation on Mate Selection," in *Dissertation Abstracts*, 1974, Order 74-26, 464.

Power, Thomas G., and M. Lynn Chapieski, University of Houston, *Developmental Psychology*, 1986, v22, no2.

Prentice, Daniel S., California State University, Hayward; Nancy E. Briggs and David W. Bradley, California State University, Long Beach, "Romantic Attitudes of American University Students," *Psychological Reports*, 1983, v53, p815.

Raschke, H. J., "The Role of Social Participation in Post-Separation and Post-Divorce Adjustment," *Journal of Divorce*, 1977, v1, p129–40.

Robin, Mitchell W., City University of New York, "Life Without Father: A Review of the Literature," *International Journal of Group Tensions*, 1979, v1–4, p169–94.

Rosow, I., and K. D. Rose, "Divorce Among Doctors," *Journal of Marriage and the Family*, 1972, v34, p587–98.

Rubin, Zick, Harvard University (later, Brandeis University), "Measurement of Romantic Love," *Journal of Personality and Social Psychology*, 1970, v16, no2, p265–73.

Saunders, Benjamin E., School of Social Work, Florida State University, "The Social Consequences of Divorce: Implications for Family Policy," *Journal of Divorce*, Spring 1983, v6, no3, p1–17.

Schachter, S., *The Psychology of Affiliation*, Stanford: Stanford University Press, 1959.

Schaninger, Charles, and W. Christian Buss, State University of New York, Albany, *Journal of Marriage and the Family*, 1986, v48, no1.

Schwab, Mary R., and David C. Lundgren, University of Cincinnati, "Birth Order, Perceived Appraisals by Significant Others, and Self-Esteem," *Psychological Reports*, 1978, v43, p443–54.

Schwartz, Pepper, University of Washington, and Janet Lever, Northwestern University, "Fear and Loathing at a College Mixer," *Urban Life*, January 1976, v4, no4, p413–31.

Shaver, Philip, and Jonathan Freedman, "Your Pursuit of Happiness," *Psychology Today*, August 1976, p26–32, 75.

Soares, Cecelia J., "The Companion Animal in the Context of the Family System," *Marriage and Family Review*, Summer 1985, v8, no3/4, p49–62.

Spanier, G. B., and R. Castro, "Adjustment to Separation and Divorce: A Qualitative Analysis," *Divorce and Separation*, George Levinger and O. C. Moles, eds., New York: Basic Books, 1979.

Stenger, John, University of Iowa, "A Study of the Relationship of Family Constellation to Work Values, Occupational Choice and Psychological Factors Among College Students," *Dissertation Abstracts*, 1975, Order 75:1269.

Sternberg, Robert, as reported in "The Three Faces of Love," by Robert J. Trotter, *Psychology Today*, September 1986, p46–54.

Stewart, Abigail J., Boston University, and Zick Rubin, Harvard University, "The Power Motive in the Dating Couple," *Journal of Personality and Social Psychology*, 1974, v34, no2, p305–9.

Strube, Michael J., and Steve Ota, University of Utah, "Type A Coronary-Prone Behavior Pattern: Relationship to Birth Order and Family Size," *Personality and Social Psychology Bulletin*, June 1982, v8, no2, p317–23.

Sutton-Smith, B., and B. G. Rosenberg, *The Sibling*, New York: Holt, Rinehart, and Winston, Inc., 1970.

Troiden, Richard R., Miami University, and Erich Goode, State University of New York at Stony Brook, *Journal of Homosexuality*, v5, no4.

U. S. Bureau of the Census, Census of the Population: 1970, Subject Reports, Final Report, PC(2)-3A, *Women by Number of Children Ever Born*.

Voith, V. L., "Behaviors, Attitudes and Interactions of Families with Their Dogs," paper presented at the Conferences on the Human-Animal Bond, Irvine, Calif., and Minneapolis, Minn., June 1983.

Weiss, R. S., "The Emotional Impact of Marital Separation," *Journal of Social Issues*, 1976, v32, p135–45.

White, Gregory L., University Of Maryland, "Jealousy and Partner's Perceived Motives for Attraction to a Rival," in *Social Psychology Quarterly*, 1981, v44, no1, p24.

Wille, R. L., "Study of the Relationship Between Pet Companionship and Health Status," paper presented at the Conferences on the Human-Animal Bond, Irvine, Calif., and Minneapolis, Minn., June 1983.

Wright, Patricia, Duke University, as reported in *National Wildlife* and by the *Chicago Tribune* syndicate, and published in *Centre Daily Times* (State College, Pa.), May 10, 1987.

Zajonc, Robert B., University of Michigan, *Motivation and Emotion*, v11, no4.

Zaphiris, Alexander G., Graduate School of Social Work, University of Houston, quoted in "The Child Victim of Incest," Michael deCourcy Hinds, *The New York Times*, June 15, 1981.

Zillman, Dolf, Institute for Communication Research, Indiana University, *Journal of Personality and Social Psychology*, as reported in "Science Watch," *The New York Times*, September 16, 1986.

CHAPTER 6: YOUR PERSONALITY TYPE

Antill, J. K., and J. D. Cunningham, "Self-Esteem as a Function of Masculinity in Both Sexes," *Journal of Consulting and Clinical Psychology*, v47, 1979, p783–85.

Arffa, Naomi B., and Michael J. Strube, Washington University, *Journal of Applied Psychology*, v16, p277–86.

Bar-On, Dan, Ben Gurion University, Israel, *Human Relations*, 1987, v39, p917–31.

Bem, Sandra L., "The Measurement of Psychological Androgyny," *Journal of Consulting and Clinical Psychology*, v42, 1974, p155–62.

Brody, Jane E., "Modifying 'Type A' Behavior Reduces Heart Attacks," *The New York Times*, August 7, 1984.

Broverman, Inge K., Worcester State Hospital; Susan Raymon Vogel, Brandeis University Mental Health Center; Donald M. Broverman and Frank E. Clarkson, Worcester State Hospital; and Paul S. Rosenkrantz, College of the Holy Cross, "Sex-Role Stereotypes: A Current Appraisal," *Journal of Social Issues*, 1972, v28, no2, p59–78.

Carlsson, Marianne, and Eva Magnusson, "Construct Validation of the Bem Sex Role Inventory," *Scandinavian Journal of Psychology*, 1980, v21, p27–31.

Carver, Charles, University of Miami, and Michael Scheier, Carnegie-Mellon

University, as reported by Tara Bradley Steck, Associated Press, in " 'Global Perspective' Influences Health," *Centre Daily Times* (State College, Pa.), July 26, 1987.

Chesney, M. A., and R. H. Rosenman, "Type A Behavior in the Work Setting," in *Current Concerns in Occupational Stress*, C. L. Cooper and R. Payne, eds., London: Wiley, 1980.

Collins, Barry E., University of California, Los Angeles, "Four Components of the Rotter Internal-External Scale," *Journal of Personality and Social Psychology*, 1974, v29, no3, p381–91.

Darden, Donna K., University of Arkansas, Fayetteville, "Values and Policy, the Case of Legal Services," *Basic and Applied Social Psychology*, March 1983, v4, p29–37.

De Fronzo, James, and Frances Boudreau, University of Connecticut, "Further Research into Antecedents and Correlates of Androgyny," *Psychological Reports*, 1979, v44, p23–29.

Doherty, William J., Oklahoma University Health Science Center, and Cynthia Baldwin, University of Iowa, "Shifts and Stability in Locus of Control During the 1970s: Divergence of the Sexes," *Journal of Personality and Social Psychology*, 1985, v48, no4, p1048–53.

Fischman, Joshua, "Type A on Trial," *Psychology Today*, February 1987, p42–50.

Francis, Leslie, Paul R. Pearson, Marian Carter, and William K. Kay, "Are Introverts More Religious?," *British Journal of Social Psychology*, 1981, v20, p101–4.

Furnham, Adrian, University College, London, "Personality and Values," *Personality and Individual Differences*, 1984, v5, no4, p483–85.

Gastorf, John W., University of Alabama College of Community Health Sciences, "Time Urgency of the Type A Behavior Pattern," *Journal of Consulting and Clinical Psychology*, April 1980, v48, p299.

Gibb, Gerald D., and Thomas T. Lambirth, Eastern Illinois University, "Who Are the Equal Rights Amendment Defenders and Opposers?" *Psychological Reports*, 1982, v51, p1239–42.

Goleman, Daniel, "Feeling of Control Viewed as Central in Mental Health," *The New York Times*, October 7, 1986.

Goleman, Daniel, "Psychology Analyzes Humbug-Sayers," *The New York Times*, December 25, 1984.

Graziano, William G., and Alice Bernstein Feldesman, University of Georgia; and Donald F. Rahe, University of Minnesota, "Extroversion, Social Cognition, and the Salience of Aversiveness in Social Encounters," *Journal of Personality and Social Psychology*, 1985, v49, no4, p971–80.

Holmes, David S., and Michael J. Will, University of Kansas, "Expression of Interpersonal Aggression by Angered and Nonangered Persons with the Type A and Type B Behavior Patterns," *Journal of Personality and Social Psychology*, 1985, v48, no3, p723–27.

Howard, J. H., D. A. Cunningham, and P. A. Rechnitzer, "Work Patterns Associated with Type A Behavior: a Managerial Population," *Human Relations*, 1977, v30, p825–36.

Hunt, Darlene M., David Lester, and Nancy Ashton, Richard Stockton State

College, "Fear of Death, Locus of Control and Occupation," *Psychological Reports*, 1983, v53, p1022.

Kobasa, Suzanne C., University of Chicago (now at City University of New York), "Stressful Life Events, Personality, and Health: An Inquiry into Hardiness," *Journal of Personality and Social Psychology*, January 1979, v37, no1, p1–11.

Major, Brenda, State University of New York at Buffalo, as reported by the Associated Press in the *Centre Daily Times* (State College, Pa.), February 10, 1988.

McGee, Mark G., and Mark Snyder, University of Minnesota, "Attribution and Behavior: Two Field Studies," *Journal of Personality and Social Psychology*, 1975, v32, no1, p185–90.

McKelvie, Stuart J., and Leonard Daoussis, Bishop's University, Lennoxville, Canada, "Extroversion and Attitude towards Capital Punishment," *Personality and Individual Differences*, 1982, v3, p341–42.

McLaughlin, Steven, and Michael Micklin, Battelle Human Affairs Research Center, in *Journal of Marriage and the Family*, v45, no1, cited in *Psychology Today*, September 1983.

Orlofsky, Jacob L., and Michael T. Windle, University of Missouri, St. Louis, "Sex-Role Orientation, Behavioral Adaptability and Personal Adjustment," *Sex Roles*, 1978, v4, no6, p801–11.

Rotter, J. B., "Generalized Expectancies for Internal versus External Control of Reinforcement," *Psychological Monographs*, 1966, v80, Whole No. 609.

Rotter, J. B., M. Seeman, and S. Liverant, "Internal vs external locus of control of reinforcement: a major variable in behavior theory," in N. F. Washburne (ed.), *Decisions, Values, and Groups*, London: Pergamon, 1962.

Rubin, Zick, Brandeis University, "Does Personality Really Change After 20?," *Psychology Today*, May 1981, p18–27.

Seligman, Martin E. P., *Helplessness*, San Francisco: Freeman, 1975.

Smith, D. I., Alcohol and Drug Authority, West Perth, Australia, and R. W. Kirkham, University of Western Australia, "Relationship Between Some Personality Characteristics and Driving Record," *British Journal of Social Psychology*, 1981, v20, p229–31.

Strube, Michael J., Washington University, and Carol Werner, University of Utah, "Relinquishment of Control and the Type A Behavior Pattern," *Journal of Personality and Social Psychology*, 1985, v48, no3, p688–701.

Trotter, Robert J., "Stop Blaming Yourself," *Psychology Today*, February 1987, p31–39.

Yarnold, Paul R., Kim T. Mueser, and Laurence G. Grimm, University of Illinois at Chicago, "Interpersonal Dominance of Type A's in Group Discussion," *Journal of Abnormal Psychology*, 1985, v94, no2, p233–36.

Zenker, Sanford I., and Ann K. Wolfgang, State University of New York at Oneonta, "Relationship of Machiavellianism and Locus of Control to Preferences for Leisure Activity by College Men and Women," *Psychological Reports*, 1982, v50, p583–86.

INDEX

BERNARD ASBELL has spent thirty-five years writing books and magazine articles and recently joined the English faculty of Pennsylvania State University to teach the writing of nonfiction and biography. Two of his books, *When F.D.R. Died* and *The Senate Nobody Knows*, appeared on the best-seller list, and his magazine articles have earned many awards. He has served as president of the American Society of Journalists and Authors, and lives in State College, Pennsylvania, with his wife, Jean Brenchley.